D1112266

IN PERFECT BALANCE

IN PERFECT BALANCE

SPENCER J. CONDIE

Bookcraft
Salt Lake City, Utah

Library of Congress Catalog Card Number: 93–72855
ISBN 0–88494–902–8

First Printing, 1993

Printed in the United States of America

To Brigitte, Stefanie, Heidi, Christel, and Craig
for keeping my life off balance

and

To Dorothea, Josie, and Spencer C., who have
tried so hard to restore that balance

Nearly two thousand years ago a perfect Man walked the earth—Jesus the Christ. He was the Son of a Heavenly Father and an earthly mother. He is the God of this world, under the Father. In his life, all the virtues were lived and kept **in perfect balance**; he taught men truth—that they might be free; his example and precepts provide the great standard—the only sure way—for all mankind.

—Ezra Taft Benson

Contents

ACKNOWLEDGMENTS

I am very grateful to one of the Brethren for his gentle encouragement to undertake the preparation of this manuscript. He shall remain anonymous lest his urging be considered by others to have been misguided.

My gratitude also goes to Patrizia Pianea, not only for her proficient typing of the final drafts but also for her helpful insights. I also wish to thank my daughter Stefanie for her meticulous editing and her extremely candid comments. She loved me enough to tell me the truth.

I am indebted to the many teachers who have influenced my life for good throughout the years. Many of the insights contained in this volume are undoubtedly the result of many years of germination of seeds planted by many faithful souls in various classes, quorum meetings, sacrament meetings, and general conferences. To each and every one of them I am most grateful.

I appreciate the *Ensign* and the *New Era* for permission to reprint modified versions of previously published articles and Brigham Young University for permission to publish revisions of addresses given previously.

Finally, I am grateful to Cory Maxwell and the editorial staff of Bookcraft for their encouragement and invaluable assistance in bringing this project to a successful completion.

Notwithstanding the substantial influence of others, the author alone bears the responsibility for the content of this book, and it should not be construed as an official statement of The Church of Jesus Christ of Latter-day Saints.

Introduction

THE QUEST FOR BALANCE

"And there stood one among them that was like unto God, and he said unto those who were with him: We will go down, for there is space there, and we will take of these materials, and we will make an earth whereon these may dwell;

"And we will prove them herewith, to see if they will do all things whatsoever the Lord their God shall command them;

"And they who keep their first estate shall be added upon; and they who keep not their first estate shall not have glory in the same kingdom with those who keep their first estate; and they who keep their second estate shall have glory added upon their heads for ever and ever" (Abr. 3:24–26).

From these three brief yet glorious verses from the Pearl of Great Price, we learn the very purpose of the creation of this beautiful earth upon which we live, and we learn *why* we were sent here to live. We have come to earth to be tried and tested, to prove to a loving Heavenly Father that we are willing to keep His commandments and to do His will.

Father Lehi explained in great detail *how* this testing is to occur and why it is that Heavenly Father created a plan through which our moral agency, the freedom to choose, can be maximized. Lehi taught his son Jacob: "For it must needs be, that there is an opposition in all things" (2 Ne. 2:11). He did not forewarn his young son that there *might* be opposition, or that there *could* be opposition, or even that there *would* be opposition. Lehi clearly taught that, in keeping with the very purpose of the plan, there *must* be opposition. He explained further that this opposition was in all things. Opposition is an inherent, indispensable ingredient in all things. He continued his explanation by teaching that if this were not so, "righteousness could not be brought to pass, neither wickedness, neither holiness nor misery, neither good nor bad. Wherefore, all things must be a compound in one." (2 Ne. 2:11.)

It has often been said that life's most difficult decisions are not necessarily between good and evil, but rather between "two goods." When we are faced with the choice between that which is of God and that which is of Satan, even when we err we soon discover afterward that the choice was wrong, for "wickedness never was happiness" (Alma 41:10). But what of the choice between reading a doctrinal commentary about the scriptures and reading the actual scriptures, or the choice between attending an edifying choir concert or attending the temple instead?

The consequences of these choices between two goods are not trivial, especially when these activities are pursued without a sense of balance and perspective.

When we are confronted with the choice between good and evil, we will find that it is generally the case that more of one begets less of the other. The scriptures are clear that evil thoughts and behavior alienate the Spirit of the Lord; therefore, the more evil our thoughts and actions, the less spirituality and spiritual guidance we will enjoy. In a related vein, the greater our spirituality, the less likely it will be for us to have a penchant toward criticism. Conversely, the greater our inclination to continually criticize, the less spirituality we will enjoy.

But what of humility and confidence, meekness and boldness, mercy and justice, faith and works? Must these important qualities be in opposition in such a way that our confidence wanes as our humility increases, or that as we gain a greater sense of justice our inclinations to be merciful decline?

We sometimes hear a friend described as a real go-getter and as a perfectionist with the afterthought, "It's just a shame he is not a little more patient, gentle, kind, and compassionate." Or, another friend is described as meek and gentle with the postscript, "I just wish she had a little more initiative, enthusiasm, and drive." It is the intent of this book to share some insights into the resolution of these apparent either-or tensions that seem to arise from the acquisition of godly attributes. Must we sacrifice our sociable inclinations in order to become reverent? Is it really possible to be both bold and meek, just and merciful, kind and assertive, or must one be content with acquiring one set of attributes to the exclusion of all others?

The following diagram suggests that it is indeed possible to possess two different attributes that may be maintained in balance without an excessive commitment to one attribute to the exclusion of the other.

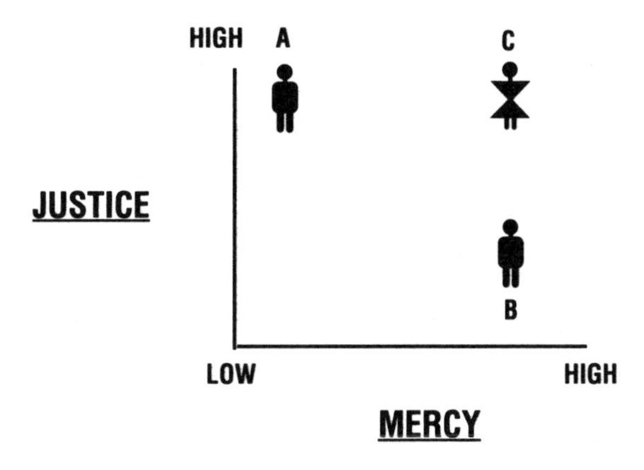

Person A has a great sense of justice but very little mercy in his heart. Person B, on the other hand, is extremely merciful but has little sense of justice, perhaps like a bishop who cannot bring himself to hold a disciplinary council for a wayward member. Person C, however, has acquired a good balance between justice and mercy, the one tempering the other.

The tension between godly attributes is ubiquitous and perpetual. This tension is not to be confused with dissension or contention, both of which are indeed ungodly and are to be avoided. At issue here is the tension inherent with an opposition in *all* things.

If our nervous system and our muscles and our skeletal frame were totally free from tension all of the time, it would be impossible for us to sit or stand or walk or lift or push or pull. However, excessive tension in our bodies can cause painful cramps and muscle spasms, and in certain cases even broken bones. Thus, muscular tensions must be kept in balance. Our bodies need exercise, but not excessive exercise that leads to total exhaustion or to the damaging of tender tissues.

We often speak of the need for a balanced diet in reference to the nourishment of our physical bodies. Our bodies need a certain amount of cholesterol, but cholesterol in excess may contribute to cardiovascular disease and eventual heart attacks. We need a large variety of minerals, such as iron, but iron in excess can lead to liver damage.

So it is with our spiritual lives. We must exercise our faith, but we must also convert our faith into works. It is a lofty goal to become a scripturalist, but we will also be judged by what we do and how we treat others, not solely by what we know or what we have read. I am reminded of the man who was asked by his quorum leader if he would be willing to accept an assignment to work on the stake welfare farm. The reply was a little disarming: "I enjoy teaching Gospel Doctrine class or giving sermons in sacrament meeting, but working on the welfare farm just isn't my thing."

We must work diligently, but we must also rely upon the Lord and recognize His hand and express our gratitude in all things. It is admirable to work hard in a successful business venture and to give generous donations to charitable causes, but it is also imperative that we become meek and lowly in heart.

The principles discussed in this book do not constitute an exhaustive list, inasmuch as each person must come to terms with living various gospel principles in balance in his or her own life.

Sometimes our quest for personal balance must be mediated by the circumstances in which we find ourselves. For example, for a marriage to be in balance it may be necessary for one partner to be thrifty in order to compensate for the other partner's generosity. One may need to be a little more "mellow" to offset the other partner's "intensity."

In a bishopric or a stake presidency, counselors must sometimes be prepared to modify some of their attitudes and behavior to provide a *collective* balance between justice and mercy, compassion and accountability, the spirit of the law and the letter of the law.

Some are concerned with generalities or the "big picture," while others are more concerned with specific details. Some leaders are bold and some are meek; some are more submissive and others are more assertive. In each instance we must strive to acquire a balance, not only in our personal lives but also within our presidency or our bishopric and within our family.

Any book with the word *perfect* in the title is apt to arouse suspicions that the author assumes he has all the answers. Actually, the inspiration for this title is traced to President Gordon B. Hinckley's closing remarks in the final session of general conference in April

1992 when he quoted President Ezra Taft Benson's observation that in the life of Jesus "all the virtues were lived and kept in perfect balance."[1]

In Perfect Balance is a quest, not the final formula. It is the musing of a struggling follower of Christ in a quest for the balanced life, a quest that most assuredly requires a lifetime.

Notes

1. Ezra Taft Benson, quoted in Gordon B. Hinckley, "Our Great Mission," *Ensign* 22 (May 1992): 89.

Chapter One

PATIENCE AND PERFECTION

Throughout the holy scriptures we are given counsel, exhortations and admonitions which, if followed, will help us to conquer our fears, overcome temptations, rise above our sorrows, transcend our trials and tribulations, and live lives of joy and fulfillment. Of all the counsel and commandments we have been given, few are more soul-stretching than the Savior's injunction: "Therefore I would that ye should be perfect, even as I or your Father who is in heaven is perfect" (3 Ne. 12:48, see also Matt. 5:48).

Because this commandment has been given to all of us, the challenge becomes two-fold in our lives: first, striving for personal perfection, and second, developing patience with ourselves and those around us who have not achieved perfection.

The story is told of the sacrament meeting speaker who began his sermon with the following provocative question: "Would all of you who are perfect please stand up?" A good brother on the back row slowly rose to his feet, and the speaker asked: "Are you *really* perfect?" "No, indeed," replied the elderly brother, "I am just standing in vicariously for my wife's first husband." Living with imperfect people can truly be one of life's greatest trials, but it is also one of life's greatest opportunities in the laboratory of life to learn patience.

Living with Imperfect People

A few years ago I met a very radiant silver-haired sister on the grounds of a temple in a foreign land. Her cheerful, Christlike countenance seemed to set her apart from those around her, and I felt inclined to ask her to explain why she looked so happy and content with life.

"Well," she said, "several years ago I was in a hurry to get married, and quite frankly, after a few months, I realized I had married the wrong man." She continued, "He had no interest in the Church as he had initially led me to believe, and he began to treat me very unkindly for several years. One day I reached the point where I felt I could go on no longer in this situation, and so I knelt down to pray, to ask Heavenly Father if He would approve of my divorcing my husband.

"I had a very remarkable experience," she said. "After praying fervently, the Lord revealed a number of insights to me of which I had been previously unaware. First of all, for the first time in my life I realized that, just like my husband, I am not perfect either. I began to work on my intolerance and my impatience with him and his lack of spirituality.

"I began to strive to become more affectionate and loving and understanding. And do you know what happened? As *I* started to change, my *husband* started to change. Instead of my nagging him about going to church, he gradually decided to come with me on his own initiative.

"Recently we were sealed in the temple, and now we spend one day each week in the temple together. Oh, he's still not perfect, but I am so happy that the Lord loves us enough to help us resolve our problems. I am just happy to be a member of this wonderful church!"

The opportunities for acquiring patience on the pathway to perfection are many and varied. Those who are married have a great opportunity to learn patience as they undergo a matrimonial merging of each other's agency. But those who remain single through no fault of their own also learn patience as their faith in the words of the Lord's prophets increases. President Joseph Fielding Smith declared:

> Through the mercy and justice of the Lord, any young woman who maintains her virtue and accepts in her heart all the commandments and ordinances of the gospel will receive the fulness of the glory and exaltation of the celestial kingdom. The great gift of eternal life will be given her. This gift the Lord has described, shall be a "fulness and a continuation of the seeds forever and ever." All the gifts of exaltation will be hers, because she has been true and faithful, and what was denied her here will be given to her hereafter.[1]

Wives married to less-active husbands learn patience that the bishop's wife may not understand, but, again, the bishop's wife and family learn patience in a laboratory that many others will not experience. Those suffering from painful arthritis or the excruciating pains of terminal cancer gain a glimpse of the Savior's suffering on the cross, and also acquire insight into the divine patience of a loving Heavenly Father who knows that "all these things shall give thee experience, and shall be for thy good" (D&C 122:7).

Though a testimony of the resurrection accompanied by a temple sealing gives us a calm assurance that we can be reunited with all our loved ones after death, death of a loved one still tries one's patience in the anticipation of the promised reunification. And when that separation through death occurs very early in life, one's patience is tried for an entire lifetime.

Married women have a marvelous opportunity to learn patience while awaiting the development and birth of a child. During this time a husband can also learn patience and compassion in dealing with his wife's morning sickness, strange eating habits, loss of energy, occasional cantankerousness, and changes in sleeping habits.

Then, after the long-awaited arrival of the infant, what a great opportunity it is to learn patience when the children are young and sputter their oatmeal all over the kitchen walls and ceiling. And when a child is seriously ill, for the parents it seems that every minute is an hour and every day an entire lifetime.

Our patience is then tried and polished by teenagers who want to quickly acquire all of the freedoms of adulthood without accepting any of the responsibilities. And when we send them on missions, although it may be the happiest time of their lives, for those of us left at home it seems they have been gone a very long time.

Children Who Stray

Not long ago a very wise and dear friend of mine passed away, leaving a grand legacy of love and service. He had served faithfully in many callings in the Church, and he had also shouldered numerous civic responsibilities within the community in which he lived. He and his wife had borne several children and had conscientiously taught them the principles of the gospel. Still, one of those children, perhaps wishing to exercise his individuality, strayed for a time from the eternal principles he had been taught and shown in his home.

Two heartbroken parents continued to serve faithfully in the Church and persisted in praying for their prodigal son. Months turned into years and the years into decades, but still they showered their son with love and affection and unbounded tolerance and mercy. Sometime before his father's death, this fine young man remembered who he really was, and he eventually became the man his parents had taught him to become.

Had those parents disowned that son, or had they been afflicted with the "curse of respectability" by dissociating themselves from him, he probably never would have returned. But as urgent as it was to bring him back into the fold, his parents patiently prayed and fasted and wrote and phoned and visited and wept, and finally he returned.

Watching our parents grow old can also be a sweet opportunity for us to develop patience in a way not previously possible. Being patient and tolerant with four-year-olds was one kind of opportunity to learn patience, but now we must learn to be patient with a loved one grown old who occasionally may act like he is age four.

Because our Heavenly Father loves us so much, He has designed a plan whereby we can become like Him and His Son. For us to do so, the lessons of life must be varied as well as repetitive, so that we may learn them all and learn them well; then "when he shall appear we shall be like him" (1 John 3:2; Moro. 7:48). To become perfect (or complete) like Him, we must also become patient like Him. The kindred traits of patience include faith, hope, humility, meekness, tolerance, kindness, long-suffering, compassion, and charity, the pure love of Christ.

The fellow travelers of impatience are arrogance, intolerance, unkindness, discouragement, temper tantrums, brutality, loss of virtue, bankruptcy, and divorce. On the collective level, impatience is manifest in mass demonstrations, a soaring national debt, revolution, or war.

Perfection Takes Time

When one thinks of righteous leaders and of a righteous people, the name of Enoch and the city of Enoch come readily to mind. In the scriptures we learn that Enoch's righteousness and his righteous influence required a great deal of time and patience. We read that Adam ordained his descendant Enoch to the priesthood when Enoch was age twenty-five, and later blessed him again when he was sixty-five, "and he walked with God three hundred and sixty-five years, making him four hundred and thirty years old when he was translated" (D&C 107:48–49). I rest my case: Perfection takes a long time! We also learn that the city of Enoch "*in process of time*, was taken up into heaven" (Moses 7:21, emphasis added).

There are great lessons in patient persistence in the lives of numerous athletes who have devoted great time and energy toward perfecting their skills. One of these was John Nabors, who pursued and won the 1976 Olympic gold medal for the swimming competition in the 100-meter backstroke. Nabors had noted the winning time of Mark Spitz in the 1972 Olympics, and he calculated that he must trim four seconds from his own current time if he was to win a gold medal.

Four seconds is a long time when you are already straining each and every muscle as hard as you can, and when your lungs and legs ache at the end of each practice session. But Nabors patiently worked out a plan based upon the following reasoning: If he trained for ten months each year, he would need to trim one-tenth of a second from his time each month. Training six days each week, he would need to reduce his time 1/300 of a second per day. He worked two hours each morning and two hours every evening, so this meant that for each hour of practice he would only have to reduce his time 1/1200 of a second, less than the time it takes to blink an eye. Over a period of four years, Nabors did reduce his time by four seconds, and he did win the gold medal.[2]

Peter's Pathway to Perfection

As previously noted, Elder Ezra Taft Benson has stated that Jesus Christ possessed all of the godly virtues and lived them in perfect balance. An example of this divine balance between patience and the quest for perfection can be found in the Savior's relationship with the Apostle Peter. Peter possessed many wonderful leadership traits in embryo, but these attributes were occasionally overshadowed by his mortal imperfections. His boldness sometimes bordered on belligerence, and his faith was strong as long as it was risk free. Nevertheless, the Savior patiently nurtured Peter, teaching him, reproving him, forgiving him, and inspiring him until the rugged fisherman truly became a compassionate fisher of men.

Peter's obedience and humility were evident as the Savior called him and his brother, Andrew, to follow Him, notwithstanding Peter's humble acknowledgment, "I am a sinful man, O Lord" (Luke 5:8). Peter and Andrew immediately accepted the divine call as "they straightway left their nets, and followed him" (Matt. 4:20).

The embryonic faith of Peter was demonstrated as the disciples were seated in a boat and one of them saw Jesus in the distance walking upon the water. Peter said, "Lord, if it be thou, bid me come unto thee on the water" (Matt. 14:28). After a faithful beginning, Peter's faith faltered and he began to sink. Foreshadowing what would occur throughout his three-year ministry with Peter, the Savior lifted Peter from the water, saying, "O thou of little faith, wherefore didst thou doubt?" (Matt. 14:31.) But He did not release Peter as the chief Apostle just because he had sunk on one occasion.

Peter's spiritual growth and increasing testimony were evidenced at Caesarea Philippi as the Savior posed the question to his disciples: "Whom do men say that I the Son of man am?" (Matt. 16:13.) It was Peter who declared: "Thou art the Christ, the Son of the living God" (Matt. 16:16).

After the miraculous feeding of the five thousand with five barley loaves and two fishes, the Savior declared, "I am that bread of life," and "no man can come unto me, except it were given unto him of my Father" (John 6:48, 65). There were many who had followed Jesus out of curiosity, hoping to see Him perform miracles, but when He challenged the people to change their lives, "From that time many of his disciples went back, and walked no more with him. Then said Jesus unto the twelve, Will ye also go away? Then Simon Peter answered him, Lord, to whom shall we go? thou hast the words of eternal life. And we believe and are sure that thou art that Christ, the Son of the living God." (John 6:66–69.)

The Savior later told his disciples of the suffering he would experience and that he would "be killed, and be raised again the third day" (Matt. 16:21). Peter, however, refused to believe that Jesus would be killed, and so he rebuked the Savior, saying, "Lord, this shall not be unto thee" (Matt. 16:22). The Savior then turned to Peter, reproving him in the very sharpest of terms: "Get thee behind me, Satan: thou art an offence unto me" (Matt. 16:23). Let it be said to Peter's credit that he accepted the Savior's sharp reproof. Peter had a lot to learn, and the Savior was always willing to teach him and to forgive him.

Somewhat later, the Savior invited Peter, along with James and John, to go with Him to a high mountain where Jesus was transfigured before them and they heard the Father testify: "This is my beloved Son, in whom I am well pleased; hear ye him" (Matt. 17:5). There, on that mount, Peter, James, and John were given priesthood keys by the Savior himself and also by Moses and Elias.[3] Peter was being prepared to lead the Church after the Savior's earthly mission had been completed. It appears that the Savior was more concerned with what Peter would be able to do in the future than with his mistakes of the past.

A short time later the Savior assembled the Twelve in an upper room where He girded himself with a towel and began to wash the disciples' feet. As He came to Peter, this chief Apostle protested: "Thou shalt never wash my feet," to which the Savior replied, "If I wash thee not, thou hast no part with me." Immediately this rugged fisherman understood that to lead is to serve, as he said: "Lord, not my feet only, but also my hands and my head." (John 13:4–9.)

After Jesus and the Apostles concluded the Last Supper together, the Savior instructed Peter: "When thou art converted, strengthen thy brethren" (Luke 22:32). One can imagine the feelings in Peter's heart after having spent three years with the Savior to be told, "When thou art converted . . . " Jesus then prophesied that Peter would deny Him three times that night, but Peter protested vehemently: "Though I should die with thee, yet will I not deny thee" (Matt. 26:35).

Jesus next invited Peter, James, and John to go to a garden called Gethsemane, and there to watch for Him as He went further into the garden to pray. It was there that He prayed earnestly to the Father to let the bitter cup pass, and it was in that garden that the weight of our sins caused Him to bleed from every pore. And as He prayed, his disciples fell asleep, so that when He returned He asked: "What, could ye not watch with me one hour? . . . The spirit indeed is willing, but the flesh is weak." (Matt. 26:40–41.) But the Savior did not release these three Apostles because of their weaknesses of the flesh.

Shortly afterward, Judas led the soldiers to Jesus and betrayed Him with a kiss. Wishing to show his loyalty to the Savior, Peter withdrew his sword and cut off the right ear of the high priest's servant, Malchus (see John 18:10). Jesus restrained Peter, saying, "All they that take the sword shall perish with the sword" (Matt. 26:52). The Savior restored the severed ear and was then led away to a trial which was to be a mockery of both Jewish and Roman law. And as He was led away, Peter "followed him afar off unto the high priest's palace" (Matt. 26:58).

That night, just as the Savior had foretold, Peter did indeed deny the Lord three times, and as he remembered what Jesus had said, "he went out, and wept bitterly" (Matt. 26:75). How much is each of us like Peter? We make sacred covenants in very holy places, and we renew covenants weekly as we partake of the sacrament, yet somehow we are sometimes quite forgetful in remembering our covenants, and, like Peter, we sink to our knees in despair, pleading for forgiveness and for a better memory.

After the Savior's resurrection and His instruction to the disciples, Peter said, "I go a fishing," and the other disciples joined him, "and that night they caught nothing" (John 21:3). The next morning they heard a voice from shore which suggested they "cast the net on the right side of the ship," and they caught one hundred and fifty-three fish (John 21:6, 11). John declared, "It is the Lord," and when Peter heard this he jumped into the water to make his way to land as fast as possible (John 21:7). This was the same Peter who, upon hearing that the Lord was risen, "ran unto the sepulchre" (Luke 24:12). His love for the Lord was so great that, notwithstanding all of his personal weaknesses, Peter longed to be in the presence of Jesus.

After eating bread and fish with the disciples, Jesus turned to Peter and asked: "Lovest thou me more than these?" (Perhaps "these" refers to the one hundred fifty-three fish in the net.) Peter responded: "Yea, Lord: thou knowest that I love thee." Then came the profound command: "Feed my lambs."

Again the Savior posed the question: "Simon, son of Jonas, lovest thou me?" And once again Peter declared: "Yea, Lord; thou knowest that I love thee." A third time the Savior asked: "Lovest thou me?" By now Peter was becoming a little agitated (the scriptures say "grieved") by these repetitive queries. But perhaps Peter needed time to review his life and the occasional lapses in faith when he slipped through the water, or when he rebuked the Lord for prophesying His crucifixion, or when he resisted the washing of the feet, or when he fell asleep outside the garden, or when he tempestuously cut off Malchus's ear, or when he denied the Savior three times.

A third time Peter declared fervently: "Lord, thou knowest all things; thou knowest that I love thee." And the Savior said once more: "Feed my sheep." (John 21:15–17.)

And Peter *did* feed the Good Shepherd's sheep. On the day of Pentecost, Peter bore such a moving testimony in the majesty of the holy apostleship, testifying of the divine mission of Jesus of Nazareth, that about three thousand people were baptized that very day (see Acts 2:22–41).

Peter continued teaching by the Spirit and he healed many, engendering such great faith in the people "that they brought forth the sick into the streets, and laid them on beds and couches, that at least the shadow of Peter passing by might overshadow some of them" (Acts 5:15).

The Savior knew all along the great potential of this great fisherman, and Jesus never gave up on Peter, and Peter never gave up on the Savior.

The Prophet Joseph Smith observed that "Peter penned the most sublime language of any of the apostles."[4] This statement is supported by a perusal of the topics of Peter's epistles. He admonishes us to be "holy in all manner of conversation" (1 Pet. 1:15) and to "love one another with a pure heart fervently" (1 Pet. 1:22). He reminds us, as children of the covenant and the inheritors of the promises of Abraham, that we "are a chosen generation, a royal priesthood, an holy nation, a peculiar people" (1 Pet. 2:9), building self-esteem on the one hand while exhorting us to be different from the world on the other.

It was the Apostle Peter who wrote of the Savior's providing the means for the spirits in prison to hear the gospel (see 1 Pet. 3:18–20; 4:6.) It was this epistle which focused the attention of President Joseph F. Smith upon the matter of redeeming the dead and prepared his mind for the revelation we find in section 138 of the Doctrine and Covenants.

And, notwithstanding an earlier life as a rugged, tempestuous man of the sea, it is Peter who, after having undergone great persecution and purification on his personal pathway to perfection, admonishes us to become "partakers of the divine nature" with the following succinct recipe for righteousness: "And beside this, giving all diligence, add to your faith virtue; and to virtue knowledge; and to knowledge temperance; and to temperance patience; and to patience godliness; and to godliness brotherly kindness; and to brotherly kindness charity." (2 Pet. 1:4–7.)

The unfolding of Peter's life after the touch of the Master's hand is a marvelous testimony of the miracle of forgiveness and the impact the gospel can have in bringing about a mighty change of heart. The change was indeed mighty, but it did not occur from one day to the next, but was rather a lifelong quest involving continual patience and constant forgiveness.

The Apostle Paul

As with Peter, the mighty change in the life of Saul of Tarsus was not instantaneous, despite the marvelous blinding vision on the road to Damascus. After receiving his sight again under the hands of Ananias, and after having been baptized and having received the gift of the Holy Ghost (see Acts 9:4–18), Paul wrote the Galatians that he next went to Arabia, and it was three years before he met with the Apostles in Jerusalem (see Gal. 1:16–18). It seems that more than an immediate change of name was necessary for Saul, and that a certain passage of time was necessary prior to his embarking on his ministry. Mighty changes of heart are often the accumulation of tiny daily changes of heart.

Efficiency

One of the greatest goals of modern, industrialized nations is efficiency. Adam Smith's classic *Wealth of Nations* describes in detail the increased efficiency possible from a division of labor characteristic of the industrial revolution, in which more and more people were employed to perform smaller and smaller specialized, repetitive tasks.

Industrialized nations become very efficient, not only in producing manufactured commodities but also in their efficient methods of birth control and abortion and their very efficient no-fault divorce laws and procedures, and their efficient networks of institutional homes for the aged, and their asylums for the village idiots. Pre-literate, non-industrial societies, on the other hand, are not so enlightened and progressive and efficient. In inefficient, developing nations families are large, extended kinship systems are very mutually supportive, and the aged, infirm, and obtuse are cared for within that supportive system.

One of the greatest challenges Adolf Hitler faced during his reign of terror in Europe was finding ever more efficient means of exterminating six million of our Jewish brothers and sisters from the earth. Wholesale shooting and burying bodies in mass graves consumed so much time and effort and were so inefficient. Efficiency was finally achieved through the gas ovens and crematoria. What a horrible price for efficiency! The efficient records maintained by Hitler's SS troops later served as unimpeachable, convicting evidence against them.

Throughout the scriptures the word *efficiency* does not appear a single time, although Satan's plan did have a certain ring of efficiency as he boasted: "I will redeem all mankind, that one soul shall not be lost" (Moses 4:1). His plan, devoid of the great eternal gift of moral agency, would have been so efficient that an atonement would not have been necessary, for no one would have sinned. Nor would mankind have had opportunities to make mistakes and to repent, and—because there would have been no suffering in the Garden, no agony on the cross—it would never have been possible for us eventually to become like our Heavenly Father and His Beloved Son.

If the only concern of the restored Church of Jesus Christ were to become more and more efficient, why is it that mission presidents are released after three years, often at the very peak of their proficiency as leaders? Or, why are young missionaries released just at the time they are most proficient with the language and with teaching the discussions? If efficiency were our major goal, and we were less concerned with developing patience leading to perfection, it would be very tempting to identify those young missionaries who are most "successful" in their work and to extend their missions a year or two longer while simultaneously sending home a year early those missionaries who just do not quite measure up. But a two-year mission for young men and an eighteen-month mission for young women is part of a much larger and longer process ultimately leading to perfection. Missionaries who learn how to teach, commit, challenge, and baptize but who do not learn humility or charity may, in the long run, not be quite as successful as they had assumed.

If efficiency were the only objective of the kingdom of God, why wasn't Moses given directions to shorten the trip from Egypt to the land of Canaan by thirty-nine years and ten months by taking the direct route? (One wag observed that men back then were just like men today—always too proud to ask for directions.)

So many times we have heard a recently released bishop or stake president exclaim: "I was just beginning to understand my calling and was finally learning what I needed to do, and then I was released." The very purpose of Church callings is for the perfecting of the Saints, and if during our brief tenure in a given calling we have blessed the lives of others and have increased in spiritual strength ourselves, then the sacred purpose has been fulfilled.

In more recent times, the circuitous saga of the Saints in moving from New York to Ohio to Missouri to Illinois to Utah to Mexico and Canada could surely have been more efficient as seen through the eyes of the world. Some have criticized the march of Zion's Camp, an attempt to reclaim the expropriated lands in Missouri, as folly, but Elder Neal A. Maxwell has aptly observed: "God is more concerned with growth than with geography. Thus, those who marched in Zion's Camp were not exploring the Missouri countryside but their own possibilities."[5] Geographical location is merely the Lord's crucible in which his children are tried and refined and purified.

Elder Marvin J. Ashton observed that "life is what happens to you while you were making other plans." For most of us, in a McDonald's society of fast foods, instant photo finishing, and one-hour dry cleaning, the desirable route is the straightest line between two points. But in the Lord's plan for our spiritual growth, the quickest, most efficient solution to our problems might rob us of patience and faith. Thus, on our way to aspiring to be president of the company or the governor of the state, the Lord may cause a detour which may lead us down an entirely different career track.

We can learn much from the miraculous creation of our bodies, especially from the assimilation of the nutrients we eat during the passage of food through an alimentary canal thirty feet long. This long circuitous process assures that a maximum amount of absorption can take place and that the greatest possible amount of energy and nutrients can be assimilated.

Our lives often unfold in circuitous ways which slow us down from achieving our initial goals but which maximize our exposure to refining experiences which prepare us for godhood. Paul stated the process well when he wrote that "we glory in tribulations also: knowing that tribulation worketh patience; and patience, experience; and experience, hope" (Rom. 5:3–4).

Be Not Weary in Well-Doing

Those who fail to arrive at a healthy balance between patience and anxious engagement have been described by Elder Neal A. Maxwell as "being over-anxious and thus underengaged." He then underscored this important counsel: "It is direction first, *then* velocity!"[6]

One of Satan's most insidious tools for inducing discouragement is planting the belief that we are always falling short of the ideal and that our efforts are invariably inadequate and ineffective. Lucifer seeks to weaken our resolve to endure to the end by nourishing the faith-weakening thought, "But when will all the blessings come?" A loving Lord who knows the thoughts of our hearts has encouraged us to "be not weary in well-doing, for ye are laying the foundation of a great work. And out of small things proceedeth that which is great." (D&C 64:33.)

To those who, in their own minds, are always falling short of their goals, or to those for whom impatience leads to the abandonment of a goal, the Lord has revealed the following comforting counsel: "Verily, verily, I say unto you, that when I give a commandment to any of the sons of men to do a work unto my name, and those sons of men go with all their might and with all they have to perform that work, and cease not their diligence, and their enemies come upon them and hinder them from performing that work, behold, it behooveth me to require that work no more at the hands of those sons of men, but to accept of their offerings" (D&C 124:49).

To the Laurel adviser who is a bit discouraged because not all of "her girls" have gotten married in the temple, and to priest advisers and bishops who have not successfully launched all of "their boys" on missions, take heart: "Behold, the Lord requireth the heart and a *willing* mind" (D&C 64:34, emphasis added). He knows the intent of our hearts and the sincerity of our well-intended actions. We are saved as individuals, not as congregations, and sometimes that saving process occurs one interview at a time, one home teaching visit or one visiting teaching visit at a time.

If we are not introspective in conducting an occasional spiritual inventory, we can experience high councilor hiatus or Primary president's paralysis. Although those who experience so-called "burnout" in their Church callings would resist the idea, the fact remains that we generally tend to feel burned out when we feel that "*I* cannot do it any longer." If the truth were known, those who feel burned out may feel that they have to do everything themselves. Feelings of burnout also reveal a certain lack of faith in the Lord's love and mercy and His willingness to provide us with inspiration and the continual companionship of the Holy Ghost in our callings. After all it is His work; therefore, He will help us accomplish it.

Regardless of the urgency of the task at hand, the Lord reminds us that "no power or influence can or ought to be maintained by virtue of the priesthood, only by persuasion, by long-suffering, by gentleness and meekness, and by love unfeigned" (D&C 121:41). All of these traits incorporate a measure of patience.

It would be well to review the counsel of beloved King Benjamin in his benedictory address as he reassures us on the one hand that "if ye should serve [God] with all your whole souls yet ye would be unprofitable servants" (Mosiah 2:21). On the other hand, Benjamin concludes with the merciful admonition: "And see that all these things are done in wisdom and order; for it is not requisite that a man should run faster than he has strength" (Mosiah 4:27).

It is always a joy to meet the bishop or Relief Society president or Young Women president or stake president or mission president who, upon being released from their current calling, continue their service in the kingdom with enthusiasm.

Goals and Aspirations

Perfection is a goal for which we all strive, but there are times when we become impatient with the daily pace of progress. Impatience can give rise to discouragement and a loss of hope, finally resulting in despair and cynicism. There is the young woman who sets a goal in her youth to become married in the temple, but with each passing birthday, that lofty goal appears to be more and more remote. Eventually goaded by impatience, she may compromise her lofty goals for the immediacy of marrying anyone under nearly any circumstances.

There is the young married couple who convince themselves that before they can begin their family they must have a suitable house for their children. And so, rather than patiently saving for a down payment on a modest home, they assume unwise heavy mortgage obligations which require both of them to work full-time. And as the years pass, somehow they become very comfortable in their affluent twosome, devoid of the responsibilities, inconvenience, and joy of having children.

One of the greatest examples of patience in obtaining a lofty goal is the story of Jacob's love for Rachel. Isaac had forbidden his son Jacob from marrying a daughter of the Canaanites among whom they lived, so Jacob left for the land where his Uncle Laban lived. Eventually he met "Rachel the daughter of Laban his mother's brother" (Gen. 29:10) and expressed to his uncle the desire to marry his daughter. But Laban, sensitive to the custom of the times, insisted that Jacob first marry his older daughter Leah, for "it must not be so done in our country, to give the younger before the firstborn" (Gen. 29:26).

After agreeing to work for Laban for seven years in order to marry Leah, Jacob then agreed to work another seven years for Rachel. Here is a great lesson in patience and how labor is lightened by love: "And Jacob served seven years for Rachel; and they seemed unto him but a few days, for the love he had to her" (Gen. 29:20).

Latter-day Saints are confronted with an interesting dilemma requiring great insight and patience in the pursuit of goals. On the one hand the restored gospel teaches us that we can and should aspire to godhood, but then we are told we should not aspire to become a Relief Society president, mission president, or stake president. There is many a good father and husband who has felt the pangs of impatience as his neighbors and friends have been ordained as high priests and he remains "just an elder." In this instance it is well to be reminded of Elder Melvin J. Ballard's statement: "Positions do not exalt, service does."

An elder holds the same Melchizedek Priesthood held by Apostles and prophets, the only distinction being the keys which the latter hold and which an elder does not. It is significant that members of the Quorum of the Twelve Apostles are referred to as "Elder."

Satan may play upon our impatience when others receive highly visible calls while we continue to serve as an invisible Scoutmaster, home teacher, or Primary teacher. Satan can plant seeds of discouragement in heads and hearts, and we lose sight of the fact that the purpose of the Church is for the perfecting of the Saints. When we stop having "an eye single to the glory of God," we begin to observe the Church as a social club or status-awarding institution instead of seeing it as the Lord's repository of priesthood keys and ordinances. And when our status needs are not met, we are tempted to look elsewhere to other organizations for investing our time and resources. But the Savior's promise in the oath and covenant of the priesthood is just as valid for elders and high priests as it is for Seventies and Apostles, that when we keep the commandments and observe our covenants, "all that [His] Father hath shall be given unto [us]" (D&C 84:38).

Wise Use of Time

Patience involves the temperate acceptance of the passage of time. Patience also requires us to optimally use the time which we have available to us, for the Lord has declared that "he who is faithful and wise in time is accounted worthy to inherit the mansions prepared for him of my Father" (D&C 72:4). The desire to use time wisely has given rise to an explosion of diversified time-management devices, daily planners, and the like. There is, of course, justifiable merit in using calendars and appointment books of various kinds to help bring order to our lives. But none of these time-management materials can help us to establish the specific *content* of our priorities. They may help us order the things which *must* be done today, and tasks that *should* be accomplished today, and activities which would be *nice to do* if time permits. However, it is up to us to allocate adequate time in reading the scriptures, in prayer and meditation, and in serving others "after hours."

Daily schedules are helpful in planning our time, but they cannot shield us from unpredictability, and this is an area in which great patience is required. The Savior's ministry was punctuated with interruptions from people who, for various reasons, needed His time and His blessing. The collision between planned protocol and spontaneous service was readily apparent when the little children were brought to Him during His teaching of the multitudes. The disciples, perhaps concerned about time schedules and the interruption of unplanned events (and opportunities for service), rebuked the crowds. "But Jesus said, Suffer little children, and forbid them not, to come unto me: for of such is the kingdom of heaven." (Matt. 19:2, 13–14.)

On another occasion, as the Savior was under way to visit the daughter of Jairus who lay ill "at the point of death," being thronged about by the people, He suddenly asked: "Who touched my clothes?"

His disciples responded: "Thou seest the multitude thronging thee, and sayest thou, Who touched me?" Little did they know that a miracle had taken place as a woman who had an "issue of blood for twelve years" touched His garment and the Savior felt "virtue had gone out of him." It was extremely important for the Savior to take the time to find the person who in great faith had touched His clothing, and when He had identified her He said: "Daughter, thy faith hath made thee whole; go in peace, and be whole of thy plague." (Mark 5:22–35.)

Daily goals and plans are extremely important in bringing order to our lives, in helping us to establish priorities, and in assisting us to use our time most efficiently, but we must be cautious that we do not "look beyond the mark" (Jacob 4:14) and become so caught up in maintaining efficient schedules that we have too little time for compassionate detours in our lives.

Patience is an important part of faith, but it is also an important part of compassion and tolerance and kindness and mercy. In the eternal scheme of things it may be much more important to develop patience with our young children, with our spouse, and with our aged parents than to play Chopin's "Minute Waltz" in less than sixty seconds.

Patience and Procrastination

Though the scriptures frequently underscore the importance of patience, there are certain areas of our lives in which patience, carried to the extreme, can be more harmful than helpful. Just as impatience can eventually lead to intolerance and unkindness, too much patience can lead to procrastination in leaving important things undone. Nephi indicted his brethren with sharpness: "Ye are swift to do iniquity but slow to remember the Lord your God" (1 Ne. 17:45).

Eli, the temple high priest, had become so patient with his wayward sons that the Lord told Samuel: "I will judge his house for ever for the iniquity which he knoweth; because his sons made themselves vile, and he restrained them not" (1 Sam. 3:13).

Alma's missionary companion, Amulek, left us a wonderful legacy of counsel regarding the establishment of priorities in the use of our time. Said Amulek: "This life is the time for men to prepare to meet God. . . . Do not procrastinate the day of your repentance . . . , if we do not improve our time while in this life, then cometh the night of darkness wherein there can be no labor performed." (Alma 34:32–33.)

There is a concern among bishops and stake presidents with certain people who seem to live their lives with a planned timetable for repentance. Young men preparing for missions often live "close to the edge" on matters of morality and the Word of Wisdom, planning to "repent" of their misdeeds in adequate time to pass their interview with the bishop. Likewise, young couples preparing for marriage sometimes intentionally plan to refrain from certain activities for a short time in order to be able to tell their bishop they are worthy to enter the temple.

Some young men and women get married outside the temple and begin to rear their families without the blessings of family prayer, scripture study, family home evening, and regular attendance at church. Then, when the children begin to leave home, the father and the mother, having grown older and wiser, begin to show an increased interest in religion. Loving home teachers and quorum leaders patiently and kindly begin to work with them, and they begin to participate in temple preparation seminars. Finally, after years of struggling, church attendance becomes regular, bad habits are laid aside, tithing is paid in full, and now they are ready to go to the temple. But the beauty of the sealing ceremony is marred by the conspicuous absence of their children, who were not reared in an active Latter-day Saint home and who have little interest in religion. Such a bittersweet experience! If only the gospel light had warmed their home twenty or thirty years earlier. Would that they had had less patience with themselves and with their inactivity during the early years when their children were still living at home.

One of the most tragic figures of the Book of Mormon is Morianton, the Jaredite king who "did do justice unto the people, but not unto himself because of his many whoredoms; wherefore he was cut off from the presence of the Lord" (Eth. 10:11).

Would that each of us could develop more patience with young children and aging parents while still retaining less patience with our own failings. Of course, too much impatience can lead to discouragement and cause us to give up and shrink from the battle, while too much patience with ourselves may be conducive to the procrastination about which Amulek warned us (see Alma 34:32–35).

There are angelic women whose wayward husbands try their patience, and some are rewarded for their endurance. I know a dear sister who had been married in the temple, and afterward her husband refused ever to return to the temple again. For thirty years she fasted one day each week that her husband's heart might be touched, and one day he decided to return to full activity in the Church, and today they are happily engaged in a good cause.

By contrast, there are men and women whose impatience with each other leads to divorce and whose impatience with their children leads to estrangement within the family.

The quest for perfection involves maintaining an appropriate amount of patience, for patience is a key ingredient in faith, hope, and charity, "and except ye have charity ye can in nowise be saved in the kingdom of God" (Moro. 10:21).

Elder Hugh B. Brown once introduced a speech with the following prayer whose authorship was unknown to him. It reflects the wisdom and mature insight gained from patiently and introspectively accepting the aging process in our lives:

> Lord, Thou knowest better than I know myself that I am growing older, and will some day be old. Keep me from the fatal habit of thinking that I must say something on every subject on every occasion. Release me from trying to straighten out everybody's affairs. Make me thoughtful, but not moody; helpful, but not bossy. With my vast store of wisdom it seems a pity not to use it, but Thou knowest, Lord, that I want a few friends left at the end. Keep my mind free from the recital of endless details, and give me wings to get to the point. Seal my lips on my aches and pains—they are increasing and love of hearing them is becoming sweeter as the years go by. I do not ask for grace enough to enjoy the tales of others of their pains, but help me to endure them with patience. I do not ask for improved memory, but for growing humility and a lessening cocksureness when my memory seems to clash with the memories of others. And teach me, O Lord, the glorious lesson that occasionally I may be mistaken. Keep me reasonably sweet. I do not want to be a saint, some of them are too hard to live with, but a sour old person is the crowning work of the devil. Give me the ability to see good things in unexpected places, and talents in unexpected people, and give me the grace to tell them so.[7]

Divine Patience

The Savior's parable of the wheat and the tares is illustrative of the divine patience which our loving Heavenly Father and His Beloved Son have for us. So significant is this parable that an entire section of the Doctrine and Covenants is devoted to unfolding its meaning. The Lord explains that the field of wheat represents the world, and the sowers of the seed are the Apostles. It is Satan who sows the tares among the wheat. And now comes the evidence of divine patience: "Behold, verily I say unto you, the angels are crying unto the Lord day and night, who are ready and waiting to be sent forth to reap down the fields; but the Lord saith unto them, pluck not up the tares while the blade is yet tender (for verily your faith is weak), lest you destroy the wheat also. Therefore, let the wheat and the tares grow together until the harvest is fully ripe; then ye shall first gather out the wheat from among the tares" (D&C 86:5–7).

Sometimes a mission president becomes impatient with an immature nineteen-year-old who does not seem to be very motivated or willing to keep mission rules or to work hard. The temptation is to send him home early. But before doing so, it would be well for the mission president to read section 86 and to reflect upon the Lord's counsel to "pluck not up the tares while the blade is yet tender (for verily your faith is weak), lest you destroy the wheat also."

Surrounding that tender blade—the missionary—may be a younger brother who is undecided about serving a mission. If the older brother is sent home early, the younger brother likely will not go on a mission. Perhaps there is a father who did not have an opportunity to serve a mission, and now his son is serving a vicarious mission for him. When the son is sent home early, the father's hopes and dreams are shattered. Likely there is a mother who prays each morning and evening, and all the day through, that her son will be protected from harm and illness and evil, and if he comes home early her heart will be broken.

Now, there certainly are times when it is better that one missionary go home early than that an entire mission become corrupted, but such decisions should be made after much, much long-suffering and patience.

Delayed Judgment Day

Outside of Paris in the city of Chartre is a beautiful cathedral noted for its beautifully preserved stained-glass windows which depict several biblical stories in detail. On a visit to this cathedral, we had a tour guide who was a very knowledgeable man and who obviously reflected a great love for the cathedral and the Bible. One of the stained-glass panels portrayed the last judgment, and the guide posed the question: "Why do you think it is that a considerable length of time passes between our death, our resurrection, and the final judgment?" He then proposed the following sobering answer to his own question: "In the Middle Ages, when this cathedral was constructed, the people believed that the judgment was delayed so as to allow time to observe the consequences of one's acts on earth. Those who had committed grievous sins would be able to see those sins played out into the third and fourth generations, and acts of kindness could likewise be compounded and imitated in subsequent generations."

This is a very solemn matter when we encounter a character flaw in our children and grandchildren, knowing that their penchant for criticism or their intolerance or their hot temper were not transmitted genetically but rather through our example. Thus, in the parable of the wheat and the tares, time is allowed to pass to permit the wheat time to become rooted in Christ, and, with time, it is hoped that the wheat can withstand the tares.

Joseph's Patient Tutelage

Divine patience is abundantly evident in the tutoring process of an embryonic prophet by the name of Joseph Smith.[8] Three and a half years passed between the First Vision in the Sacred Grove and Moroni's appearance revealing Joseph's mission to serve as an instrument in bringing forth the Book of Mormon. After that revelation on September 21, 1823, there was the long waiting period as Joseph returned to the Hill Cumorah each year for four years to examine the plates. And then, after receiving the plates in 1827, it was still not until the spring of 1830 that the Book of Mormon was published.

The preparation for the translation of the Book of Mormon, for the restoration of priesthood keys, and for the organization of the Church spanned an entire decade. But divine patience was in even greater evidence by the fact that the Father and the Son had patiently endured the Great Apostasy and the preparatory Reformation which had spanned centuries as a prelude to the Restoration and the ushering in of the dispensation of the fulness of times.

Spiritual Urgency

Notwithstanding the relationship of patience and faith, it is well to remember that, although impatience can often lead to mischief and sin, our faith is often manifest by our sense of spiritual urgency in accomplishing the tasks which the Lord has given us. Few mortal men have been given as challenging a command as that given Abraham when he was commanded to sacrifice his son Isaac. Abraham's faith in the Lord was manifest in the fact that the day after receiving that commandment "Abraham rose up early in the morning . . . and went unto the place of which God had told him" (Gen. 22:3). After receiving the commandment, Abraham did not procrastinate in attempting to fulfill it.

The angel who intervened and stayed the hand of Abraham as he was about to slay young Isaac also deserves an accolade for being trustworthy and for having ministered with a sense of spiritual urgency. My venerable former stake president, Joseph T. Bentley, once asked a group of college students what would have happened if they had been the angel dispatched to restrain the hand of Abraham. With our penchant toward procrastination or our lack of punctuality, would we have said in typical fashion, "Oh no, Tuesday morning at eight o'clock—it just slipped my mind"?

From the Book of Mormon we have the example of Alma, who had been cast out of the city of Ammonihah after the people had "withstood all his words, and reviled him, and spit upon him" (Alma 8:13). But then an angel appeared commanding him to "return to the city of Ammonihah, and preach again unto the people of the city." Despite the unfriendly treatment he had received at the hands of the residents of Ammonihah, "he returned speedily" (Alma 8:18). The demonstration of our consecration to a sacred task is found not only in our performing the task eventually but also in doing our duty when it needs to be done.

Urgent Completion of the Nauvoo Temple

As the bullet-riddled bodies of Joseph and Hyrum Smith were brought from Carthage back to Nauvoo, it was apparent even then that the persecution of the Saints would once again drive them from their homes. As early as August 6, 1842, the Prophet Joseph had prophesied that the Saints would build a mighty kingdom in the "midst of the Rocky Mountains";[9] and now at the end of June 1844 the Saints had lost their beloved Prophet, and plans would be made to move westward. But before they left Nauvoo "the Beautiful" they urgently needed to finish the temple so they could receive the Lord's promised blessings (see D&C 124:37–41). The Lord had posed the question: "How shall your washings be acceptable unto me, except ye perform them in a house which you have built to my name?" (D&C 124:37.)

In November of 1845 the members of the Church were faced with two very urgent challenges: First, completing the temple, and second, the making of preparations to leave their homes, pack their wagons, and move westward. Brigham Young, as President of the Quorum of the Twelve, personally assisted in making the temple ready for dedication, and on November 30, 1845, he dedicated the attic story of the temple for the performance of endowments.[10]

On December 10, 1845, thirty persons received their endowments. This first session began at 4:25 P.M. and lasted until 3:30 A.M.[11] Eleven hours to receive the endowment! (And sometimes we complain when we have to wait half an hour.) The whole endowment ceremony was new both to temple workers and to recipients, but with experience the time was shortened each day, and on December 15 sixty-four brothers and sisters received their endowments.

Each day, more and more people came to the temple, and so important was this work that 122 people were endowed on Christmas Eve, 107 on Christmas Day, and 268 on the day after. The work continued each and every day with an ever-increasing sense of urgency.

On January 11, 1846, the Council of the Twelve began making final arrangements to leave Nauvoo and to move west. On January 20 Brigham Young wrote that there was so much public prejudice against the Saints that the temple ordinances were administered day and night.[12]

Tuesday, February 3, Brigham Young recorded the following:

> Notwithstanding that I had announced that we would not attend to the administration of the ordinances, the House of the Lord was thronged all day. . . . But I informed the brethren . . . that we should build more Temples, and have further opportunities to receive the blessings of the Lord, as soon as the saints were prepared to receive them. In this Temple we have been abundantly rewarded, if we receive

> no more. I also informed the brethren that I was going to get my wagons started and be off. I walked some distance from the Temple supposing the crowd would disperse, but on returning I found the house filled to overflowing.
>
> Looking upon the multitude and knowing their anxiety, as they were thirsting and hungering for the word, we continued at work diligently in the House of the Lord.
>
> Two hundred and ninety-five persons received ordinances.[13]

On February 4, Brother Brigham recorded: "I continued loading up my wagons preparatory to starting west."[14]

On February 6, 512 members received their endowments, and the next day upwards of 600 people received theirs.[15]

At 3:20 P.M. on February 9 the roof of the temple was discovered to be on fire. President Young wrote: "I saw the flames from a distance, . . . and I said if it is the will of the Lord that the Temple be burned, instead of being defiled by the Gentiles, Amen to it."[16]

From these brief two months of Church history we learn the following important lessons:

First, that ordinances are far more important than buildings. As beautiful as each of the temples may be, the building is not as important as the ordinances performed therein.

Second, that no unclean persons should be permitted to come into the holy house of the Lord and pollute it (see D&C 109:20).

Third, there is a great urgency in this wonderful work as reflected in the words quoted by Moroni during each of his four visits to the Prophet Joseph in September 1823: "Behold, I will reveal unto you the Priesthood, by the hand of Elijah the prophet, before the coming of the great and dreadful day of the Lord. . . . And he shall plant in the hearts of the children the promises made to the fathers, and the hearts of the children shall turn to their fathers. If it were not so, the whole earth would be utterly wasted at his coming." (JS–H 1:38–39.)

The spirit of Elijah is seldom more evident than when children are being sealed to their parents in the house of the Lord. But the promises planted in the hearts of the children must continue to be patiently nourished so that the spirit of Elijah is found in the kitchens and the nurseries of our homes as well as in the temple. Family home evening, family prayer, and family scripture study all help to nourish the promises planted in the hearts of our children.[17]

Patience, Punctuality, and Goodwill

Related to spiritual urgency is the need to maintain a balance between patience, punctuality, and goodwill. Within the Church we have a great system of accountability, especially with regard to financial reports and ward and branch activity reports. When such reports are not punctually filled out and returned by one branch or ward clerk, the stake records fall in arrears, and if such were the case in each stake of Zion, we would have little knowledge of the actual innerworkings of the kingdom. We would have no idea whether the Saints were really being spiritually fed and whether sacred funds were being shepherded as they should.

But sometimes a ward clerk, through a wide variety of reasons, is not punctual in submitting an important report, and this becomes an excellent opportunity for a bishop, a stake clerk, and a stake president to learn and practice the perfect balance between patience, punctuality, and goodwill. Keeping records and submitting them in a timely fashion is extremely important, but we must also not forget that the worth of a ward clerk's soul "is great in the sight of God" (D&C 18:10). Providing encouragement and needed assistance several days before the report is due is far preferable to castigation after the due date, since the latter tends to breed resentment, discouragement, and eventual inactivity.

If I may be so bold as to confess my personal sins in public, I learned a very painful lesson regarding punctuality and goodwill while serving as a mission president in Austria several years ago. One of our zones in southern Austria was divided by a large mountain with a dozen missionaries on one side and another dozen on the other side. To equalize travel costs, we alternated between holding the meetings in Graz one month and Klagenfurt the next month. Whenever the meetings were held in Graz, the Klagenfurt missionaries would catch the 6:30 A.M. train in order to arrive at the Graz chapel by 9 A.M. Approximately the same schedule would be followed when the Graz missionaries traveled to Klagenfurt.

One morning we had gathered in the Klagenfurt chapel to begin our zone conference, but the Graz missionaries did not arrive on time. I became irritated at their lack of punctuality. It was obvious that someone had overslept and they had missed the 6:30 train. When they finally arrived, after having caught the next train an hour later, instead of welcoming them with the love and relief of a concerned father I chastened the tardy missionaries in front of their peers. This was the only zone conference during a period of three years where the Spirit of the Lord was not present in rich abundance. Instead, there was a spirit of discouragement, for they had incurred the wrath of their mission president. I have never forgotten that lesson, and I hope those wonderful missionaries have forgiven me. We never again had the problem of missionaries arriving late, but at what great cost!

Patience is the principle undergirding the Lord's counsel on bringing about change in others through "persuasion, by long-suffering, by gentleness and meekness, and by love unfeigned" (D&C 121:41).

Notwithstanding the need to carry out the Lord's work with a sense of spiritual urgency, patience must temper reprisals for a lack of punctuality. The Epistle to the Hebrews describes the balance well: "Let us run with patience the race that is set before us" (Heb. 12:1). Long-distance runners know much more about running with patience than sprinters do. Unlike those who excel in the hundred-yard dash, mile runners must patiently measure their energy and allocate it evenly throughout the race, lest they set a record for the fastest first lap and then fail to finish the last lap.

As priesthood leaders and parents, as mission presidents, as teachers and Scoutmasters, as nursery teachers, and ward choir directors, as home teachers and visiting teachers, we must ever remember to run the race, but we need to run with patience. Even the Son of God "received not of the fulness at first, but continued from grace to grace, until he received a fulness" (D&C 93:13).

I must confess my impatience at the slow pace of nature as we moved into our home more than two decades ago. We planted various trees and shrubs which seemed at the time to be extremely fragile and slow in growing. We were particularly anxious to grow a privet hedge around our yard. To accelerate the process, I very frequently spread large amounts of fertilizer on the tiny hedge. Unfortunately, my good intentions to encourage faster growth killed the hedge as the hot summer sun combined with the fertilizer to burn the tender plants.

There is the apocryphal account of the chicken farmer who sought to reduce the incubation time of baby chicks from the normal twenty-one days to nineteen days. He reasoned that if he began to crack the shells at nineteen days the baby chicks would have a much easier time fighting their way out of their shells, and the extra two days would increase his productivity by nearly 10 percent. But, alas, nature's timetable is rather fixed in such matters. By robbing the chicks of those two extra days and by trying to make their entry into the world much easier, the chicken farmer deprived them of the very necessary experience of persistently pecking their way through the eggshell to freedom. The baby chicks all died.

His Work and His Glory

Certain kinds of growth must simply occur in the process of time, but sometimes home teaching and missionary work can be transformed from *His* work and *His* glory to *our* work and *our* glory as names behind the numbers become ends in themselves rather than means to long-range spiritual goals. The Apostle Paul was well aware of this unfortunate tendency in many of us as he admonished the Philippians to "let nothing be done through strife [or competition] or vainglory" (Philip. 2:3). He observed that "some indeed preach Christ even of envy and strife; and some also of good will: the one preach Christ of contention, not sincerely, . . . the other of love" (Philip. 1:15–17).

Paul himself was imbued with a sense of spiritual urgency as he admonished the Corinthians: "Know ye not that they which run in a race run all, but one receiveth the prize? So run, that ye may obtain." (1 Cor. 9:24.) But in the very next verse he added: "And every man that striveth for the mastery is temperate in all things" (1 Cor. 9:25). Perhaps the proper balance between patience and urgency is captured best in Hebrews 12:1–2, cited previously: "Let us *run with patience* the race that is set before us, looking unto Jesus the author and finisher of our faith" (emphasis added).

May we all strive to soften our hearts so that we might be more receptive to the Lord's divine guidance and also be more sensitive to his holy purposes through pursuing our spiritual goals with the faith and patience of Enoch, who was 430 years old when he was finally translated (see D&C 107:48). The Lord's promise is sure: "In your patience possess ye your souls" (Luke 21:19).

Notes

1. Joseph Fielding Smith, *Answers to Gospel Questions*, comp. and ed. Joseph Fielding Smith, Jr., 5 vols. (Salt Lake City: Deseret Book Co., 1957–66), 2:36.

2. See Steven J. Danish, "Learning Life Lessons by Setting Goals in Sports," *New York Times*, Sept. 25, 1983, p. S2.

3. See *History of the Church* 3: 387; hereafter cited as *HC*.

4. *HC* 5:392.

5. Neal A. Maxwell, in Conference Report, October 1976, p. 16.

6. Maxwell, in Conference Report, October 1976, p. 14.

7. Quoted in Hugh B. Brown, *The Abundant Life*, (Salt Lake City: Bookcraft, 1965), p. 84.

8. For an excellent discussion of the tutoring process, see H. Donl Peterson, "Moroni— Joseph Smith's Tutor," *Ensign* 22 (January 1992): 22–29.

9. *HC* 5:85.

10. See *HC* 7:534.

11. See *HC* 7:542–43.

12. See *HC* 7:570.

13. *HC* 7:579.

14. *HC* 7:580.

15. See *HC* 7:580.

16. *HC* 7:581.

17. The section in this chapter on the Nauvoo Temple is a revision of remarks given at the rededication of the Swiss Temple, October 23, 1992.

Chapter Two

MERCY AND JUSTICE

The mission president had driven a considerable distance to interview a married couple who were contemplating baptism. They had previously been involved in a very serious transgression which came to light during the district leader's interview, and he felt inclined to invite the mission president to also interview the couple involved. He would determine if, after having learned of the restored gospel, they understood the seriousness of the transgression and had truly repented.

After listening to their account of a decision which they had made hastily and had painfully regretted ever since, the mission president felt inclined to approve their baptism. They knew they had committed a grievous sin, and now, after having acquired additional light and knowledge, their hearts were truly broken and their spirits contrite. In fact, the president was concerned that the couple in question seemed unwilling to accept the fact that they could *ever* be forgiven, even after their baptism. The truths of the plan of salvation which they had recently learned caused great anxiety and guilt, rather than filling their hearts with hope and joy. It seemed to the mission president that, even though they might be forgiven of the Lord, they could not forgive themselves.

Together they began to read in the Gospel of Luke the account of the Savior's visit to the house of Simon, one of the Pharisees. As Jesus was seated at the dinner table a woman who was known to be a sinner "began to wash his feet with tears, and did wipe them with the hairs of her head, and kissed his feet, and anointed them with the ointment" (Luke 7:38).

The host, Simon, thought to himself: "This man, if he were a prophet, would have known who and what manner of woman this is that touched him: for she is a sinner" (Luke 7:39). Then Jesus, discerning the thoughts of Simon, said:

> There was a certain creditor which had two debtors: the one owed five hundred pence, and the other fifty.
>
> And when they had nothing to pay, he frankly forgave them both. Tell me therefore, which of them will love him most?
>
> Simon answered and said, I suppose that he, to whom he forgave most. And he said unto him, Thou hast rightly judged.
>
> And he turned to the woman, and said unto Simon, Seest thou this woman? I entered into thine house, thou gavest me no water for my feet: but she hath washed my feet with tears, and wiped them with the hairs of her head.
>
> Thou gavest me no kiss: but this woman since the time I came in hath not ceased to kiss my feet.
>
> My head with oil thou didst not anoint: but this woman hath anointed my feet with ointment.
>
> Wherefore I say unto thee, Her sins, which are many, are forgiven; for she loved much: but to whom little is forgiven, the same loveth little.
>
> And he said unto her, Thy sins are forgiven.
>
> And they that sat at meat with him began to say within themselves, Who is this that forgiveth sins also?
>
> And he said to the woman, Thy faith hath saved thee; go in peace. (Luke 7:41–50.)

After a long pause to contemplate the message they had read together, the mission president looked into the tear-stained faces of the guilt-ridden baptismal candidates. "I have driven all the way from the mission home some distance from here, just to reassure you that your Heavenly Father loves you, and that His Only Begotten Son suffered for your sins if you will but repent and be baptized and continue to keep His commandments."

The tears were dried, and a few days later this fine couple was baptized. They had brought forth the fruits of repentance, a contrite spirit and a broken heart, and they were beginning to experience a mighty change of heart which would help them escape from the self-inflicted bondage and pain which they had experienced for the past four years. Had mercy robbed justice? Shouldn't they have to suffer longer for their sins?

The Savior himself declared: "For behold, I God, have suffered these things for all, that they might not suffer if they would repent; But if they would not repent they must suffer even as I; which suffering caused myself, even God, the greatest of all, to tremble because of pain, and to bleed at every pore, and to suffer both body and spirit" (D&C 19:16–18).

"Being filled with compassion towards the children of men; standing betwixt them and justice" (Mosiah 15:9), the Savior, through His atoning sacrifice, brought the scales of justice back into balance for the children of men upon condition of their sincere and complete repentance. The Savior's promise is very explicit. He suffered, "that they might not suffer *if* they would repent; but *if* they would *not* repent they must suffer even as I."

Nevertheless . . .

President Howard W. Hunter has reminded us that the element of free agency runs like a golden thread throughout the entire plan of salvation.[1] Moral agency was the deciding factor between the two opposing plans presented in the premortal Council in Heaven. Satan's plan was one of no choice, no risk, no growth, and no opportunity to become like our Heavenly Father. The Father's plan fulfilled by the Savior granted us freedom of choice and endless opportunities for growth, notwithstanding the possibility of our making many mistakes and committing many sins.

Moral agency, as discussed in that premortal council, was introduced to man on earth through our first parents, Adam and Eve, as they were placed in the Garden of Eden. The Lord commanded them: "Of every tree of the garden thou mayest freely eat, but of the tree of the knowledge of good and evil, thou shalt not eat of it, *nevertheless*, thou mayest choose for thyself, for it is given unto thee; but, remember that I forbid it, for in the day thou eatest thereof thou shalt surely die" (Moses 3:16–17, emphasis added).

I am so grateful that a loving Heavenly Father included this important "nevertheless" in his instruction to Adam and Eve, for

> if Adam had not transgressed he would not have fallen, but he would have remained in the garden of Eden. And all things which were created must have remained forever, and had no end.

> And they would have had no children; wherefore they would have remained in a state of innocence, having no joy, for they knew no misery; doing no good, for they knew no sin. . . .
>
> Adam fell that men might be; and men are, that they might have joy. (2 Ne. 2:22–23, 25.)

The prophet Alma further expanded our knowledge of the purpose of our mortal existence and our moral agency:

> And we see that death comes upon mankind, yea, the death which has been spoken of by Amulek, which is the temporal death; *nevertheless* there was a space granted unto man in which he might repent; therefore this life became a probationary state; a time to prepare to meet God; a time to prepare for that endless state which has been spoken of by us, which is after the resurrection of the dead (Alma 12:24, emphasis added).

In the premortal council, the Savior agreed to fulfill the Father's plan to come to earth and to take upon Himself the sins of the world. As the hour drew near for the Savior to atone for our sins, He came to a place called Gethsemane, and He "began to be sore amazed, and to be very heavy," and He said, "My soul is exceedingly sorrowful unto death" (Mark 14:33–34). He then pleaded with the Father: "Father, if thou be willing, remove this cup from me: *nevertheless* not my will, but thine be done" (Luke 22:42, emphasis added). The divine answer of His Father required that He go through this excruciating ordeal, but in the next verse we read: "And there appeared an angel unto him from heaven, strengthening him" (Luke 22:43).

Sometimes in our personal lives, we, too, pray that the bitter cups—and sometimes gallon jugs—may be removed, but if we are to become like the Savior, then we, too, must have experiences similar to His. If we are ever to overcome the natural man, we must be "willing to submit to all things which the Lord seeth fit to inflict upon [us], even as a child doth submit to his father" (Mosiah 3:19). And through it all, His promise is sure: "I will not leave you comfortless" (John 14:18).

Again, I am grateful for the Savior's "nevertheless" in the Garden of Gethsemane for the reasons explained by Amulek in the Book of Mormon:

> And thus he shall bring salvation to all those who shall believe on his name; this being the intent of this last sacrifice, to bring about the bowels of mercy, which overpowereth justice, and bringeth about means unto men that they may have faith unto repentance.
>
> And thus mercy can satisfy the demands of justice, and encircles them in the arms of safety, while he that exercises no faith unto repentance is exposed to the whole law of the demands of justice; therefore only unto him that has faith unto repentance is brought about the great and eternal plan of redemption. (Alma 34:15–16.)

Section 1 of the Doctrine and Covenants "is the Lord's Preface to the revelations which He has given to this Dispensation of the Fulness of Times."[2] The purpose of a preface to any book is to prepare one's mind for the information one is about to read. Thus, the messages of this prefatory section are extremely important as a "voice of warning" given to all the earth's inhabitants. It was actually received after sections 2 through 66 had been revealed. In verse 31 of section 1 the Lord gives us a particularly sober warning: "For I the Lord cannot look upon sin with the least degree of allowance; . . ."

If this were the end of the scripture, there would be virtually no hope for me because of the many sins I have committed during my half century on this earth. If there were no allowance for sin, I would fall hopelessly short of ever attaining eternal life. However, this scripture ends with a *semicolon* rather than a *period*, and so the next verse continues: "*Nevertheless*, he that repents and does the commandments of the Lord shall be forgiven" (D&C 1:32).

Once again, that wonderfully important "nevertheless" to our rescue!

The Lord explains how we might avail ourselves of the Atonement in our lives: "Behold, he who has repented of his sins, the same is forgiven, and I, the Lord, remember them no more. By this ye may know if a man repenteth of his sins—behold, he will confess them and forsake them." (D&C 58:42–43.)

In *The Miracle of Forgiveness*, President Spencer W. Kimball outlines in great detail how each of us may partake of the Savior's loving atonement, a blessing founded on our realizing full well "that it is by grace we are saved, after all we can do" (2 Ne. 25:23). And there is so much that we can do and should do to demonstrate our gratitude for our moral agency, for the atonement of Christ, for the opportunity to make mistakes and still gain forgiveness of our sins. If we are to become partakers of the Savior's mercy, then we, too, must become more merciful to others.

The Unmerciful Servant

The spirit of the Atonement and the judicious balance between justice and mercy is captured well in the Savior's parable of the unmerciful servant. This parable had been prompted by Peter's question: "Lord, how oft shall my brother sin against me, and I forgive him? till seven times?" You will, of course, recall the Savior's answer: "I say not unto thee, Until seven times: but, Until seventy times seven." (Matt. 18:21–22.)

Typical of the Master Teacher, Jesus then proceeded to unfold the following profound parable:

> Therefore is the kingdom of heaven likened unto a certain king, which would take account of his servants.
>
> And when he had begun to reckon, one was brought unto him, which owed him ten thousand talents.
>
> But forasmuch as he had not to pay, his lord commanded him to be sold, and his wife, and children, and all that he had, and payment to be made.
>
> The servant therefore fell down, and worshipped him, saying, Lord, have patience with me, and I will pay thee all.
>
> Then the lord of that servant was moved with compassion, and loosed him, and forgave him the debt.
>
> But the same servant went out, and found one of his fellowservants, which owed him an hundred pence: and he laid hands on him, and took him by the throat, saying, Pay me that thou owest.
>
> And his fellowservant fell down at his feet, and besought him, saying, Have patience with me, and I will pay thee all.
>
> And he would not: but went and cast him into prison, till he should pay the debt.
>
> So when his fellowservants saw what was done, they were very sorry, and came and told unto their lord all that was done.
>
> Then his lord, after that he had called him, said unto him, O thou wicked servant, I forgave thee all that debt, because thou desiredst me:
>
> Shouldest not thou also have had compassion on thy fellowservant, even as I had pity on thee?
>
> And his lord was wroth, and delivered him to the tormentors, till he should pay all that was due unto him.

So likewise shall my heavenly Father do also unto you, if ye from your hearts forgive not every one his brother their trespasses. (Matt. 18:23–35.)

In latter-day revelation the Lord reiterated the main point of this parable when he said: "I the Lord will forgive whom I will forgive, but of you it is required to forgive all men" (D&C 64:10). We cannot expect to gain forgiveness for our sins against the Lord if we are unable to forgive those who have trespassed against us.

It is very easy to discuss forgiveness as an abstract principle, but when one has been bilked out of one's life's savings, or been the object of an unjust lawsuit, or been the victim of untrue gossip, or become the physically handicapped victim of an accident caused by a drunken driver, or been the victim of child abuse, then forgiveness is no longer an ethereal, abstract principle. It is then that the requirements of the Atonement, the tempering of justice with mercy, can have a great impact in our lives in freeing us from the bondage of hatred and revenge by cleansing our souls through the miracle of forgiveness.

The Prophet Joseph's Magnanimous Heart

There are few individuals who suffered more for the sake of the kingdom of God than the Prophet Joseph Smith. His perpetual persecution began shortly after receiving the First Vision while only in his fifteenth year, and this persecution continued without surcease for the next two dozen years, culminating in his martyrdom.

Although the Saints had settled in Nauvoo, and notwithstanding their submission to the extermination and expulsion orders of Governor Boggs of Missouri, there were still those living in Missouri whose venomous hatred would not be satisfied. One such man was Joseph H. Reynolds, the sheriff of Jackson County. In June of 1843 Reynolds conspired with another mean-spirited man, Harmon T. Wilson, the constable in Carthage, Illinois, to arrest the Prophet Joseph Smith while he was visiting the Saints in Dixon, Illinois.

In describing his surprise arrest, the Prophet wrote that Constable Wilson "accosted me in a very uncouth, ungentlemanly manner, when Reynolds stepped up to me, collared me, then both of them presented cocked pistols to my breast, without showing any writ or serving any process." Reynolds then began assailing the Prophet with vile profanity, threatening to shoot him.

The Prophet's narrative continues: "They then hurried me off, put me in a wagon without serving any process, and were for hurrying me off without letting me see or bid farewell to my family or friends. . . . They still continued their punching me on both sides with their pistols. . . . The officers held their pistols with the muzzles jamming into my side for more than eight miles." This abusive treatment of continually punching Joseph's sides severely bruised the Prophet's flesh "about eighteen inches in circumference on each side."[3]

Through an appeal to the people in Dixon, the Prophet was successful in obtaining a writ of habeas corpus "granted by the Master in Chancery at Dixon [which] was made returnable to the nearest court having jurisdiction," which just happened to be Nauvoo.[4] When the Prophet and his ill-tempered escorts arrived in Nauvoo, the Prophet invited them to dine with his family and about fifty of his friends. Reynolds and Wilson were invited to be seated at the head of the table while Emma served them "the best that the table afforded."[5]

The hospitality of Joseph and Emma stood in sharp contrast to the treatment these unruly men had given a prophet of God. Nevertheless, Joseph lived the gospel that he preached (see 1 Cor. 9:14). He believed and exemplified the Savior's teachings in the Sermon on the Mount: "Love your enemies, bless them that curse you, do good to them that hate you, and pray for them which despitefully use you, and persecute you. . . . For if ye love them which love you, what reward have ye? do not even the publicans the same?" (Matt. 5:44, 46.)

Annaroesli Birsfelder

While living in Germany we became acquainted with a marvelous couple from Switzerland, Brother and Sister Birsfelder. They had served in the Swiss Temple and later served missions at the visitors' center in Freiberg and in the Frankfurt Temple, and Brother Georg Birsfelder had been a counselor in the temple presidency in the Swiss and Frankfurt temples.

In February 1991 after the end of their temple shift, Brother and Sister Birsfelder were taking a little stroll together down one of the little streets in Friedrichsdorf near the Frankfurt Temple. All of a sudden an elderly man drove his car around the street corner, over the curb, and onto the sidewalk where the Birsfelders were walking. The momentum of the car hurled Sister Birsfelder through a thick plate-glass door of a store. She was very critically injured and was rushed to the hospital, where she was treated for a double skull fracture, a severe concussion, and a severely injured eye.

For seven weeks she lay in a coma, totally unaware of her surroundings. Her loyal husband stayed at her bedside patting her hand gently and speaking to her in softened tones of love and encouragement. Though many of us feared the worst, we were heartened by Brother Birsfelder's faith and undaunted optimism. Finally she opened her eyes. At eight weeks she could begin to speak and sit up and eat solid food. We visited her in the hospital ten weeks after the accident, and she could stand up and take a few steps and could converse in English, German, and French. It was a miracle! Our prayers had been answered.

She still experienced considerable pain, and it was apparent that she had permanently lost the sight of her right eye. Three months after the accident, the careless driver of the car came to visit her in the hospital. Filled with anxiety and fear of legal reprisals, he looked at Sister Birsfelder in her hospital bed and asked: "Do you hate me for what I have done to you?" He was not prepared for her reply. She returned the question: "Do you know who I am? I am a Mormon. In our religion we learn to love one another. I am convinced you didn't intentionally harm me. I am glad I am still alive for your sake, because if I had been killed, the burden would have been awful for you. No," she said, "I don't hate you. I love you and forgive you and feel sorry for you."

This elderly man had a heavy burden lifted that day, for he knew that his erratic driving had nearly cost a human life. But now he had received forgiveness from the person he had seriously injured. He was so relieved he went to the minister of the local Huguenot church in Friedrichsdorf and told him of the magnanimous heart of Sister Birsfelder. For various reasons, there had been some tension between the Huguenot citizens of Friedrichsdorf and the Mormons who frequently came on bus excursions to visit the Frankfurt Temple. It was a little irritating to some of the neighbors to have so many strangers visit their little village so often. The Huguenot minister told his congregation of Sister Birsfelder's forgiving heart, and how this dear Latter-day Saint sister had been an example to all of us by tempering justice with mercy. Now relations between the Mormons and the Huguenots are excellent, in large part because of Sister Birsfelder.

If

Though poetry is not scripture, there are many poets whose insights, eloquently expressed, inspire us to better our lives. One such example is Rudyard Kipling's classic poem which captures well the principles of mercy and enduring to the end:

If—

If you can keep your head when all about you
Are losing theirs and blaming it on you;
If you can trust yourself when all men doubt you
But make allowance for their doubting too;
If you can wait and not be tired by waiting,
Or, being lied about, don't deal in lies,
Or, being hated, don't give way to hating,
And yet don't look too good, nor talk too wise;

If you can dream—and not make dreams your master;
If you can think—and not make thoughts your aim;
If you can meet with triumph and disaster
And treat those two imposters just the same;
If you can bear to hear the truth you've spoken
Twisted by knaves to make a trap for fools,
Or watch the things you gave your life to, broken
And stoop and build 'em up with wornout tools;

If you can make one heap of all your winnings
And risk it on one turn of pitch-and-toss,
And lose, and start again at your beginnings
And never breathe a word about your loss;
If you can force your heart and nerve and sinew
To serve your turn long after they are gone,
And so hold on when there is nothing in you
Except the Will which says to them: "Hold on!";

If you can talk with crowds and keep your virtue,
Or walk with kings—nor lose the common touch;
If neither foes nor loving friends can hurt you;
If all men count with you, but none too much;
If you can fill the unforgiving minute
With sixty seconds' worth of distance run—
Yours is the Earth and everything that's in it,
And—which is more—you'll be a Man, my son![6]

The Miracle of Forgiveness

In this dispensation the Lord has revealed that in the ordinances of the priesthood, "the power of godliness is manifest. And without the ordinances thereof, and the authority of the priesthood, the power of godliness is not manifest unto men in the flesh." (D&C 84:20–21.)

The ordinances of the priesthood serve to link heaven and earth as covenants are made and renewed and priesthood power is manifest or demonstrated to mortal men on earth. The Prophet Joseph taught that the atonement of Jesus Christ is the fundamental, central principle of the entire gospel, and that "all other things which pertain to our religion are only appendages to it."[7] It is noteworthy that the Atonement also lies at the heart of many of the sacred ordinances of the gospel. For example, the Apostle Paul taught the Romans that the ordinance of baptism by immersion symbolizes the death and resurrection of Christ. "If [through baptism] we have been planted together in the likeness of his death, we shall be also in the likeness of his resurrection: knowing this, that our old man is crucified with him, that the body of sin might be destroyed, that henceforth we should not serve sin" (Rom. 6:5–6). At the heart of baptism is the miracle of forgiveness: "Though [our] sins be as scarlet, they shall be as white as snow" (Isa. 1:18).

When we participate in the ordinance of the sacrament, once again the Atonement is at the center. As we drink of the water, we commemorate the drops of blood shed for us in Gethsemane by Him who was the source of the living water (see John 4:10–14). As we partake of the broken bread, we commemorate the broken body, hung upon the cross, of Him who testified, "I am that bread of life" (John 6:48).

When the elders bless the sick through the power of the priesthood, the person who is ill is anointed with a few golden drops of pure, consecrated olive oil. And why do we use olive oil to anoint the sick and afflicted? At the very close of his earthly ministry Jesus took with him Peter, James, and John to a garden which in Hebrew is called *Gathshemanim*, the place of the oil press. To extract the oil from the olive takes tremendous pressure, and it was in Gethsemane that the weight of your sins and mine exerted such great pressure that even the Son of God bled from every pore. These tiny drops of golden liquid can be seen as symbolizing the Atonement and its power to heal.

Marriage in the temple, the sealing of a couple for time and all eternity, is an ordinance so sacred we cannot discuss it in any detail outside of the house of the Lord. But once again, as a couple kneel across the altar from each other, the Atonement, the miracle of forgiveness, lies at the center of this ordinance. And the miracle of forgiveness is found in every happy, successful, eternal marriage and in the center of every happy family. If we wish to be forgiven of our sins, we must be readily willing to forgive our marriage partners, our children, and our parents of their offenses toward us.

The Spirit of "Nevertheless"

Although there was a great risk involved in giving us our moral agency, *nevertheless* all the children of a loving Heavenly Father can be free "to act for themselves and not to be acted upon" (2 Ne. 2:26). We have been given magnificent examples of men and women who have undergone great hardships in life but who, *nevertheless*, have remained true to the faith. The ultimate example was the Savior's suffering in Gethsemane and on the cross at Calvary.

We also gain courage from accounts of the trials and tribulations of those great missionaries, Paul and Alma. In our own dispensation we are inspired by the Prophet Joseph's prayerful endurance in Liberty Jail and by the faith of the survivors of the Willie and Martin handcart companies. We are heartened by the perseverance of modern prophets and Apostles who, notwithstanding the observable weakening of their physical tabernacles, *nevertheless* persist in doing the work of the Lord to the very limits of their physical strength and energy.

"Nevertheless" can and should have a powerful, positive impact upon our thoughts and actions. For example:

I am very busy this month; *nevertheless*, I will find time to visit the temple.

I am going on vacation this month; *nevertheless*, I will assure that my families are carefully home taught.

Our family budget is a bit tight during this time of the year; *nevertheless*, I will pay an honest tithing and a generous fast offering.

I feel very tired and would like to spend some time alone just relaxing; *nevertheless*, my family needs my attention and care.

Our young children tend to try my patience; *nevertheless*, I will give them the love and attention and tolerance they deserve.

I would like to retire near a golf course and play a few rounds of golf each day; *nevertheless*, my wife and I are pleased to serve a mission for the Lord.

I would rather persist in my unrelenting sense of justice and in my lengthy list of prejudices, grievances, and grudges; *nevertheless*, I will overcome them that I might be filled with Christlike love, "that when he shall appear [I] shall be like him, . . . that [I] may be purified even as he is pure" (Moro. 7:48).

And how can we acquire this Christlike love? Mormon tells us we must "pray unto the Father with all the energy of heart, that [we] may be filled with this love" (Moro. 7:48).

Chief Blue

Sometimes it is difficult to realize what is required by "all the energy of heart," but Chief Sam Blue learned that lesson well. Sam had joined the Church as a young man, and through hard work and keeping the commandments he won the admiration and respect of many of his friends among the Catawba Indians in North Carolina. Eventually he was elected to be the chief or tribal chairman of the Catawbas.

One day, as Chief Blue drove into town to buy groceries for the family, some of the Catawba young men invited Sam Blue's ten-year-old son to accompany them on a squirrel hunt. His son's job was to climb the tree and scare the squirrels onto the extremities of the branches where the other young men could shoot them down with their shotguns.

The young men were having a great time together and were having a good deal of success, but one of the young men was especially jealous of Chief Blue's position and tribal authority. It was he who suggested that Sam's little boy climb up into the tree and flush out the squirrels, but just as the little boy was climbing down from the tree this young man opened fire on the lad and filled him with buckshot from his groin to his chin.

Two of the young men laid the limp little body in the shade of the tree, another young man ran for the doctor, and still another ran into town to fetch Chief Blue. As he arrived in town he shouted, "Sam, you've got to come home. Your son has been shot." Sam's first reaction was that it was one of his older married sons who had been hurt, but when he arrived at the scene he found his little boy's nearly lifeless body. The physician arrived at about the same time, and he said, "Sam, there's very little I can do. He has lost so much blood and the injuries are so severe, all I can do is give him a shot of morphine to ease the pain. He won't last long."

The doctor was right. Within a few minutes this brave little warrior slipped to the other side, and Sam tenderly carried him back home in his arms. As he arrived home a large crowd had gathered to offer their condolences to the Blue family. But above the crowd Sam could hear the raucous voice of the young man who had pulled the trigger on his son. His voice had no sympathy. In fact, it was almost as if he were bragging or making light of his deathly deed. At that moment Sam Blue seemed to hear a voice within his head: "Sam, if you do not avenge the death of your son, you are a coward."

Sam had been a member of the Church for many years, and he knew that killing the young man who shot his son would be a grievous sin, even if under tribal law it might be permissible under these circumstances. Sam laid his son's body on the bed and then excused himself to retire to a little forest not far away where he often went to pray and meditate about tribal matters. He knelt down and asked Heavenly Father to please remove these unclean and unkind feelings of hatred and revenge from his heart.

After a period of time he felt much better, so he arose from his knees and returned home, but as soon as he spied the young man who had killed his son, he again heard that voice: "Sam Blue, you're a coward." A second time he went back to his private grove of trees and poured out his heart to the Lord. After a while he again felt better and he returned home. But once again, as soon as he set eyes on his son's malefactor his heart and mind overflowed with feelings of vengeance and hatred.

A third time he returned to the forest, and this time he prayed with all the energy of his heart that a loving Heavenly Father might remove his feelings of hurt and revenge and hatred. He stayed on his knees a long, long time, but eventually he felt a sweet Spirit distill upon him, the cleansing, purifying, comforting Spirit of the Holy Ghost, and soon his heart was filled with love.

Chief Blue returned home a third time, and as he saw the man who shot his son he extended his hand and said: "I forgive you, and I love you." Had mercy robbed justice? I think not, for that day Chief Sam Blue became a free man, free from hatred and vengeful feelings, and that day as his heart became purified he became a little more like the Savior.[8]

Mormon admonished us not only to pray to *have* love in our hearts, but also to pray that our hearts would be *filled* with love (see Moro. 7:47–49). Indeed, in this dispensation the Lord has revealed that "no one can assist in this work except he shall be humble and full of love" (D&C 12:8). A heart filled with love has no room for hatred, envy, discouragement, or revenge, because a heart full of love is full.

Notes

1. See Howard W. Hunter, "The Golden Thread of Choice," *Ensign* 19 (November 1989): 17–18.

2. *History of the Church* 1:222; hereafter cited as *HC*.

3. *HC* 5:439–42.

4. *HC* 5:461.

5. *HC* 5:460.

6. Rudyard Kipling, "If—," in *The Golden Treasury of Poetry*, ed. Louis Untermeyer (New York: Golden Press, 1959), p. 314.

7. *HC* 3:30.

8. See Marion G. Romney, *The Power of God unto Salvation*, Brigham Young University Speeches of the Year (Provo, 3 February 1960), p. 6.

Chapter Three

FAITH AND WORKS

Life Is a Stage

In two of Shakespeare's plays he reiterates the metaphor that life, the world, is a stage. In one of those plays a character states, "All the world's a stage,"[1] and in the other another character observes that the world is "a stage, where every man must play a part."[2] It may be illustrative to continue this metaphor in comparing our lives to a three-act play. Act 1 occurred in the presence of our Heavenly Father, where we, as His spiritual offspring, participated in a premortal council in which the plan of salvation and the purpose of earth life were explained.

Two opposing plans were presented in that council, and we chose the one which would allow us to come to earth and inherit mortal bodies which would clothe our spirits with flesh. We would also be given moral agency on earth, the opportunity to choose for ourselves, to make mistakes, to repent of our sins, and to partake of the miracle of forgiveness, the atonement of Jesus Christ. We were so pleased with this wonderful opportunity for growth eventually leading to godhood that we "shouted for joy" (Job 38:7).

As we left that premortal sphere and were born to earthly parents, the curtain descended on act 1, and much of our memory of act 1 has been lost. But there are many times when we, with Wordsworth, experience intimations that

> Our birth is but a sleep and a forgetting:
> The Soul that rises with us, our life's Star,
> Hath had elsewhere its setting,
> And cometh from afar:

Not in entire forgetfulness,
And not in utter nakedness,
But trailing clouds of glory do we come
From God, who is our home:
Heaven lies about us in our infancy![3]

The truth of the statement that "heaven lies about us in our infancy" hit me all of a sudden while visiting the Saints in Cairo, Egypt. Before the meeting started I introduced myself to each of the nearly one hundred expatriates attending the meeting. These are faithful saints from various parts of the world, most of whom work for international business concerns in Egypt. I asked each of them where they called home. They indicated they came from California, or Arizona, or Utah, or Ghana, or the Philippines.

When I asked a little tot where she came from, she simply replied: "Fwom Hebenly Fatho." And that explains, in large part, the purity of little children, for it has been so recent a time when they did, in fact, dwell in the presence of their Heavenly Father.

Where's My Script?

Notwithstanding the intimations of our premortal existence, we now find ourselves onstage in act 2, our mortal life on earth, and somewhere we need to find a script so that we can, indeed, prove ourselves by keeping the Lord's commandments. But where is this script to be found? Is it not more than coincidental (at least in English) that the words "script" and "scripture" are derived from the same etymological roots?

A script is, of course, a detailed description of actions and dialogues that occur among actors and is a unique form of literature. Unlike poetry, novels, history, or biographies which inspire, entertain, inform, or enlighten us, a script consists of prescriptions for behavior and words to be spoken and descriptions of actions to be taken in concert with other actors. Scripts tell us what to say and describe how we are to treat other people and how we should react to their actions. Such is one of the important functions of the scriptures, and Nephi has promised us that when we "feast upon the words of Christ . . . , the words of Christ will tell [us] all things what [we] should do" (2 Ne. 32:3).

The scriptures also contain poetry, and historical and biographical information, but most important, they testify of the divinity of Jesus Christ. The Old Testament foreshadows His birth and ministry, and the New Testament contains the account of His earthly ministry. The Book of Mormon is another witness of Jesus Christ. The Doctrine and Covenants is yet another testament and a detailed script for the governance of His kingdom on earth. The Pearl of Great Price is an additional body of scripture to testify of the divinity of the gospel and to enlighten us regarding our premortal existence, in addition to containing many other important truths.

Latter-day Saints are so fortunate to have access to several scriptures which serve as our "lifescripts." Though we sometimes refer to the Savior of the world as our Elder Brother, there are vast differences between His life and ours as mortal men and women. He was the Only Begotten Son of the Father in the flesh. Furthermore, He alone led a perfect life on earth. That is to say, He is the only person to have lived on earth who followed the divine script perfectly. He acknowledges this fact in reference to His relationship with His Father in Heaven: "I do always those things that please him" (John 8:29), and therein lies such a great difference between His life and our lives. All too often we forget our lines and depart from the divine script, but He always did those things that pleased His Father.

That the Savior himself was given a script to follow is made abundantly clear in the Gospel of John as He humbly declared, "I can of mine own self do nothing" (John 5:30). Notwithstanding all of the miracles He performed, the Savior acknowledged that "the Son can do nothing of himself, but what he seeth the Father do" (John 5:19), "for I came down from heaven, not to do mine own will, but the will of him that sent me" (John 6:38). After preaching beautiful, profound, and inspiring doctrine, the Savior meekly, yet boldly, assured his listeners: "My doctrine is not mine, but his that sent me. If any man will do his will, he shall know of the doctrine, whether it be of God, or whether I speak of myself." (John 7:16–17.)

Rehearsing Our Parts

Within nearly every family there will be occasions when one or both parents and some of the children will stray from the script. Invariably, when one or the other is extremely tired, or feeling ill, or under considerable stress, there is bound to be some overreaction to the spilt milk of an innocent child. There may also be teenagers who wish to assert their independence through various forms of civil disobedience or passive resistance. Parents and children would do well to remind themselves that parents are practicing to become better parents, and teenagers are practicing becoming adults. Each of us must be given a little rehearsal time.

The current president of the Frankfurt Temple, at this writing, is my good friend Johann Wondra. For a quarter of a century Brother Wondra had worked as the general secretary of the Burgtheater (the National Theater) of Austria. He is a very talented man with considerable experience in producing and directing great theatrical works. Prior to his present calling, his employment often required him to travel throughout Europe to observe various actors who might be engaged to perform in the Burgtheater in Vienna.

He returned home one evening after an extended trip of several days. His lovely wife, Ursula, greeted him with a rather casual, "Oh, hello, Hans." Each of the children also gave him a rather lukewarm welcome, sort of what one would expect after an absence of an hour at the supermarket. Brother Wondra, a man of great spirituality with a warm sense of humor, called his family together in the living room. "Each of you has played the scene all wrong," he said. "The father has been away from home for several days. During his absence the mother of the family missed him terribly and she can hardly wait until he walks through the door. Each of the children has longed to see their father's cheerful face again, and when he returns home with a suitcase full of presents, they can hardly contain the love and joy they feel upon his return."

Brother Wondra continued: "Now, I'm going to take my suitcase and go out the door and walk around the block, and when I return in ten minutes, I would like you to play the scene right this time."

True to his word, in ten minutes the doorbell rang. In ecstacy Ursula exclaimed: "Oh, Hans, I'm so glad you're home again!" She then gave him an affectionate embrace and kissed him. Then, each of the children said, in turn: "Oh, Daddy, Daddy, we missed you soooooooo much!" They, too, hugged and kissed their daddy enthusiastically.

After the second performance, with a satisfied grin, Brother Wondra replied, "That was much, much better. Now, let's unlock the suitcase and open the presents I brought for each of you."

The plan of salvation provides each of us with countless opportunities to practice living the principles of the gospel as found in the Holy Script, and when we forget our lines on the stage of life, we are granted additional rehearsal time to get the scene right.

Not only parents and children but also bishops and stake presidents and mission presidents occasionally wish they could have the opportunity to practice their parts one more time and to play the same scene over again with a flawless performance. And here is where faith and works can converge to bless the lives of all concerned. When our priesthood leader fails to handle a situation with the wisdom and finesse we had anticipated, it is incumbent upon us to retain our faith that he was called of God, and he is still our leader, warts and all.

Conversely, when members of the Church do not initially perform well as home teachers and visiting teachers and in other callings in the kingdom, it is well to continue coaching them with their lines, helping them with their parts until they experience the joy of following the script. To quickly dismiss them from the stage without a few patient rehearsals does a disservice to the process of perfecting the Saints.

Following the Script

President Marion G. Romney once wryly observed that attorneys never discuss cases they lost. Most of us are also reticent to speak in public about the times we have strayed from the admonitions of the scriptures. I trust you will pardon a few personal heart petals, however, which will hopefully illustrate what happens when we do not follow the script provided by the scriptures. When we are "stagestruck" from life's anxieties and vicissitudes or when we "forget our lines," it is always well to review the script. Nephi was inspired to promise us that "the words of Christ will tell [us] all things what [we] should do," and sometimes that which we should do is to change our attitude.

My German-born wife enjoyed our Church assignments in Vienna, Austria, and Frankfurt, Germany, very much because she had no trouble conversing with Church members and friends in their native language. But when we were called to move to France on a new assignment, her enthusiasm for living in Europe began to wane. And when we moved into a little house in the country far removed from neighbors who were members of the Church, this became a trial of her faith. Shopping in a foreign country in a foreign language was mildly traumatic, to say the least. Then one day as she was reading the Book of Mormon, she came upon a verse in Alma 48:12 which describes Captain Moroni as "a man whose heart did swell with thanksgiving to his God, for the many privileges and blessings which he bestowed upon his people."

Somewhat similar to Joseph Smith's experience in reading the first chapter of James, she began to make some important connections in her own mind and heart. She began thinking: Moroni lived at a time when he had no electricity, no hot running water, no oven or microwave, no refrigerator, freezer, washer or dryer, no radio, television, or stereo system. He had no convenient supermarkets or department stores. He had no automobile for convenient and comfortable transportation. And still his "heart did swell with thanksgiving." Since that day of reading that passage of scripture, Sister Condie's attitude changed remarkably and she developed a great love for France and Switzerland and for the French-speaking people. She was at peace with herself and with the world in which she lived.

I, too, had a similar experience. We had lived for seven of the previous nine years in Austria, Germany, and France, and one day in particular I was almost overcome with feelings of homesickness for our four lovely daughters. One was serving a mission in Japan, another was on a mission in Austria, another daughter lived in Seattle, and yet another was living in Boston. I also missed my elderly parents, and I was beginning to wax nostalgic about America.

Then one night as we were reading the New Testament together we came across a verse we had read several times before but which had not jumped from the page as it did on this evening: "And every one that hath forsaken houses, or brethren, or sisters, or father, or mother, or wife, or children, or lands, for my name's sake, shall receive an hundredfold, and shall inherit everlasting life" (Matt. 19:29). Since that time we still longed to see our loved ones, but the pain was totally and completely removed with that marvelous promise of the Savior.

Hearers and Doers

As mentioned earlier, unlike poetry or novels, the scriptures, like the script in a theater, impel us to act in certain ways. It was never intended that the scriptures should be read and analyzed as one would dissect a novel in a comparative literature class, notwithstanding great insights that can be gained from studying the Bible as literature. The scriptures are not to be treated like history books or biographies which are read and then whose content is only stored in our memory. It is abundantly clear that the scriptures impel us to act and to become "doers of the word, and not hearers only" (James 1:22).

The Savior himself taught: "Not every one that saith unto me, Lord, Lord, shall enter into the kingdom of heaven; but he that doeth the will of my Father which is in heaven" (Matt. 7:21). Pursuant to these scriptures, it is interesting that a modern-day prophet, President Spencer W. Kimball, when he was a member of the Quorum of the Twelve Apostles, suggested a change in one of the verses to "I Am a Child of God." He was quite taken by the words accompanied by the beautifully simple melody of this little song, but then he heard the phrase: "Teach me all that I must *know* to live with him someday." This kindly Apostle gently suggested that the verse would be more correctly sung if it were changed to: "Teach me all that I must *do* to live with him someday." The lyricist gladly made the change, and that is how we sing it today.

Martin Luther and some of the other early Reformers were impressed by Paul's Epistle to the Romans in which he wrote: "Therefore we conclude that a man is justified by faith without the deeds of the law" (Rom. 3:28). Luther felt so strongly about the importance of faith expressed in this verse that he translated it into German with a word added—"justified by faith *alone*." This, of course, created a great controversy among the Catholic theologians of the day, who held to the notion that the sacraments or ordinances of the Church were necessary for salvation.

Legend has it that as Luther was translating the New Testament and came upon James's epistle, he declared that this epistle was "straw," for James declared: "Even so faith, if it hath not works, is dead, being alone" (James 2:17).

The tension between faith and works, grace and ordinances, is readily resolved in Nephi's teaching "that it is by grace that we are saved, after all we can do" (2 Ne. 25:23).

Faith, Works, and the Handcart Companies

The history of the early Christian church and the more recent history of the restored Church are punctuated by scores of faith-promoting stories of those who were willing to risk their very lives for the gospel of Jesus Christ. The martyrdom of the early Apostles and the subsequent martyrdom of Joseph, Hyrum, David W. Patten, Parley P. Pratt, and many others give us pause to contemplate the depth of our own commitment to building the kingdom.

There may, perhaps, have been no more faithful group of individuals who demonstrated their faith through their works than those Saints in the ten handcart companies who crossed the plains between June 9, 1856, and September of 1860. Between 1849 and 1855 about sixteen thousand Saints from Europe had emigrated to Utah, supported in part by the Perpetual Emigration Company. But as financial resources became extremely scarce, in September of 1855 Brigham Young was led to conclude: "We cannot afford to purchase wagons and teams as in times past. I am consequently thrown back upon my old plan—to make hand-carts, and let the emigration foot it, and draw upon them [the carts] the necessary supplies, having a cow or two for every ten. They can come just as quick, if not quicker, and much cheaper."[4]

Each company left from Iowa City and required about four months to reach the Salt Lake Valley. All of the companies left the Midwest in May or June with two exceptions: the Willie company departed on July 15, 1856, and the Martin company left two weeks later on July 28 of the same year. Hindsight indicated that this was very late in the summer to begin a four-month trek which would cause them to travel during very inclement winter weather.

Both the Willie and Martin companies encountered severe snowstorms and freezing weather causing many of their number to die from exposure. Unfortunately, news of their plight did not reach the Valley until October 4. The next day was general conference. Brigham Young, in typical, practical eloquence, introduced the conference with the following stirring counsel:

> I will now give this people the subject and the text for the Elders who may speak to-day and during the conference. It is this. On the 5th day of October, 1856, many of our brethren and sisters are on the plains with handcarts, and probably many are now seven hundred miles from this place, and they must be brought here, we must send assistance to them. The text will be, "to get them here."[5]

President Young then gave the bishops the charge to recruit sixty mule teams and twelve to fifteen wagons and to take with them twelve tons of flour. He continued: "I will tell you all that your faith, religion, and profession of religion, will never save one soul of you in the Celestial Kingdom of our God, unless you carry out just such principles as I am now teaching you. *Go and bring in those people now on the plains.*"[6]

On November 3, the Martin company reached the Sweetwater River, which was filled with floating ice.

> Three eighteen-year-old boys belonging to the relief party, came to the rescue; and to the astonishment of all who saw, carried nearly every member of that ill-fated handcart company across the snow-bound stream. The strain was so terrible, and the exposure so great, that in later years all the boys died from the effects of it. When President Brigham Young heard of this heroic act, he wept like a child, and later declared publicly, "That act alone will ensure C. Allen Huntington, George W. Grant, and David P. Kimball an everlasting salvation in the Celestial Kingdom of God, worlds without end."[7]

It had been seven weeks since general conference, and once again the Saints were assembled on a Sunday in the Tabernacle on November 30. President Young announced the imminent arrival of the bedraggled Martin company:

> When those persons arrive I do not want to see them put into houses by themselves; I want to have them distributed in the city among the families that have good and comfortable houses; and I wish all the sisters now before me, and all who know how and can, to nurse and wait upon the new comers and prudently administer medicine and food to them. To speak upon these things is a part of my religion, for it pertains to taking care of the Saints. . . .
>
> The afternoon meeting will be omitted, for I wish the sisters to go home and prepare to give those who have just arrived a mouthful of something to eat, and to wash them and nurse them up.[8]

During a period of five years a total of 2,962 Saints crossed the plains in handcart companies, with a mortality rate of about 250.

Few of us will ever be called upon to make the same sacrifices as those of our pioneer forebears, but we can demonstrate our faith by our diligence as home teachers and visiting teachers, by our tithes and offerings, by our willingness to share the gospel with others, by our family history research and temple work, and by the way we treat our Heavenly Father's children.

What Faith Is Not

In his benedictory general conference address shortly before his death, Elder Theodore Tuttle spoke on the need for faith in the Lord Jesus Christ, not positive thinking but bedrock faith in the Lord.[9]

Elder Tuttle's concerns and counsel are wellfounded. We often glibly recite the first principles and ordinances of the gospel as faith, repentance, baptism, and receiving the gift of the Holy Ghost. But the first principle is not just faith, but faith in the Lord Jesus Christ. Many individuals make shaky business investments "on faith," when in fact their decision is based more on wishful thinking. Sometimes we even confuse inspiration with desperation, mistaking temptation for revelation.

True faith in the Lord Jesus Christ engenders preparation, patience, and effort. This was a disappointing lesson Oliver Cowdery learned as he sought to translate the golden plates without any prior effort on his part (see D&C 9).

The Savior posed a great soul-searching question for each of us: "And whosoever doth not bear his cross, and come after me, cannot be my disciple. For which of you, intending to build a tower, sitteth not down first, and counteth the cost, whether he have sufficient to finish it? Lest haply, after he hath laid the foundation, and is not able to finish it, all that behold it begin to mock him, saying, This man began to build, and was not able to finish." (Luke 14:27–30.)

Too often we fail to realize that His ways are not our ways. In this day and age of instant photocopies, instant breakfast, instant credit, and instant weedkiller, we have become conditioned to expect immediate results to our requests and our prayers. But instant answers do not always build patience or faith, unless, of course, we are willing to pay the price of sacrifice and consecration.

Lorenzo Snow in Italy

Young Elder Lorenzo Snow was one who exerted his faith and his patience in achieving a given goal and who was willing to pay whatever price was necessary to attain that goal.

It was fall of 1850, and Elders Snow, Stenhouse, and Toronto were anxious to bring the gospel to the people of northern Italy. Lorenzo Snow recorded in his journal:

> It was no small tax on my patience, to be weeks and even months in the midst of an interesting people without being actively and publicly engaged in communicating the great principles which I had been sent to promulgate. But, as I felt it was the mind of the Spirit that we should proceed at first with slow and cautious steps, I submitted to the will of heaven.
>
> September 6th.—This morning, my attention was directed to Joseph Grey, a boy of three years of age—the youngest child of our host. Many friends had been to see the child, as to all human appearances his end was near. I went to see him in the afternoon; death was preying upon his body—his former healthy frame was now reduced to a skeleton, and it was only by close observation we could discern that he was alive. As I reflected upon the peculiarity of our situation, my mind was fully awakened to a sense of our position. For some hours before I retired to rest, I called upon the Lord to assist us at this time. My feelings on this occasion will not easily be erased from my memory.
>
> September 7th.— This morning I proposed to Elder Stenhouse we should fast and retire to the mountains and pray. As we departed, we called and saw the child—his eyeballs turned upwards—his eyelids fell and closed—his face and ears were thin, and wore the pale marble hue, indicative of approaching dissolution. The cold perspiration of death covered his body as the principle of life was nearly exhausted. Madam Grey and other females were sobbing, while Monsieur Grey hung his head and whispered to us, "*Il meurt! il meurt!*" (He dies! he dies!)
>
> After a little rest upon the mountain, aside from any likelihood of interruption, we called upon the Lord in solemn, earnest prayer, to spare the life of the child. As I reflected on the course we wished to pursue, the claims that we should soon advance to the world, I regarded this circumstance as one of vast importance. *I know not of any sacrifice which I can possibly make, that I am not willing to offer, that the Lord might grant our requests* [emphasis added].
>
> We returned about three o'clock in the afternoon, and having consecrated some oil, I anointed my hand and laid it upon the head of the child, while we silently offered up the desires of our hearts for his restoration. A few hours afterward we called, and his father, with a smile of thankfulness, said, "*Mieux beaucoup! beaucoup!*" (Better, much, much!)
>
> September 8th. The child had been so well during the past night the parents had been enabled to take their rest, which they had not

> done for some time before; and to-day they could leave him and attend to the business of the house. As I called to see him, Madam Grey expressed her joy in his restoration. I, in turn remarked, "*Il Dio del cielo ha fatto questa per voi.*" (The God of heaven has done this for you.)[10]

This miraculous reliance upon holy priesthood power became the means through which interest in the Church was generated and which led to the humble beginnings of the Church in Italy.

At the conclusion of his mission Elder Snow made the following poignant entry in his journal:

> Arriving at my home in Salt Lake City, the long anticipated oasis of this portion of my life-journey—the beacon light which succeeded my arduous missionary labors, and shone with a brighter beam than all other earthly luminaries, the happiness of once again meeting my loved and loving family would have been full, but alas! there was a sad vacancy. A lovely one was not; one who ever met me with a smiling face and a loving heart, was not there to respond to love's sacred call; Charlotte, my dear wife, had been stricken down by death, and her beautiful form lay mouldering in the silent tomb. Yet there was consolation in the thought that her pure spirit was mingling with holy beings above.[11]

In her biography of her brother Lorenzo Snow, Eliza R. Snow wrote of this event:

> On the mountain in Italy which was subsequently named "Mount Brigham," on the same memorable day in which the Church of Jesus Christ of Latter-day Saints was there organized, Lorenzo, in the force of his spirit, aroused by intense interest in the work devolving upon him, which seemed shrouded in darkness, and probably without realizing the weight of his covenant, told the Lord that he knew of no sacrifice he could possibly make he was not willing to offer, that the Lord might grant a request concerning the mission before him. When I received a copy of the report of the proceedings of the day, in which the above was included, I was deeply struck with the coincidence. Just at this time, as nearly as I could calculate by comparing dates and distances, the Lord removed, by the hand of death, from my brother's family circle, one of the loveliest of women.
>
> Charlotte died very suddenly. I was with her and saw her draw the last breath; her beloved husband was very far away, but his name was on her dying lips. She loved truly for she loved sincerely; and as she loved, so was she beloved by all who knew her.[12]

This poignant account of one man's quest to accomplish the Lord's work in a foreign land is a graphic example of faith in the Lord Jesus Christ. But this incident also demonstrates the power of faith coupled with works. Elders Snow and Stenhouse did not just pray for the well-being of little Joseph Grey. They fasted in preparation for a special supplication to the Lord, and Elder Snow expressed his willingness to make any sacrifice he would be called upon to make. They then administered to the little boy and his healing began to open the doors of the residents of northern Italy in a way which had previously not been achieved.

There are times in each of our lives when our faith wavers and we lose our humility and begin to concentrate upon how "hard hit" we are by the uncooperative vicissitudes of life. In such moments we begin to feel that we are truly picked on by our surrounding circumstances. We begin to wonder why other people get all the breaks, and why certain people never have to undergo the trials which we must experience. At such times it would be well to reflect upon the life of President Lorenzo Snow and realize that he experienced trials because the Lord loved him and wanted to strengthen him. Strength and faith come through testing, not resting.

Intentions and Actions

In the Book of Mormon those two great missionaries Alma and Amulek encountered a very obstreperous lawyer who wished to contend with them. In the course of their presentation to him, Amulek taught him that after death we will "be judged according to our works" (Alma 12:12), and Alma added that "our words will condemn us, yea, all our works will condemn us . . . and our thoughts will also condemn us" (Alma 12:14).

Bruce Hafen explains that in a court of law, intentions are often a crucial part of the final judgment. For example, a victim may be killed at the hand of another person, but depending upon the actual intentions of the person charged with murder, the judgment may be first-degree murder involving pre-meditation and planning, or it may be judged as second-degree murder or perhaps involuntary manslaughter, negligent homicide, or murder in self-defense. The final verdict of a jury will have little impact upon the deceased, but for him who is being judged, the relationship between intentions and actions is absolutely crucial.

The Apostle James explains in his epistle the sequential relationship between thoughts and actions: "Let no man say when he is tempted, I am tempted of God: for God cannot be tempted with evil, neither tempteth he any man: but every man is tempted, when he is drawn away of his own lust, and enticed. Then when lust hath conceived, it bringeth forth sin: and sin, when it is finished, bringeth forth death." (James 1:13–16.)

Real Intent

The book of Proverbs also addresses the importance of the intent of our hearts, for "as he thinketh in his heart, so is he" (Prov. 23:7). The Book of Mormon also makes it very clear that "if a man being evil giveth a gift, he doeth it grudgingly; wherefore it is counted unto him the same as if he had retained the gift" (Moro. 7:8).

We are all familiar with the old adage that "the road to hell is paved with good intentions." But as King Benjamin urged the Saints of his day to be generous with their means in helping the poor, he instructed the poor to "say in [their] hearts that: I give not because I have not, but if I had I would give" (Mosiah 4:24). In other words, it may well be that the road to heaven is also paved with good intentions. But James contends that these intentions must, for the most part, be translated into actions, for "faith without works is dead" (James 2:26).

There are many religions that encourage their adherents to pray openly, even ostentatiously, several times each day, but Mormon warns us that it is "counted evil unto a man, if he shall pray and not with real intent of heart; yea, and it profiteth him nothing, for God receiveth none such" (Moro. 7:9).

In the final chapter of the Book of Mormon, Moroni also gives us instructions regarding how each of us might determine for ourselves if that book truly contains the word of God. It is an act of faith transformed into work on our part to read this Book, and after having done so we are then qualified to receive a personal revelation regarding its truth when we but "ask with a sincere heart, with real intent, having faith in Christ" (Moro. 10:4). Elder Dallin H. Oaks instructed a group of missionaries in Porto, Portugal, regarding the importance of "real intent," adding that when we pray with real intent we are willing to accept the consequences of the answer we receive. That is to say, we are willing to assume the responsibility of that confirmation we receive by undergoing a mighty change of heart and, in most cases, undergoing a mighty behavioral and attitudinal change in our lives.

The Lord's Tenth

About fifteen years ago I was in the process of conducting tithing settlement the week before Christmas. This is always a wonderful time of year when a bishop can express his gratitude and appreciation to each member of the ward as each, in turn, declares his or her payment of an honest tithing.

A young married couple with three small children came into the bishop's office. He was struggling with a small business enterprise he had founded and was barely earning enough to support their growing family. As faithful Latter-day Saints they had come to see the bishop to ensure that their tithes and offerings had been properly recorded. After ensuring that our records and receipts were in agreement, I asked them if their donations constituted a full and honest tithing for the year.

Their eyes began to fill with tears as they explained that they did, in fact, need to pay two hundred dollars more to make this an honest tithe. With quivering voices they explained that this was all the money they had left, and if their family were to have Christmas at all, this money would need to be used for much-needed shoes and other clothing, with a little left over for toys for the children.

My heart ached for this fine young couple who wanted so badly to pay an honest tithe, but who were torn by their obligation to provide their children with a little of the spirit of Christmas.

Two nights later I received a phone call in the bishop's office. It was this young father. He wanted to drop by the office to revise his previous declaration as a part-tithe payer. He and his wife had prayed about the matter and discussed it at great length: it was more important to be full-tithe payers than to have a commercial Christmas. They had been married in the temple, and their children were born in the covenant. If they were to remain a forever family, then they must abide by the covenants they made to keep the commandments.

We filled out a new tithing receipt and he declared that he and his eternal companion were now full-tithe payers. This time he left the office with a radiant countenance, knowing he had done that which was pleasing before the Lord. This time it was the bishop who had tears in his eyes.

Two days before Christmas the phone rang again. It was my friend again. He had just received word of a new job offer with a much higher salary, and he could start work immediately. The windows of heaven had begun to open.

The goal of our earthly existence is to become like Jesus Christ, and if we are to become like Him then we must practice in our daily lives the principles which He taught and lived. He willingly paid for our sins in the Garden of Gethsemane and died on the cross that we might live. His sacrifice was total and complete. We may not be asked to die for the gospel's sake, but we are commanded to pay an honest 10 percent of our income that we might gain a glimpse of the Lord's love for us. Through this small sacrifice we become more like Him. Tithing is not paid with money. Tithing is paid by faith and by our love for the Lord.

Intent of the Heart

Georg Birsfelder was a young man in Switzerland who wooed and won the hand of a pretty Mormon girl named Annaroesli. They were married in August of 1950, and in May of the following year he was baptized a member of the Church. A year or so later a great test of their faith occurred. Georg recorded this series of events as follows:

> One morning I came into the branch house just as the mission president was speaking with a brother from the Malix Branch. As he saw me, he explained that he had just extended a call to this young man to be the first missionary from Switzerland. He then turned to me, laid his hand on my shoulder, and said: "And you will be the second!"
>
> What a great feeling came over me! I, a missionary for the Church of Jesus Christ? How wonderful! I immediately spoke with Annaroesli.
>
> "But that's impossible," she said. "They don't call married men."
>
> "But that's what he said," I protested. "Yes, why not? It has to be all right."
>
> We discussed the matter together. We could give up our apartment, and Annaroesli could live with her parents. We then checked to see if

> she could assume my job as a clerk in the government office where I worked. She had already helped us there on a part-time basis. Yes, that was possible. Now we could finance my mission.
>
> There was a long waiting period, but the mission president did not contact us, and we began to get nervous.
>
> One day, about six weeks after the mission president's call, I saw him again and asked when my mission would start. At first he could not remember what I was referring to, and then he laughingly said: "But, Brother Birsfelder, I was only kidding."
>
> What a disappointment that was for Annaroesli and me! We were so well-prepared and now I couldn't go. But from then on we decided that someday we would definitely fulfill a mission together.

And fulfill a mission together they did, not once but twice.

There is within the Church a large number of brethren who, as young men, would have loved to serve a full-time mission. In fact, many of the General Authorities of the Church were denied this opportunity because of the untimely intervention of World War II and the Korean War. There is also a somewhat younger generation whose opportunities for missionary service were limited by the Vietnam War, during which time only one young man from each ward was able to serve at a given time. But regardless of their current age or past circumstances, many of these brethren quietly served as missionaries in uniform. Some of them assisted in the teaching and conversion process of pioneer members of the Church in the countries of Japan, Korea, and Vietnam. Others were faithful examples to their comrades in arms and were instruments in the Lord's hands in bringing their military buddies into the kingdom.

One of these great missionaries is my long-time friend Herman Moessner. Herman was born in Stuttgart, Germany, and joined the Church as a young man. When World War II began he was drafted into the German army. During the course of the war he was captured by the British army and taken to England as a prisoner of war. Moved by the Spirit, and wishing to use his time wisely, Herman began to share the gospel with his fellow German soldiers. They had plenty of time to be taught, and though Herman had not been called and set apart as a full-time missionary, he was a missionary nevertheless. During that period of time, several of his friends were baptized into the Church in a makeshift baptismal font.

Brother Moessner also used this opportunity to learn English as he conversed with his British prison guards. He practiced his English on any British guard who was willing to converse with him. His soft voice and cheerful spirit endeared him to the British, and at the conclusion of the war his English had become so proficient that he later served as an interpreter for the visiting General Authorities who came to Germany. He was called as the first stake president of the Stuttgart Stake after having served as a counselor to several successive mission presidents. He later served in the presidency of the Swiss Temple. For Herman Moessner, time in a British prisoner-of-war camp had not been lost time, but rather a time of preparation for future service in the kingdom.

The Intent of Single Adults

There is within the Church an ever-burgeoning number of single adults who, for a variety of reasons, are making their way through life as unmarried, divorced, or widowed individuals. As I have attended numerous gatherings of young adults and single adults, I have been impressed by their faith, their seemingly boundless talents, their zest for life, and their perseverance, sometimes amid great opposition.

In the divine justice and mercy of an omniscient, loving, and wise Heavenly Father, all worthy women will be eligible for the blessings of priesthood ordinances, and those women who are denied the power of motherhood in this life will receive eternal compensation if they remain true and faithful. Of that, modern prophets have borne witness.[13]

Single men who, in Western culture, have the responsibility to initiate marital agreements were candidly challenged by President Ezra Taft Benson to, in the words of Lehi, "arise from the dust, my sons, and be men" (2 Ne. 1:21). In short, he admonished them to get with the program and get married. Still, these brethren who are reticent to assume the obligations of marriage will be judged by the intent of their hearts, and there are some who would like to marry if they could ever get a favorable response to their proposals of marriage.

Sincere Intent to Serve God

After the Savior's ascension into heaven, the Apostles experienced success in spreading the word of God. Then, as now, not everyone who was baptized received that ordinance with real intent. Apparently such an one was Simon the sorcerer, who held himself up to the people as "some great one" (Acts 8:9). He heard the gospel preached by Philip and joined the Church.

Shortly thereafter Peter and John arrived from Jerusalem and conferred the gift of the Holy Ghost upon the newly baptized members by the laying on of hands. Having observed this ordinance, Simon offered the Apostles money for the power to perform this same ordinance "that on whomsoever I lay hands, he may receive the Holy Ghost" (Acts 8:19). "But Peter said unto him, Thy money perish with thee, because thou hast thought that the gift of God may be purchased with money" (Acts. 8:20). The chief Apostle had discerned the real intent of Simon the sorcerer's heart. His desire for the priesthood power was not so much to bless as to impress.

By contrast, while the Savior was still with them one of His Apostles, John, said: "Master, we saw one casting out devils in thy name, and he followeth not us: and we forbad him, because he followeth not us. But Jesus said, Forbid him not: for there is no man which shall do a miracle in my name, that can lightly speak evil of me. For he that is not against us is on our part." (Mark 9:38–40.) It would seem that it is the intent of the heart which distinguishes Simon the sorcerer from him who would do good only for the sake of serving others.

Knowledge and Service

The balance between faith and works is reflected in how well we translate what we know into what we do. But before we can do His will, we must know His will. Therefore, Nephi admonishes us to search the scriptures and then to liken the scriptures to ourselves (see 1 Ne. 19:23). While it is tragic that so many people in the world do not know His will, it is an even greater tragedy to know His will and not do it.

Three years after the Church had been organized, a number of the presiding brethren of the Church had evidently invested so much time and energy in their Church callings, they had neglected their families. On May 6, 1833, after revealing some very profound doctrinal truths, the Lord then took the occasion to reprove several of the brethren, including the Prophet Joseph, for neglecting the teaching of and caring for their families. Joseph was told that his "family must needs repent and forsake some things, and give more earnest heed unto your sayings, or be removed out of their place" (D&C 93:48). Fredrick G. Williams, a Counselor in the First Presidency, was chastened for not having taught his children "light and truth, according to the commandments" (D&C 93:41–42), and Sidney Rigdon, another Counselor, was reproved because "in some things he hath not kept the commandments concerning his children." Continuing, the Lord told Sidney: "Therefore, first set in order thy house." (D&C 93:44.) Newel K. Whitney, a righteous man and bishop of the Church, was also chastened and commanded to "set in order his family" (D&C 93:50).

Sometimes those who are engaged in the Lord's work have the faith that their service as a bishop or stake president or mission president or Seventy (true confession time) will compensate for failing to assume their (our) responsibilities as a parent and husband and grandfather. King Benjamin's counsel is valid for all parents, regardless of their occupational responsibilities or ecclesiastical callings: "And ye will not suffer your children that they go hungry, or naked; neither will ye suffer that they transgress the laws of God, and fight and quarrel one with another, and serve the devil. . . . But ye will teach them to walk in the ways of truth and soberness; ye will teach them to love one another, and to serve one another." (Mosiah 4:14–15.)

Paul said it well: "They which preach the gospel should live the gospel" (1 Cor. 9:14).

Notes

1. *As You Like It*, act 2, scene 7, line 39.

2. *The Merchant of Venice*, act 1, scene 1, line 78.

3. William Wordsworth, "Ode: Intimations of Immortality from Recollections of Early Childhood," in Stanley B. Greenfield and A. Kingsley Weatherhead, eds., *The Poem: An Anthology* (New York: Appleton-Century-Crofts, 1968), pp. 163–68.

4. Quoted in LeRoy R. Hafen and Ann W. Hafen, *Handcarts to Zion: The Story of a Unique Western Migration, 1856–1860* (Glendale, California: Arthur H. Clark Co., 1960, pp. 29–30.

5. Quoted in Hafen and Hafen, *Handcarts*, p. 120.

6. Quoted in Hafen and Hafen, *Handcarts*, p. 121.

7. Solomon F. Kimball, "Belated Emigrants of 1856," *Improvement Era*, 17:288, cited in Hafen and Hafen, *Handcarts*, pp. 132–33.

8. Quoted in Hafen and Hafen, *Handcarts*, p. 139.

9. Theodore Tuttle, "Developing Faith," *Ensign* 16 (November 1986): 72–73.

10. In Eliza R. Snow Smith, *Biography and Family Record of Lorenzo Snow* (Salt Lake City: Deseret News Co., 1884), pp. 128–29.

11. In Eliza R. Snow Smith, *Biography and Family Record*, p. 232.

12. Eliza R. Snow Smith, *Biography and Family Record*, p. 233.

13. See Harold B. Lee, *Ye Are the Light of the World* (Salt Lake City: Deseret Book Co., 1974), p. 292. See also Joseph Fielding Smith, *Answers to Gospel Questions*, comp. and ed. Joseph Fielding Smith, Jr., 5 vols. (Salt Lake City: Desert Book Co., 1957–66), 2:34–38.

Chapter Four

Risk and Security

It was the end of May in 1964, and all of the prospective graduates of Brigham Young University were seated in the George Albert Smith Fieldhouse as President Hugh B. Brown of the First Presidency conducted the commencement exercises. America's foremost newscaster, Lowell Thomas, was the main speaker.

Thomas was an adventurer and author as well as a radio announcer, a person equally familiar with the ski slopes of Switzerland, Alaska, Utah, and Katmandu. He had been on jungle safaris and in the middle of war zones. He was a friend of presidents and prime ministers, kings and queens throughout the world. We all waited in anticipation of his sage advice on how we could succeed in life. I remember his words as if he had spoken them yesterday. In essence, he counseled the graduates not to be too caught up in the quest for security but to enjoy life's adventures.

The Quest for Security

There I sat. In a few days Dorothea and I were going to be married in the Idaho Falls Temple; we were then moving into a basement apartment; I was beginning graduate school in two weeks and did not yet have a job—and Lowell Thomas said not to worry about security. At that time in my life I craved security so much that I remember first discounting Lowell Thomas's counsel and then becoming a bit irritated at his flippant remarks about something so important as security.

There seemed to be sound spiritual grounds for yearning for

security, perhaps best reflected in a refrain from the beautiful hymn "How Gentle God's Commands":

> Beneath his watchful eye,
> His Saints securely dwell;
> That hand which bears all nature up
> Shall guard his children well.[1]

Ah yes, how sweet it would be if his Saints did all securely dwell, but for many of them, security is an extremely elusive state of being. There are many parents throughout the world for whom life is a constant struggle just to adequately feed and clothe their children. There are many youth who, sometimes through no original intent of their own, fall prey to drug abuse and become hooked in an earthly hell characterized by constant anxiety and fear. There are also many of the aged for whom the scepter of chronic illness and encroaching death robs them of peace of mind and tranquility of soul.

There are many individuals for whom absolute, total, complete security has become a continuous lifelong quest, even an obsession, if you will. Many of the generation who went hungry during the Great Depression vowed later that they would never suffer from financial insecurity again. And many of them have achieved their goal—at least for the time being. Their large and lovely homes are paid for; they have excellent retirement programs reflecting prudent previous planning; and they enjoy good health, with the added security of medical insurance that includes comprehensive coverage against catastrophic illness.

Risks to Be Taken

Some of these Saints may, perhaps, dwell too securely, for when the bishop extends an invitation for them to teach a Sunday School class, they point out that it would be a shame if their thirty-foot motor home were not put to good use on the interstate highways of the land. A steady calling in the Church would, of course, preempt that option.

Still other older couples in good health, with complete financial security, decline an invitation to serve full-time missions because they worry about the care of their home, they would miss their grandchildren, they might get ill, or they might receive a call from the prophet to go to an area which would not suit them well.

At the younger end of the continuum are young men who have a priesthood obligation and privilege to serve a full-time mission, but some of them, too, are unwilling to take any risks. If I am called on a mission, they think to themselves, what if my girlfriend doesn't wait for me? What if I can't get back into my academic program in college? What if I'm called to Hong Kong, or Russia, or Montana? And in the wake of what if, what if, what if, their current quest for security robs them of blessings and opportunities for spiritual growth which can be gained in no other way.

There are other young men who have taken the risk of serving a mission—and most of them have served faithfully and well—but upon returning home they have a difficult time "leaving father and mother" and the security of home. Yes, marriage can be a risky business, as evidenced by the soaring divorce rates in our society. But like missions, and getting an education, and taking diving lessons, and playing football, and performing in band or choir concerts, those who take the risks will have experiences not possible for those who are addicted to security.

Risks

Nearly thirty years have passed since that commencement address by Lowell Thomas, and though we have not been to Katmandu, Kilamanjaro, or Hong Kong like Lowell Thomas, we have had some interesting adventures as a family, and each of them involved taking risks and sacrificing a bit of security. In fact, many of our greatest adventures have occurred as we have taken risks rather close to home.

It was a risk to become the parents of two wonderful daughters while we were still in graduate school without a firm guarantee of employment at the end. There was also considerable risk involved in taking out a mortgage on our house at a time when mortgage rates had nearly doubled over a period of four years. There were risks involved in having the children learn how to swim, and risks involved in running rapids in mountain streams. There have been risks involved in responding to Church calls to Austria and Germany and France and having to leave college-age daughters behind. But those risks have been accompanied by guardian angels—two elderly grandparents—whose lives have been continually interrupted and blessed by those stray kittens who always knew where to go for a taste of security and a warm, free meal.

The very plan of salvation hinges upon our striking a balance between risk and security. The scriptures tell us that before this world was created, God said: "We will make an earth whereon these may dwell; and we will prove them herewith, to see *if* they will do all things whatsoever the Lord their God shall command them" (Abr. 3:24–25, emphasis added). The word *if* is seldom used in a statement describing security, but it is used rather frequently in situations involving risk.

When our loving Heavenly Father granted us moral agency, the power to make right and wrong choices, he equipped us with the ability to take risks, to make mistakes, to repent, and to grow until we become similar even to God himself.

Satan's alternative plan was one of absolute security, no risks, no moral agency, no sin, no repentance, no growth, and no opportunity for godhood.

The Savior himself literally risked—and willingly gave—His life for us. The history of the restored Church is fraught with incidents in which men and women took risks during their continual quest for a place where the Lord's Saints could securely dwell. A reading of Church history leads us to conclude that the Prophet Joseph Smith's entire life involved taking risks while sacrificing security. Indeed, each risk was a demonstration of his faith in the Lord Jesus Christ.

Each of the brethren who left families behind to preach the gospel took great risks, but the blessings which accrued to their lives and the lives of their children are immeasurable.

The general membership of the Church, those who remained behind, were also left at great risk. Persecution of the Saints persisted long after Palmyra, Kirtland, Jackson County, and Nauvoo. Hardly had the Saints settled in the Valley of the Great Salt Lake than Johnston's army threatened to destroy their peace. In the modern era, before the collapse of communism in Eastern Europe there were hundreds of faithful Saints who risked their jobs, chances for advancement, and housing opportunities all for their membership in the Church. In other areas of the world today there are faithful Saints who continue to risk much for the blessings of the kingdom.

Risks Not to Be Taken

The word *risk* is mentioned only two times in all of holy writ. Alma counsels his wayward son, Corianton, to "not risk one more offense against your God upon those points of doctrine, which ye have hitherto risked to commit sin" (Alma 41:9).

Elder Boyd K. Packer has described our wicked world in which "with ever fewer exceptions, what we see and read and hear have the mating act as a central theme."[2] With the desecration of what should be a secret and sacred act, even the most carnally minded persons are now plagued with fears of having taken the risks also taken by Corianton. Indeed, the prolific references to so-called "safe sex" in newspapers and in instructions in sex education classes in public schools are merely a placebo to postpone the pain of Paul's proclamation to the Romans that "the wages of sin is death" (Rom. 6:23).

During the centuries prior to the discovery of penicillin and other antibiotics, the fear of contracting venereal disease exacted a price from those who took the risks of infidelity and promiscuity. With the discovery of powerful antibiotics, the fears of physically paying a price for sensuality were postponed. But now, with the emergence of AIDS, a scourge is raging throughout the world which is projected to afflict 120 million people by the year 2000.[3]

There are many innocent victims of AIDS who have contracted this cruel disease through absolutely no fault of their own, such as by receiving a transfusion of contaminated blood. They will suffer a physical death as a result of undergoing the risks of transfusion. But there are others whose deaths have even sadder consequences, for they will suffer not only physical death but also the consequences of the greater risks included in Alma's counsel to Corianton—the risk of losing eternal life.

Alma said it well: "Wickedness never was happiness" (Alma 41:10).

In trying to prepare a degenerate nation for the eventual visit of Jesus Christ to their continent, Samuel the Lamanite prophet observed that the Nephites in 6 B.C. "sought for happiness in doing iniquity, which thing is contrary to the nature of that righteousness which is in our great and Eternal Head" (Hel. 13:38). Some risks, those involving sin, simply must not be taken. Other risks, such as leaving homes for missions, getting married or getting re-married, rearing families, enrolling in language courses at age fifty, accepting a Church calling for which we feel totally inadequate, are risks borne of faith, and risks which assure happiness in the doing and compound interest after the accomplished fact.

A political scientist once observed that the Constitution of the United States guarantees the *pursuit* of happiness, *not* happiness. He then added, "Sometimes we must be content with the happiness of pursuit." And so it is in our quest for life eternal.

Elder Russell M. Nelson has reminded us that while we lived in the Father's presence as spirit beings, we looked forward to coming to this sphere of existence and even "wanted the risks of mortality. . . . But we regarded the returning home as the best part of that long-awaited trip, just as we do now. Before embarking on any journey, we like to have some assurance of a round-trip ticket."[4] While living in this probationary state we must not carelessly take risks which would jeopardize that round-trip ticket.

Those who are sexually promiscuous run the risk of ruining marriages, the risk of losing their membership in the Church, and the risk of forfeiting their priesthood and temple blessings, in addition to the risks of venereal disease and AIDS. Those who continue to smoke run the risk of lung cancer, emphysema, and pulmonary heart disease, and of exposing their loved ones to the same diseases through so-called "secondary smoke" from living in the same household.

Those who persist in drinking alcohol run the risk of cirrhosis of the liver. The renowned Harvard psychologist and philosopher William James said that a loving wife and compassionate children and a merciful Father in Heaven may forgive the repentant alcoholic of his sins, but his liver cells will never forgive him!

In another chapter we drew the distinction between what some people call faith and faith in the Lord Jesus Christ. There are some who confuse faith with poor judgment in the taking of risks. There are myriad accounts of well-meaning individuals who, often with lofty goals in mind, risk their life's savings or home equity for get-rich-quick schemes involving promises of unrealistic returns on their investments. Such risks are not of the kind referred to earlier. Not all risks are sins. Some are simply mistakes in judgment, but they are not based on faith in the Lord Jesus Christ, and taking such risks does little to help build His kingdom.

The Quest for Celestial Security

Nephi warned us of one of Satan's great strategies of pacifying people and then lulling them "away into carnal security" (2 Ne. 28:21). When people are secure, or feel entirely secure in terms of the acquisition of the physical comforts of the world, their faith tends to dwindle. This is what Hugh Nibley refers to as the "Nephite disease" which is so recurrent throughout the Book of Mormon.

Evidence of this same feeling continues today. Throughout the world as one compares the rate of growth of the Church in various countries it is abundantly clear that, generally speaking, the lower the per capita income, the greater the growth of the Church. Conversely, the wealthier a nation is, the slower the growth will be in the kingdom of God. Carnal security tends to anesthetize people to the things of the Spirit, just as Nephi warned us.

But what are the consequences of spiritual security or insecurity? It was while in a state of great spiritual insecurity that the young Joseph Smith prayed for a divine confirmation of his standing before the Lord. It was the evening of September 21, 1823, three and a half years after Joseph's first vision of the Father and the Son. By Joseph's own account:

> I was left to all kinds of temptations; and mingling with all kinds of society, I frequently fell into many foolish errors, and displayed the weakness of youth, and the foibles of human nature; which, I am sorry to say, led me into divers temptations, offensive in the sight of God. In making this confession, no one need suppose me guilty of any great or malignant sins. A disposition to commit such was never in my nature. But I was guilty of levity, and sometimes associated with jovial company, etc., not consistent with that character which ought to be maintained by one who was called of God as I had been. . . .
>
> In consequence of these things, *I often felt condemned for my weakness and imperfections*; when, on the evening of the above-mentioned twenty-first of September, after I had retired to my bed for the night, I betook myself to prayer and supplication to Almighty God for forgiveness of all my sins and follies, and also for a manifestation to me, that I might know of my state and standing before him; for I had full confidence in obtaining a divine manifestation, as I previously had one. (JS–H 1:28–29, emphasis added.)

You will recall how the angel Moroni appeared to Joseph three times that evening and a fourth time the following morning to prepare him for the coming forth of the Book of Mormon and the restoration of the keys of the sealing power held by Elijah.

This account tells us so much about the young man Joseph Smith. It reveals his absolute honesty and candor in publicly confessing his weaknesses to the world. Here was no hypocrite, no charlatan, but rather a humble, honest, sincere young man in search of spiritual security. And we learn of his great faith as he confesses: "I had full confidence in obtaining a divine manifestation." Sometimes we fail to recognize a certain element of risk in our prayers. Sometimes we fail to plead with the Lord for fear that His answer will not be to our liking. The Savior's prayer in Gethsemane should be the pattern for our personal prayers: "Nevertheless not my will, but thine, be done" (Luke 22:42).

There were others during the early history of the Church who also sought a divine manifestation to bolster their faith. Through the Prophet Joseph, the Lord told Oliver Cowdery: "Verily, verily, I say unto you, if you desire a further witness, cast your mind upon the night that you cried unto me in your heart, that you might know concerning the truth of these things. Did I not speak peace to your mind concerning the matter? What greater witness can you have than from God?" (D&C 6:22–23.)

Lyman Sherman was another troubled brother who came to the Prophet for some assurance of his standing before the Lord. Brother Sherman had previously served as one of the Presidents of the Seventy and had been released the previous month. In his behalf the Prophet Joseph received the following revelation: "Verily thus saith the Lord unto you, my servant Lyman: Your sins are forgiven you, because you have obeyed my voice in coming up hither this morning to receive counsel of him whom I have appointed. Therefore, let your soul be at rest concerning your spiritual standing, and resist no more my voice." (D&C 108:1–2.)

Would that each of us could have such seemingly ready access to a living prophet who could be the Lord's mouthpiece in speaking such comforting words of assurance to us. But as Elder Boyd K. Packer has reminded us on two separate occasions, "Vienna and Geneva are just as close to heaven as Salt Lake City." In the quiet closets of our own homes we can draw upon the powers of heaven to be with our families and to comfort our occasionally troubled hearts.

Spiritual security is ours for the asking, ours for the taking, and ours for the making. Perhaps there is no more succinct passage outlining required risks and ultimate security in the eternities than the Savior's injunction: "He that findeth his life shall lose it: and he that loseth his life for my sake shall find it" (Matt. 10:39). Here is the balance to be found between risk and security.

We must risk carnal security for spiritual security, and we must be willing to risk the treasures of this earth for the treasures of heaven. We must "lose" minutes and hours in the service of others in order to gain eternal life.

President Harold B. Lee recounted an experience with a friend whose father had been a stake patriarch. His son had served as his father's scribe in recording patriarchal blessings. President Lee's friend shared his observation that each patriarchal blessing was based upon certain conditions, that they were, in the words of this friend, "iffy" blessings. His friend spoke anonymously of individuals who had received wonderful and marvelous promises if they lived true and faithful and kept the commandments of God. Unfortunately, there were some who did not keep the commandments nor abide by the conditions of their blessings, and so these blessings were forfeited. Patriarchal blessings can be a great source of spiritual security when we abide by the conditions outlined therein.[5]

The Risks and Security of a Mission

Gwendolyn Robison was a seventeen-year-old nonmember of the Church living in England in 1937. She had a number of good Latter-day Saint friends who had encouraged her to attend Church meetings with them, and they had also pressed her into service in making preparations for a jubilee pageant commemorating one century since the arrival of Heber C. Kimball, and the other missionaries in Liverpool in 1837.

The Monday before the pageant found Gwendolyn busily painting the backdrop on the makeshift stage at one end of a large warehouse where the festivities would take place later in the week. After painting the cloudy sky and the waves of the sea near the port where the first missionaries landed, Gwendolyn's eye caught sight of an elderly, distinguished-looking man seated in the rear of the hall. He had a kindly countenance framed by a white beard, and Gwendolyn felt impelled to speak with him.

In her strong British accent she said: "Ya know, sir, it's not a good thing fer a man yer age to be just sittin' around. Ya need to activate yerself. Now I need some help up here a-paintin' the bushes and trees and the rest of the scenery. Now here's an extra brush, and I'd like ya to come help me."

The elderly gentleman graciously declined the offer, insisting he was enjoying himself just watching the activity of the others.

After a few hours Gwendolyn again approached the elderly gentleman with some cotton batting, the kind used in making quilts. She looked at him and said: "If ya don't want to paint, at least ya can help us make some beards. We're havin' a play here this weekend, and it's got prophets in it, and, of course, prophets have got to have beards."

Again the bearded gentleman declined her invitation to get involved. But, undaunted, she continued to pester him: "Then if ya won't help us out, at least ya can walk with me to the lake where we can feed the ducks [rhymes with "looks"]. Ya really need to activate yerself." So, after she had finished painting and had cleaned her brushes, she grabbed the elderly man by the hand, and he somewhat reluctantly strolled with her to a little pond in the middle of a park where they fed the ducks some stale bread she had brought along.

Tuesday the scene repeated itself. At the end of a day of painting scenery Gwendolyn grabbed the elderly man's hand, and this time he more willingly joined her in feeding the ducks. On Wednesday he actually looked forward to the event and immensely enjoyed their stroll through the park.

Thursday morning she saw him again, seated at the rear of the hall. By now they were becoming fast friends. "Now, this afternoon," she said, "we can't feed the ducks because I'm going to get myself baptized a member of the Mormon church, and I'd like ya to be there." He replied, with a twinkle in his eye, "I would enjoy that very much, young lady."

After her baptism someone with an accordion style camera took a photo of petite Gwendolyn standing next to this stately gentleman. After the photo had been taken, he looked at her and said, "Gwendolyn, when this picture is developed, I would like you to write on the back of it, 'From the last to the highest ordained.'" Gwendolyn was very puzzled by his cryptic statement and asked him for a clarification.

He smiled benevolently at her and said, "You do not know who I am, do you?" She replied somewhat sheepishly, "Now that ya mention it, I've been doin' all the talkin' this past week, and I fergot to ask ya." "Well," he said, "my name is Heber J. Grant, and I am the President of the Church."

This was Gwendolyn's first encounter with a member of the First Presidency, but it was not to be her last. Forty-seven years later, in the summer of 1984, Gwendolyn and her Polish-born husband, Stanley Mazur, arrived in Warsaw, Poland, to reopen missionary work in that country. Other faithful missionaries had preceeded them in previous years, but due to the political instability of the country they had not been able to remain there.

Though Gwendolyn and Stanley Mazur had been married for many years, he had only recently joined the Church a few years prior to their mission call, and so his knowledge of the gospel and Church administration was naturally quite limited. But he did speak fluent Polish. Gwendolyn, on the other hand, had been a member of the Church for nearly half a century, but, unfortunately, she spoke no Polish. The two of them exemplified the Lord's latter-day revelation in which he said, "Wherefore, I call upon the weak things of the world, those who are unlearned and despised, to thrash the nations by the power of my Spirit" (D&C 35:3; see also 1 Cor. 1:27).

They lived in a very small apartment on one of the main streets of Warsaw. The apartment had only a small wash basin and no bathtub, and their combination bedroom-kitchen had only a hot plate for cooking. At that time there was a rather critical food shortage in Poland, so their diet consisted largely of boiled eggs, boiled potatoes, boiled onions, and boiled cabbage.

It so happened that Elder Thomas S. Monson, then first contact of the Twelve for Europe, visited the mission home in Vienna while the Mazurs were there for a missionary couples' conference with the other couples serving in Greece, Yugoslavia, Austria, and Hungary. Elder Monson heard the Mazur's report on the hardships the Polish people were facing with a shortage of food and clothing, and he was filled with compassion. When they concluded their report he said: "Elder and Sister Mazur, I brought two suits with me on this trip, and I would like to give one of them to you to take back to Poland with you. When you find someone my size, please give him the suit with my love."

It was interesting to observe Sister Mazur holding Elder Monson's suit bag, because he is such a large man, and she is not quite five feet tall.

Elder and Sister Monson returned home and the Mazurs returned to Poland, and each week when I called, I would ask her if she had given away the Apostle's suit. One week she replied, rather testily: "No, I ain't given it away, nor am I gonna. Sometimes I get so tired of eatin' nothin' but potatoes and onions, and I get feelin' down in the dumps [pronounced "doomps"] from Stanley teachin' these people in Polish and I can't understand 'em, that I go get the Apostle's suit coat out of the closet [with the sleeves nearly touching the ground] and I sing 'Coom, Coom, Ye Saints' till I'm not in the doomps no more. So ya see, President Condie, I ain't never gonna give the suit away."

Well, time passed, and a few months later Stanley and Gwendolyn did find someone who could wear the suit of a caring, compassionate Apostle. Before they concluded their mission, Brother and Sister Mazur had brought thirty-four people into the Church in Poland.

The Mazurs were followed by another British-Polish combination, Elder Juliusz and Sister Dorothy Fussek. They were called for eighteen months but ended up staying on their mission for five years. President Monson commended them for their service during general conference in April 1992.

Alonzo and Renae Plumb were called for a year and a half to Athens, Greece, but they stayed for three years, rendering yeoman's service in establishing the fledgling Church there. They were there when the first young elders were called to Greece in the spring of 1986, and they were assisted by several other valiant couples who preceded and followed them.

Elder William and Sister Barbara Williams served a mission in Zagreb, Yugoslavia, went home for a while, were called back to Beograd, Yugoslavia, and finally completed their second mission as pioneers in Bulgaria. Elder Joseph and Sister Melba Padovich also served faithfully and well on two different missions to Yugoslavia.

Elder Hyrum and Ruth Ciezlak served two missions in Germany, a third mission in Austria, and a fourth mission to Poland. There are hundreds of others, all of whom *should* be mentioned in this book, whose concern for eternal security far outweighed any risks involved in temporarily setting aside concerns for temporal security.

Balance involves determining which risks should further be taken after we took that first risk of leaving our heavenly home. Our quest for security should involve seeking for those things which do not wear out or fade, or which do not have to be replaced or repaired, or which cannot be stolen or destroyed. Celestial security involves taking temporal risks like paying a full tithing even when Christmas shopping money is tight, or giving a blessing to someone in the hospital at the risk of missing a ballgame, or taking the risk of not seeing a new grandbaby blessed because we are serving a mission.

His Saints can and should and will "securely dwell" when they exercise their faith in risking that which is of temporary worth to establish that which is of eternal worth.

Notes

1. Philip Doddridge, "How Gentle God's Commands," *Hymns*, 1985, no. 125.

2. Boyd K. Packer, "Our Moral Environment," *Ensign* 22 (May 1992): 66.

3. See "Grim Global Outlook on AIDS," *International Herald Tribune*, June 4, 1992, p. 1.

4. Russell M. Nelson, "Doors of Death," *Ensign* 22 (May 1992): 72.

5. See Harold B. Lee, "Admonitions for the Priesthood of God," *Ensign* 3 (January 1973): 107–8.

Chapter Five

FORM AND CONTENT

Having a Form of Godliness [1]

Several years ago, while our family was blessed to live in the beautiful city of Vienna, we often enjoyed going to the Kunsthistorisches Museum (Museum of Art History). This massive, ornate structure, fashioned in a neo-Baroque style, houses more than a thousand of the world's greatest paintings and other art treasures. In many respects it embodies much that is "virtuous, lovely, or of good report or praiseworthy."

Even devoid of its masterworks, this building would be a work of art in its own right. The grandeur of its architectural symmetry, its beautifully sculptured columns, and its ornate ceilings evoke feelings of awe and appreciation for the talents of the builders and those who gave of their means to help construct this beautiful building.

On one occasion as we visited this museum, I reflected upon the words of the Savior to a young farm boy in a grove of trees in the spring of 1820: "They draw near to me with their lips . . . , having a form of godliness, but they deny the power thereof" (JS–H 1:19; see also 2 Tim. 3:5).

Each time I revisited this museum or the Musikverein concert hall or the famous Vienna State Opera House, I felt inspired by the talents of others, all of whom had been given the Light of Christ (Moro. 7:12–16), and many of whom lived as best they could within the light they had been given. But in each of these buildings returned the reverberating theme, "They have a form of godliness, but they deny the power thereof."

And then, on a sudden, I was struck with a three-hundred-kilovolt question: "Bibbed and tuckered in your white shirt and blue serge suit, with your spit-shined shoes and your missionary haircut, you perhaps sometimes have a form of godliness, but does your personal life really reflect the power of the priesthood of God?"

For one of the few times in my life, I gained a glimpse into the depths of my own soul, and I did not like everything I saw. Like Enos, the son of Jacob, I have observed through personal experience the egocentricity of sin. As Enos went hunting and his soul began to hunger for the things of the Spirit, his first recorded thoughts were upon his *own* soul. It was not until he had prayed all day long and into the night and had received a confirmation of forgiveness of his own sins that his heart was next turned to thoughts of others.

Through personal experience I have found that when one does not have the Spirit of the Lord, any service within the Church becomes extremely arduous. On the other hand, when our spirits are in tune, the powers of heaven can and do distill upon us, drenching us with joy in serving the Lord through service to others. It is then that our confidence waxes strong before God and the Holy Ghost becomes our constant companion. (See D&C 121:45–46.)

King David

There are few examples more poignant than the life of King David in illustrating a corrosion of confidence in the sight of the Lord. As a naive shepherd boy filled with faith and confidence, he slew Goliath while his compatriots cowered in the background. As a poet-king, anointed to that position under the hands of the prophet Samuel, he exemplified a form of godliness as he wrote of green pastures, still waters, and paths of righteousness. Filled with faith he humbly, yet confidently, proclaimed: "Yea, though I walk through the valley of the shadow of death, I will fear no evil: for thou art with me; thy rod and thy staff they comfort me" (Ps. 23:4). In his very next recorded psalm he asserted that those who shall ascend unto the hill of the Lord must have "clean hands, and a pure heart" (Ps. 24:3–4).

But some time later, after becoming the king of all Israel, David, the shepherd boy grown tall, "lifted up his soul unto vanity" (Ps. 24:4), and following the lusts of a heart no longer pure, he committed a sin for which forgiveness is difficult, and then compounded it by committing an even greater sin.

The Psalms of David provide us with an excellent barometer of his spirituality, just as our personal journals reflect the strengths and weaknesses of our respective lives. Thus, it is of interest to read David's journal entry shortly after his encounter with Bathsheba. Racked with unrelenting remorse, he no longer possessed a faith which fears no evil, for David's green pastures had become deserts of despair.

Without divine guidance, how was he going to lead Israel and defend her borders? In 1 Chronicles we learn that Satan placed in David's heart the desire to take a census of all his people. His chief commander, Joab, was a bit distressed at David's request, for had not God always helped his chosen people regardless of their numbers? (See 1 Chr. 21:1–3.) Had not Jehovah trimmed Gideon's troops from 32,000 to 300 to prove that it was the Lord's power and not sheer numbers which was responsible for the victory over the Midianites? (See Judg. 7.) Had not David the shepherd boy been a majority of one in single-handedly defeating the Goliath-led Philistines? Little wonder that Joab questioned his king's sudden striving to find safety in numbers.

President Harold B. Lee, upon becoming the President of the Church in July, 1972, said: "The safety of the Church lies in the members keeping the commandments."[2] And what of the safety of a nation? Is our nation any less exempt from the blessings of obedience and the consequences of disobedience? Were the matter not so serious, I could chuckle at the similarities between David's census of the Israelites and our own nation's compulsive counting of nuclear warheads. How many missiles does it take to protect a nation in which abortion is currently the most frequently performed operation in hospitals and clinics throughout this land?[3]

Is national security possible for a country whose citizens are addicted by the millions to movies, magazines, and television programs which vividly portray Satan's smutty smorgasbord on a daily basis? In my humble view, parity in nuclear numbers may numb our fears, but it is a sad substitute for spiritual strength and security. Sometimes, even within the Church, an undue concern with numbers can impair human relationships as people become pawns in a quantitative quest for perfection. But what of *qualitative* perfection? Do our statistical reports sometimes have a form of godliness and yet lack any godly power?

Elder Dean L. Larsen reminds us that "the qualities of the spirit are susceptible to assessment, but they must be assessed by spiritual means."[4] Paul's counsel to the Corinthians may be helpful to us in this regard: "The letter killeth, but the spirit giveth life" (2 Cor. 3:6); and I suppose the secular equivalent to this statement is the sage observation that "too much rigor often leads to mortis."

Means and Goals

I make no claims to being a theologian, but with my limited knowledge and perspective, it appears to me that in the eternal economy of things, the methods we use to achieve our eternal goals are often as important as the goals themselves.

In the fourth chapter of Moses we learn of the Council in Heaven wherein Satan proposed what appears to be a very laudable goal: "I will redeem all mankind, that one soul shall not be lost, and surely I will do it" (Moses 4:1). Now, what could possibly be wrong with such a lofty goal to absolutely assure eternal salvation to all mankind? The Lord himself answers this question: "Because that Satan rebelled against me, and sought to destroy the agency of man, . . . I caused that he should be cast down" (Moses 4:3).

As we continually contemplate this vital relationship between mortal means and eternal goals, it may be well to reflect upon the fact that the Savior called Peter and Andrew to be "fishers of men," not hunters (Matt. 4:19). Whereas hunters pursue their quarry, assailing them with slings and arrows, the fishers of men are to use the methods of "persuasion, long-suffering, gentleness, meekness, and love unfeigned" (D&C 121:41). It is well to remember that fishing requires that the fish must take some of the initiative in order to swim into the gospel net, therein finding the eternal meaning of life.

Sunday Neurosis

In his book *Man's Search for Meaning*, Viktor Frankl discusses individuals whose lives have no sense of meaning. He refers to this empty feeling, or existential vacuum, as a "Sunday neurosis," a kind of depression "which afflicts people who become aware of the lack of content in their lives when the rush of the busy week is over and the void within themselves becomes manifest."[5] In other words, who are we and what are we on Sundays when we don't go to work to perform the roles of accountant, electrician, truck driver, beautician, or nurse? Or, who are we after we have been released as bishop or Relief Society president? Or, who are we on Sunday when we're not in church? Is the Sabbath day a day of spiritual regeneration or one of emptiness and boredom, devoid of celestial content?

Sunday Nostalgia

A few years ago I visited a priests quorum meeting in one of the wards in our stake. I had been touched by the lesson given to prospective missionaries preparing to preach the gospel. The adviser's quiet yet firm testimony reminded me once again that the gospel really is true. As I journeyed home that day I felt no Sunday neurosis; it was more of a Sunday nostalgia, a sense of longing for a celestial home. I was reminded of a familiar song:

> Yet ofttimes a secret something
> Whispered, "You're a stranger here,"
> And I felt that I had wandered
> From a more exalted sphere.[6]

President Spencer W. Kimball gave us the solution to resolving feelings of emptiness in our lives as he said:

> When we are engaged in the service of our fellowmen, not only do our deeds assist them, but we put our own problems in a fresher perspective. When we concern ourselves more with others, there is less time to be concerned with ourselves. In the midst of the miracle of serving, there is the promise of Jesus, that by losing ourselves, we find ourselves. (See Matt. 10:39.)
>
> . . . The more we serve our fellowmen in appropriate ways, the more substance there is to our souls. . . . Indeed, it is easier to "find" ourselves because there is so much more of us to find![7]

Form and Content

The importance of finding the contents beneath the form was brought forcefully home to me while I shopping in an Austrian supermarket. I was perplexed to observe two cans of mushrooms of identical size with different labels and very discrepant prices.

I asked one of the clerks what the difference was between the cans for 13 schillings and the ones for 27 schillings. With a smile the clerk replied: "The ones for 27 are guaranteed not to be poisonous!"

The Viennese social critic Karl Kraus wrote a biting satire on the glorification of war in his play *The Last Days of Mankind.* At the outbreak of World War I, Kraus described the situation in Berlin as "serious but not hopeless, whereas in Vienna things were hopeless, but not serious."[8]

The Viennese took their operas and their arts very seriously. In the Kaffee houses of Vienna, fighting was not uncommon. And what was the source of these heated debates? Whether Wagner was a greater composer than Brahms! But war—that was different. Music should be taken seriously, but not war. That was a matter of pomp and glory and of good, heroic fun. Little mention was made of death and destruction. And so, an army of two and a half million soldiers marched to the glorious front, never to return from battle.

I suspect that sometimes in our personal lives we, too, may sometimes take the wrong things seriously and make light of sacred covenants which should be taken most seriously. Martin Duberman's description of the "bit" technique illustrates this problem:

> The "bit" technique goes like this: At all costs one must avoid the stigma of being too serious; to do so, you stick a self-mocking label on any scene in which you might be caught displaying deep emotion. Thus: I don't want to do the "engaged-couple bit," but . . . or I don't want to do the "expectant-father bit," but . . . Doing "bits" with people is the "in" way of establishing fellowship. They allow one to show affection while ridiculing it, to be sentimental while appearing tough.[9]

Perhaps King Saul did the "sacrifice bit" when the prophet Samuel commanded Saul to slay all of the Amalekites and all of their animals. When Saul returned home from battle, Samuel was distraught to discover that Saul had brought several animals back with him, supposedly to sacrifice them upon his arrival home. Saul learned the hard way that "to obey is better than sacrifice, and to hearken than the fat of rams" (1 Sam. 15:22).

I hope the youth of Zion will not engage in the "dress-standards bit" or the "missionary bit" or the "temple-marriage bit" or any other "bits" which may have a form of godliness but deny the power thereof. When we make covenants in the temple, they are to be valid for time and all eternity—period.

Consider the following practices, some of which have a form of godliness and some of which have both the form and the power:

Do we appreciate the difference between fasting and skipping breakfast?

Is there a crucial distinction in our lives between praying and saying prayers?

Do we know the difference between consecration and contribution?

Can we discriminate between music which edifies and that which debases? The amplification of three basic guitar chords through sixteen-inch speakers still begs the question of whether some music is good and loud or just loud.

Some well-meaning producers of instructional films have assumed that to convey important information to the younger generation, we must "meet them halfway" by presenting sacred or serious information accompanied by soft rock music so that the message will be more palatable to the youth. Unfortunately, the asymmetry between the serious content of the message and the very casual form of the musical sound track may generate considerable uncertainty in the minds of young listeners who take the message casually and the soundtrack seriously. If eternal gospel messages are combined with avant garde music, the rising generation may assume that the Church is based upon soft rock instead of the rock of revelation.

The form should always match the content. Psalm 137 eloquently addresses this concern as the children of Israel, while living in captivity, posed the poignant question: "How shall we sing the Lord's song in a strange land?" (Ps. 137:4.)

Faith vs. Fear

Form and content meet head-to-head in the matter of obedience. Can we discern between obedience based on faith versus obedience based on fear? Elder Theodore M. Burton provided some very interesting insights in this regard:

> Some members of the Church have said to me, "Why should we keep a store of food on hand? If a real emergency came in this lawless

world, a neighbor would simply come with his gun and take it from us. What would *you* do if a person came and demanded *your* food?" I replied that I would share whatever I had with him, and he wouldn't have to use a gun to obtain that assistance either.

"I wouldn't," replied one man. "I have a gun, and I wouldn't hesitate to use it to defend my family. Anyone would have to kill me first in order to get food away from me! After all, they bring their own misery upon themselves by not being prepared!"

Elder Burton, with a twinkle in his eye, continued: "Well, one way to solve this problem is to convert your neighbors to become obedient Latter-day Saints with their own supply of food."[10]

Of course, another solution to this "drawbridge mentality" is obedience to the counsel of the Lord: "If ye are prepared ye shall not fear" (D&C 38:30); and, "Inasmuch as ye have done it unto one of the least of these my brethren, ye have done it unto me" (Matt. 25:40).

Activity vs. Devotion

It has been interesting to note the extremely widespread use of the words *active* and *inactive* to describe members of the Church. If people show up for most of their meetings we call them "active." On the other hand, if they miss most of their meetings, we label them "inactive." Over the years it has been interesting to observe how many so-called "active" Saints seldom contribute fast offerings or attend the temple. By contrast, there are Saints whose neighbors call them "inactive" but who contribute generous fast offerings.

It seems that the words *active* and *inactive* do not adequately capture the dimensions of devotion, consecration, commitment, and godliness. For example, the sons of Eli regularly officiated in the temple, despite the fact that they were impure and desecrated the sacrifices of those who had come to worship (see 1 Sam. 2–3). By today's statistical standards they were "active," because they showed up at the temple each day.

Power vs. Form

There are many organizations and activities which compete for our time, our means, and our loyalty. Many of these are what Robert

Bellah calls "civil religion," for they have the form of a religion.[11] For example, there are civic organizations and learned societies which have a hierarchical structure complete with high councils and other presiding officers. They solicit contributions in proportion to one's income and hold regional and general conferences. Their purposes are generally lofty, and membership in such organizations is to be encouraged. But after all is said and done, in an eternal perspective, often more is said than done, for the priesthood of God is absent from such organizations.

The training and self-discipline of athletic competition does much to remind us that our bodies are the temples of our spirits (see 1 Cor. 3:16). But for some, interest in athletics, either as participant or spectator, takes on a sacred aura which has a form of religious devotion. But what of the power of God? A million-dollar baseball contract pales in comparison to the priesthood promises contained in the oath and covenant of the priesthood in section 84 of the Doctrine and Covenants.

Patriotism, misused and misdirected, may also assume a form of godliness devoid of godly power as we have seen in various countries of the world. In Austria we visited the Nazi concentration camp at Mauthausen, and our souls were subdued by this memorial to the high costs of hatred and the wreckage of patriotism gone awry. What began with exclusionary ethnic epithets grew into vicious vandalism and eventually ended in mass murder. After that visit I made a promise that I was going to refrain from telling ethnic jokes and that I was going to try harder to substitute charity for criticism. I am still wrestling with that promise.

I fear that many of us, like Saul, are more willing to sacrifice other people's possessions than to sacrifice our own sins. This was the sacrifice which the father of King Lamoni made when he prayed: "O God, . . . I will give away all my sins to know thee" (Alma 22:18). This kind of sacrifice is precisely the price that must be paid to know Him and to enter into His presence. I sense that sometimes as Latter-day Saints we are often too ready to sacrifice and too slow to obey. I sometimes question how much of what we call sacrifice really constitutes a sacrifice on our part. For example, if we invest several thousand dollars in long-term savings certificates with the intent of gaining a rich return on our investments, do we ever refer to such investments as a sacrifice? I have heard of stock brokers, realtors, and investment counselors, but I have never heard of sacrificial account executives.

Then what of financial contributions to the kingdom? And what of the time we spend in preparing Primary lessons, singing in ward choirs, or taking a troop of Boy Scouts to Camp Poison Sumac for a week's retreat on the shores of Mosquito Lake? Do these contributions constitute a major sacrifice, or are they eternal investments in a paradisiacal portfolio promising divine dividends that "all that [our] Father hath shall be given unto [us]"? (D&C 84:38.)

In section 84 we learn from the words of the Lord that "without the ordinances thereof, and the authority of the priesthood, the power of godliness is not manifest unto men in the flesh" (D&C 84:21). It is in the priesthood, not in numbers, that the power of godliness is manifest.

Godliness and Perfection

Elder Bruce R. McConkie has identified as fallacious the belief that "we must be perfect to gain salvation."[12] I was heartened by his observation, for I have counseled with many students who have disclosed their distress in having failed to reach perfection by the second semester of their junior year; or, they are discouraged because they failed to return home from a mission perfect; or, they were married in the temple to a "perfect" companion, when they themselves were not perfect.

Elder McConkie's statement is true: we will not achieve perfection in this life. The Savior himself is the only one to accomplish this goal on this earth. But, if we are to become like the Savior, we would do well to follow the admonition of Moroni in the final verses of the Book of Mormon: "Come unto Christ, and be perfected in him, and deny yourselves of all ungodliness; and if ye shall deny yourselves of all ungodliness and love God with all your might, mind and strength, then is his grace sufficient for you, that by his grace ye may be perfect in Christ; and if by the grace of God ye are perfect in Christ, ye can in nowise deny the power of God" (Moro. 10:32).

The pathway to perfection will always be punctuated with painful and unpleasant events. After all, Lehi instructed Jacob that "it must needs be, that there is an opposition in all things" (2 Ne. 2:11). He did not say "there could be" or "there might be" or even that there "would be" opposition. Lehi said "it must needs be, that there is an opposition in all things." Opposition is indispensable to the plan of salvation and for the eternal experiences and growth afforded therein.

The pathway to perfection and godhood begins with the acquisition of godly attributes such as those described in section 4 of the Doctrine and Covenants: "faith, virtue, knowledge, temperance, patience, brotherly kindness, godliness, charity, humility, [and] diligence" (D&C 4:6). In our personal striving, and in assisting those who are lost or faltering to obtain the power of godliness, may we keep in mind the Savior's thrice-given injunction to Peter to "feed my sheep" (John 21:15–17). It seems significant that the Lord said "feed my sheep," not "herd them." Means are often as important as goals.

It is my prayer that each of us may begin each day with a firmer resolve to cultivate the attributes of godliness, having both the form of godliness *and* the power thereof.

Notes

1. This chapter is a revision of a devotional address given at Brigham Young University, July 28, 1981.

2. *Church News*, July 15, 1972, p. 3.

3. See *Statistical Abstracts of the United States*, Washington, D.C., U.S. Department of Commerce, 1992.

4. Dean L. Larsen, "Some Thoughts on Goal-Setting," *Ensign* 11 (February 1981): 62–65.

5. Viktor E. Frankl, *Man's Search for Meaning* (New York: Simon and Schuster, 1963), p. 169.

6. Eliza R. Snow, "O My Father," *Hymns*, 1985, no. 292.

7. Spencer W. Kimball, "Small Acts of Service," *Ensign* (December 1974): 2.

8. Karl Kraus, *Die letzen Tage der Menscheheit* (Muenchen: Koesel, 1957).

9. Martin Duberman, *New York Times Book Review*, Sept. 19, 1965, pp. 60–61.

10. Theodore M. Burton, in Conference Report, April 1974, p. 91.

11. Robert N. Bellah, "Civil Religion in America," *Daedalus*, 1976, pp. 1–21.

12. Bruce R. McConkie, "The Seven Deadly Heresies," in *1980 Devotional Speeches of the Year* (Provo, Utah: BYU Press, 1981), p. 78.

Chapter Six

The Spirit and the Letter of the Law

There are few gospel principles which are in greater tension than the spirit of the law and the letter of the law, and resolving this tension is by no means an easy task. Those who prefer broad and general interpretations of scripture are fond of quoting Paul's statement to the Corinthians, "For the letter killeth, but the spirit giveth life" (2 Cor. 3:6, see also Rom. 9:31–2; D&C 88:34). Jacob also warned of the danger of rule followers who look "beyond the mark," like those who adhered to the law of Moses in such meticulous detail that they failed to recognize the Messiah whose coming had been anticipated by the law (Jacob 4:14).

Those who gravitate toward a rule-following mentality are fond of quoting the Book of Mormon description of Helaman's faithful two thousand and sixty stripling warriors, who "did obey and observe to perform every word of command with exactness" (Alma 57:21). A kindred scripture, often quoted out of its complete context, is, "I, the Lord, cannot look upon sin with the least degree of allowance" (D&C 1:31).

The Savior, ever exemplifying the perfect balance between eternal principles, chastened the scribes and Pharisees of His day with the following unvarnished candor: "Woe unto you, scribes and Pharisees, hypocrites! for ye pay tithe of mint and anise and cummin, and have omitted the weightier matters of the law, judgment, mercy, and faith: these ought ye to have done, and not to leave the other undone" (Matt. 23:23). Herein lies the key: they needed to incorporate within their lives the weightier matters of the Spirit but not overlook the requirements of the law in the process.

Law of Moses

Although today we no longer adhere to the law of Moses in all of its details as it was revealed to the children of Israel, it is very insightful and instructive, nevertheless, to examine the purpose of that law as seen through the eyes of Book of Mormon prophets. We shall not go into great detail regarding the specific feast days and fast days and rites and rituals of the law, but suffice it to say that one crucial element of the law included the sacrifice of the unblemished lamb, the firstling of the flock pointing to the atonement of the Lamb of God, the Only Begotten of the Father.

All of the Book of Mormon prophets prior to the coming of Christ taught the law of Moses. Nephi recorded that "notwithstanding we believe in Christ, we keep the law of Moses, and look forward with steadfastness unto Christ, until the law shall be fulfilled. For, for this end was the law given." (2 Ne. 25:24–25.)

Jacob explained that "for this intent we keep the law of Moses, it pointing our souls to him; and for this cause it is sanctified unto us for righteousness, even as it was accounted unto Abraham in the wilderness to be obedient unto the commands of God in offering up his son Isaac, which is a similitude of God and his Only Begotten Son (Jacob 4:5).

Jacob's grandson Jarom recorded four centuries before Christ that prophets, priests, and teachers of his day taught the people the law of Moses with "the intent for which it was given; persuading them to look forward unto the Messiah, and believe in him to come as though he already was" (Jarom 1:11).

During King Benjamin's reign about 124 years before Christ, the people "took of the firstlings of their flocks, that they might offer sacrifice and burnt offerings according to the law of Moses" (Mosiah 2:3).

When the prophet Abinadi came into the kingdom of wicked Noah, he chastened Noah's priests for not having applied their "hearts to understanding" (Mosiah 12:27). Then, after having taught them the Ten Commandments, he said:

> And now ye have said that salvation cometh by the law of Moses. I say unto you that it is expedient that ye should keep the law of Moses as yet; but I say unto you, that the time shall come when it shall no more be expedient to keep the law of Moses.

> And moreover, I say unto you, that salvation doth not come by the law alone; and were it not for the atonement, which God himself shall make for the sins and iniquities of his people, that they must unavoidably perish, notwithstanding the law of Moses. . . .
>
> Therefore there was a law given them, yea, a law of performances and of ordinances, a law which they were to observe strictly from day to day, to keep them in remembrance of God and their duty towards him.
>
> But behold, I say unto you, that all these things were types of things to come. (Mosiah 13:27–28, 30–31.)

Abinadi's teachings were supported by Amulek's excellent summary statement of the purpose of the law when he said: "This is the whole meaning of the law, every whit pointing to that great and last sacrifice; and that great and last sacrifice will be the Son of God, yea, infinite and eternal" (Alma 34:14).

When we partake of the sacramental emblems of the broken bread and water, we do so in *remembrance* of the atonement of Jesus Christ. The children of Israel and the ancient Nephites sacrificed the firstling of the flock and shed the blood of the unblemished lamb in *anticipation* of the atonement of Christ. Hence, Paul's declaration to the Galatians that "the law was our schoolmaster to bring us unto Christ" (Gal. 3:24).

More Excellent Way

In the book of Ether, Moroni gives us a marvelous sermon on faith, teaching us, among other important things, that "by faith was the law of Moses given. But in the gift of his Son hath God prepared a more excellent way; and it is by faith that it hath been fulfilled." (Ether 12:11.)

Paul uses this expression to introduce his eloquent and inspiring discourse on charity. Both Paul and Moroni viewed the law of Moses as an excellent way to bring people unto Christ, but charity, the pure love of Christ, is an even more excellent way because the quest for charity leads us to become like Christ.

Paul teaches us that "charity suffereth long, and is kind; charity envieth not; charity vaunteth not itself, is not puffed up, doth not behave itself unseemly, seeketh not her own [i.e., does not strive for exclusivity, shutting others out of one's own social circle], is not easily provoked, thinketh no evil; rejoiceth not in iniquity, but rejoiceth in the truth; beareth all things, believeth all things, hopeth all things, endureth all things. Charity never faileth." (1 Cor. 13:4–8.)

In his record Moroni included his father's teachings on charity, which conclude with this important statement on how we can obtain this love: "Wherefore, my beloved brethren, pray unto the Father *with all the energy of heart*, that ye may be filled with this love, which he hath bestowed upon all who are true followers of his Son, Jesus Christ; that ye may become the sons of God; that when he shall appear we shall be like him, for we shall see him as he is; that we may have this hope; that we may be purified even as he is pure. Amen." (Moro. 7:48, emphasis added.)

When Principles Collide

Fast Offerings. In the Doctrine and Covenants the Lord teaches us two important principles regarding the care of the poor. First, "thou wilt remember the poor, and consecrate of thy properties for their support," and second, "he that is idle shall not eat the bread nor wear the garments of the laborer" (D&C 42:30, 42). In brief, bishops are to succor the needs of the worthy poor, those who are not idle, those who are trying to support their families but have fallen into economic difficulty. But what of the Jonsen family in which the father is idle, perhaps even an alcoholic who has been fired from several jobs because of his absenteeism due to drinking? His wife and four children under the age of ten are committed to keeping the commandments. They pray together and attend Church meetings together, but they have depended upon their husband and father for support. Should fast offering assistance and food from the bishops' storehouse be denied them because the head of the household is unworthy?

To resolve the tensions between the spirit and the letter of the law, the bishop has at his disposal several resources. The ward welfare committee—consisting of the bishopric, the Relief Society presidency, the elders quorum presidency, and the high priests group leader—can prayerfully discuss alternative solutions to the problem facing the Jonsen family.

Contact should be made with Brother and Sister Jonsen's extended family members, their parents, brothers and sisters, and any aunts or uncles who may be in a position to assist in resolving the problem. Immediate assistance may be needed in the form of fast-offering funds to pay utility bills and rent, and an order from the bishops' storehouse and Deseret Industries may alleviate critical needs for food and clothing. But this type of assistance should be short-term with a specific goal in mind of making the family self-sufficient as soon as possible.

Perhaps alcoholic rehabilitation is needed, followed by some short-term assistance in obtaining additional job training. The ward and stake employment specialists can assist in finding better employment for Brother Jonsen and perhaps some work opportunities for Sister Jonsen within the home.

Through combining the resources of the extended family, the priesthood quorum, compassionate Relief Society members, and devoted home teachers, the tension between the letter of the law and the spirit of the law is resolved as each and every member follows the course of the more excellent way.

Fasting. Much has been written and spoken about the law of the fast. Those who speak of following the law with exactness are quick to proclaim that fasting involves twenty-four hours (not twenty-two or twenty-three hours) of complete abstinence from food and drink. These same individuals may believe that the only valid fast is from evening to evening, that is to say, one must fast a whole day through in order for the fast to be valid.

That great prophet Isaiah teaches the true principles of fasting in the following very clear, eloquent and insightful way:

> In the day of your fast ye find pleasure, and exact all your labours.
>
> Behold, ye fast for strife and debate. . . .
>
> Is it such a fast that I have chosen? a day for a man to afflict his soul? is it to bow down his head as a bulrush, and to spread sackcloth and ashes under him? wilt thou call this a fast, and an acceptable day to the Lord?
>
> Is not this the fast that I have chosen? to loose the bands of wickedness, to undo the heavy burdens, and to let the oppressed go free, and that ye break every yoke?
>
> Is it not to deal thy bread to the hungry, and that thou bring the poor that are cast out to thy house? when thou seest the naked, that thou cover him; and that thou hide not thyself from thine own flesh? [Isaiah refers here to our willingness to help our extended families in need, i.e., our "own flesh."]
>
> Then shall thy light break forth as the morning, and thine health

> shall spring forth speedily: and thy righteousness shall go before thee; the glory of the Lord shall be thy rereward.
>
> Then shalt thou call, and the Lord shall answer; thou shalt cry, and he shall say, Here I am. . . .
>
> And the Lord shall guide thee continually, and satisfy thy soul in drought, and make fat thy bones: and thou shalt be like a watered garden, and like a spring of water, whose waters fail not. (Isa. 58:3–9, 11.)

In the scriptures we read of the Savior and of Moses and of Elijah fasting for forty days. Perhaps reading the accounts of their fasting will put counting the minutes in a broader, eternal perspective. We would do well to follow the spirit of Isaiah's teachings regarding the true purposes and spiritual consequences of the fast rather than making of fasting an athletic event of endurance.

In the Doctrine and Covenants the Lord commands us to keep the Sabbath day holy: "And on this day thou shalt do none other thing, only let thy food be prepared with singleness of heart that thy fasting may be perfect, or in other words, that thy joy may be full" (D&C 59:13).

President Joseph F. Smith shared the following wise insights with the Saints of his day:

> The law to the Latter-day Saints, as understood by the authorities of the Church, is that food and drink are not to be partaken of for twenty-four hours, "from even to even," and that the Saints are to refrain from all bodily gratifications and indulgences. Fast day being on the Sabbath, it follows, of course, that all labor is to be abstained from. In addition, the leading and principal object of the institution of the fast among the Latter-day Saints was that the poor might be provided with food and other necessities. . . .
>
> Now, while the law requires the Saints in all the world to fast from "even to even" and to abstain both from food and drink, it can easily be seen from the Scriptures, and especially from the words of Jesus, that it is more important to obtain the true spirit of love for God and man, "purity of heart and simplicity of intention," than it is to carry out the cold letter of the law. The Lord has instituted the fast on a reasonable and intelligent basis, and none of his works are vain or unwise. His law is perfect in this as in other things. Hence, those who can are required to comply thereto; it is a duty from which they cannot escape; but let it be remembered that the observance of the fast day by abstaining twenty-four hours from food and drink is not an absolute rule, it is no iron-clad law to us, but it is left with the people as a matter of conscience, to exercise wisdom and discretion.[1]

Wisdom and discretion, for example, may dictate that the Saints living in warm climates during the hot summer months may occasionally need to drink water to avoid dehydration during a period of fasting.

Young missionaries expend great energy in riding bicycles and climbing stairs and walking long distances to teaching appointments. Thus, they are counseled to use wisdom in fasting. They are encouraged to observe a proper fast each fast Sunday but are counseled generally to avoid extended fasting during the rest of the month, for to do so excessively may deprive them of the health and energy they so urgently need to do the work of the Lord. Extended and too frequent fasting may also make missionaries more susceptible to illness. Occasional fasting for a specific purpose is, of course, within the realm of "wisdom and discretion."

President Smith then deals with those who may not be in a position to live the law of the fast quite so meticulously:

> Many are subject to weakness, others are delicate in health, and others have nursing babies; of such it should not be required to fast. Neither should parents compel their little children to fast. I have known children to cry for something to eat on fast day. In such cases, going without food will do them no good. Instead, they dread the day to come, and in place of hailing it, dislike it; while the compulsion engenders a spirit of rebellion in them, rather than a love for the Lord and their fellows. Better teach them the principle, and let them observe it when they are old enough to choose intelligently, than to so compel them.
>
> But those should fast who can, and all classes among us should be taught to save the meals which they would eat, or their equivalent, for the poor. None are exempt from this; it is required of the Saints, old and young, in every part of the Church.[2]

President Smith advocated donating the equivalent of the cost of meals foregone during fasting as a fast offering. The word *equivalent* has for many years been a spiritually sensitive discriminator between the spirit and the letter of the law. It was President Spencer W. Kimball who energetically taught the more excellent way as he encouraged the Saints who are able to do so to contribute "much more—ten times more."[3] There are countless Saints whose faithful consecration has brought them a realization of Isaiah's promise: "Then shalt thou delight thyself in the Lord" (Isa. 58:14).

Tithing. There are countless principles of the gospel which can be a great blessing in our lives when we keep the spirit of the principle and the prescriptions of the principle in balance. As a bishop during tithing settlement in a ward of nearly eight hundred members from all walks of life, I found it a very interesting experience to observe what constituted a "full tithing" in the minds of the members. The scriptures and the *General Handbook of Instructions* are clear that tithing is "one-tenth of all their interest annually" (D&C 119:4); this is interpreted as income.

Some Saints feel at peace with themselves in declaring 10 percent of their net income as tithing, while others pay 10 percent of their gross income. Some pay 10 percent on everything but Social Security and retirement investments, with the justification that they will continue to pay tithing when they begin receiving their retirement income. There are even a few folks who pay tithing on ten percent of "what's left over," a variation of the gross versus net issue.

Certainly those engaged in the professions and various businesses with fixed costs for building overhead, employee wages, and so forth must arrive at some fair formula for determining an appropriate tithe. It may be advisable to consider how we would like to receive our blessings for having paid our tithes. That is to say, would we like all our blessings only after retirement, and would we like carefully calculated blessings or a more generous calculation when the "windows of heaven" are opened?

Temple Interviews. The spirit and letter of temple worthiness interviews is yet another area in which balance is absolutely crucial. I recall being interviewed in the living room of a member of the stake presidency with members of his family sitting in the same room watching television. He asked me only one question: "Have you been a good kid lately?" Had there been a need for me to discuss some detailed concerns with my personal worthiness, that would certainly not have been the time nor the place.

To provide some gentle guidance for priesthood leaders, the Brethren have outlined a series of more than a dozen questions which bishops and members of stake presidencies should ask their members in an assessment of personal worthiness. There are hundreds of questions which could be asked, including those addressed in Alma 5 of the Book of Mormon. They are excellent questions, but there must be a balance, and so local leaders are counseled to ask only the questions printed in the front of the temple recommend book and to refrain from asking questions beyond those prescribed.

The spirit of the interview should be an opportunity for edifying and uplifting. The assessment of worthiness on the part of the common judge of Israel is a matter of vital importance. Worthiness is not synonymous with perfection, and one would hope that candidates for temple recommends become more worthy with each succeeding year. If we are not judicious, and if we do not balance mercy with justice, our interviews can be sources of frustration and discouragement rather than being inspirational and purifying experiences. "The letter killeth, but the spirit giveth life." Whatever the outcome of any interview, the individual being interviewed should know he or she is loved by the bishop and loved of the Lord. Interviews should include expressions of gratitude and should inspire improvement.

Notes

1. Joseph F. Smith, *Gospel Doctrine* (Salt Lake City: Deseret Book Co., 1939), pp. 243–44.

2. Smith, *Gospel Doctrine*, p. 244.

3. Spencer W. Kimball, *The Teachings of Spencer W. Kimball*, ed. Edward Kimball (Salt Lake City: Bookcraft, 1982), p. 146.

Chapter Seven

STEADFASTNESS AND CHANGE

After teaching the ancient Nephites the principles and ordinances of His gospel, the Savior declared: "I am the Lord, I change not" (3 Ne. 24:6). Central to the gospel of Jesus Christ is the concept that God is omniscient and His truths are eternal. Thus, throughout holy writ the followers of Christ are admonished to remain steadfast and to "be not moved away from the hope of the gospel" (Col. 1:23).

In the marvelous Olive Leaf, or section 88 of the Doctrine and Covenants, the Lord revealed the greeting which was to be used by the brethren participating in the School of the Prophets in Kirtland: "I salute you in the name of the Lord Jesus Christ, in token or remembrance of the everlasting covenant, in which covenant I receive you to fellowship, in a determination that is fixed, immovable, and unchangeable" (D&C 88:133). The admonition is clear: having accepted the gospel of Jesus Christ, and having received the blessings of gospel ordinances in our lives, each of us is expected to stand in "holy places and be not moved" (D&C 87:8; see 45:32).

All of us must continually wrestle with our personal imperfections, unrighteous thoughts and desires, and the subsequent sins which often follow. But the challenge of the Book of Mormon is that we are to undergo a "mighty change of heart" in our lives, not just make a few timid, tiny changes, notwithstanding the fact that the mighty change generally involves an entire lifetime. The tension between steadfastness and change can best be resolved when we determine what and who must change and what and who must not change.

Most Latter-day Saints faithfully repeat the ninth article of faith: "We believe all that God has revealed, all that He does now reveal, and we believe that He will yet reveal many great and important things pertaining to the Kingdom of God." For some members of the Church it is easy to accept and sustain the notion of continuous *revelation;* they just have a problem accepting *change*. But change is an inevitable consequence of continuous revelation.

Throughout the modern-day history of the restored Church, there have been those who remain so steadfast in certain ideas, they have been unable to accept change resulting from continuous revelation. They are akin to those described by Jacob who look "beyond the mark" (Jacob 4:14), being so engrossed in observing the letter of the law that they overlook the very purposes for which the law was given.

There were those who refused to leave Kirtland when the Saints were asked to move to Missouri. Others refused to leave Missouri, and still others refused to leave Nauvoo. These are they who fail to realize that earth life is a journey, not a destination; mortality is a process, not an immutable condition.

Principles, Policies, and Procedures

The policies and procedures of the Church have been and ever will be based upon eternal principles, principles which are fixed and immovable. These principles are based upon the words of living prophets and the scriptures. From time to time, various handbooks are published to provide a current interpretation of Church policies in light of eternal principles. These policies are then subsequently implemented in the wards and branches and families throughout the world.

Problems sometimes arise when local leaders and members conclude that because their area of the world is different and cultural traditions are different it will, therefore, be necessary for them to modify policies to fit their current situation. The challenge is to determine what can and should be modified and what cannot. Any procedures which constitute departures from policy must have the approval of the First Presidency of the Church.

For example, there are certain parts of the world where the predominant religion has set aside Friday as a holy day. In another part of the world Saturday is considered to be the Sabbath. In many of these countries there are faithful Latter-day Saint families who work in embassies and other government offices or who are employed by international business concerns and are required to observe the deeply ingrained customs of the country. Thus, Friday or Saturday is the religious day and Sunday is considered to be just another working day.

It was determined several years ago by the First Presidency that members of the Church living within a country which has a weekly holy day other than Sunday may be permitted to hold Church services on the holy day of the country in question. While the day of the "Sunday" meetings may change, the format and content of the meetings remain steadfast. These scattered units throughout the world steadfastly follow the prescribed format of sacrament meeting and fast and testimony meeting. The sacrament prayers are the same throughout the Church. The number of Sunday School classes is flexible, determined by the size of the branch, the age constellation of the members, and the number of available classrooms, but the course of study is immovably centered upon the scriptures.

Ordinances

The sacred ordinance of baptism is performed in many different locations throughout the world, ranging from a quiet lagoon in the Pacific Ocean to a baptismal font in a stake center. But regardless of the location, this holy ordinance is performed by immersion in water, using perfectly prescribed words, with two witnesses present. On occasion, under unusual circumstances, some individuals have been baptized without the benefit of two witnesses. But in these exceptional cases, certain principles still remained fixed and immovable: the person performing the ordinance held the office of a priest in the Aaronic Priesthood or he held an office in the Melchizedek Priesthood. The mode of baptism (immersion) and the priesthood authority required will never change, even if the location may change from a river to a baptismal font.

After we are baptized we renew our baptismal covenant through partaking of the sacrament. Nearly five months after the Church had been organized the Prophet Joseph Smith received a revelation regarding the actual elements used for the sacred symbols of the sacrament. In keeping with principles expressed in the Lord's instructions to the Prophet in this revelation (see D&C 27), in later years it became the practice in the Church to use water instead of wine in the sacrament.

Today there are some well-meaning priesthood leaders who reason in their own minds that white bread must be used for the sacrament because white is a symbol of purity. Other well-meaning members reason that only whole-wheat bread should be used for the sacrament because whole wheat is favorably sanctioned by the Word of Wisdom.

The Savior revealed to Joseph "that it mattereth not what ye shall eat or what ye shall drink when ye partake of the sacrament, if it so be that ye do it with an eye single to my glory—remembering unto the Father my body which was laid down for you, and my blood which was shed for the remission of your sins" (D&C 27:2). The *General Handbook of Instructions* refers only to "the unbroken bread" without a specific description of whether the bread is to be brown or white. The important issue is not the texture or color of the bread but whether we partake of the sacrament worthily (see 3 Ne. 18:28–30).

Procedures should never be subject to the whims and eccentricities of an individual leader. While creativity and initiative are not to be stifled, there are some core principles, policies, and procedures to which we should adhere with steadfastness. There are other areas in which considerable latitude may be given. The quest is determining which things may change and which things must not.

Accepting New Leaders

"I am the Lord, I change not" (Mal. 3:6), and if we are to become like Him, then we must change, and the Book of Mormon prophets teach us that this must be a mighty change (see Mosiah 5:2, see also Alma 5:7,12–14, 26; Alma 19:33; Hel. 15:7). There are many who are so concerned with changes in the *Church*, they fail to realize that the whole purpose of the Church is to change *them*, for as Paul taught, the Church is for the "perfecting of the saints" (Eph. 4:11–14).

Perhaps there may have been no greater challenge to accepting change in the Church than when the Prophet Joseph met a martyr's death, leaving the Church in need of a new prophet. Considerable dissension arose as Sidney Rigdon, one of the Prophet's Counselors, laid claim to the office of the President of the Church. In an impassioned, inspiring address to the Saints, Brigham Young, then President of the Quorum of the Twelve, preached the following:

> Here is President Rigdon, who was counselor to Joseph. I ask, where are Joseph and Hyrum? They are gone beyond the veil; and if Elder Rigdon wants to act as his counselor, he must go beyond the veil where he is.
>
> . . . If the people want President Rigdon to lead them they may have him; but I say unto you that the Quorum of the Twelve have the keys of the kingdom of God in all the world. . . .
>
> . . . You cannot appoint a prophet; but if you let the Twelve remain and act in their place, the keys of the kingdom are with them and they can manage the affairs of the church and direct all things aright.[1]

Elder George Q. Cannon described a marvelous transformation that occurred during President Young's address to the Saints:

> If Joseph had arisen from the dead and again spoken in their hearing, the effect could not have been more startling than it was to many present at that meeting. It was the voice of Joseph himself; and not only was it the voice of Joseph which was heard, but it seemed in the eyes of the people as though it was the very person of Joseph which stood before them.
>
> A more wonderful and miraculous event than was wrought that day in the presence of that congregation we never heard of. The Lord gave His people a testimony that left no room for doubt as to who was the man He had chosen to lead them.[2]

Those Saints who were in tune with the Spirit received a confirmation that Brother Brigham was to become the successor to the Prophet. Those who did not receive such a manifestation, or who later denied it, chose not to follow President Young as he led the Saints to the safety of the Salt Lake Valley. These are they who stayed in Nauvoo or who founded or joined splinter groups led by various leaders who did not have the keys of which Brigham Young spoke.

Word of Wisdom

Although eternal principles do not change, their method of implementation does involve change, often in response to local circumstances and cultural constraints. The Word of Wisdom was given in

1833, long before the discovery of electricity and the invention of canning techniques or refrigeration. Thus, the counsel to eat "every fruit in the season thereof" should certainly not discourage us from eating bottled peaches in December or frozen strawberries in February. However, the proscriptions against tobacco, alcohol, and hot drinks (that is, tea and coffee) remain steadfast.

There appear to be some people who have a difficult time distinguishing between what can and cannot be changed or what is and is not included in the Word of Wisdom. To these people President Gordon B. Hinckley has said: "Some have even used as an alibi the fact that drugs are not mentioned in the Word of Wisdom. What a miserable excuse. There is likewise no mention of the hazards of diving into an empty swimming pool or of jumping from an overpass onto the freeway. But who doubts the deadly consequences of such? Common sense would dictate against such behavior."[3]

Welfare Program

Throughout the scriptures the Lord has given his children an injunction to care for the poor and the needy, the widow and the orphan. This eternal principle remains steadfast, immovable, and unchanging. However, the method of caring for the poor has been adapted throughout the years. There was a period when the Saints lived the law of consecration in a united order of sharing their goods with others. Tithing and fast offerings were paid in kind in a predominantly agrarian society, and bishops' storehouses became the collecting center for these tithes and offerings in the form of agricultural produce. The storehouse was also the distribution center for these commodities, which were given for the use of those in need. More recently, welfare farms and other production facilities have been used to provide the commodities previously acquired through the payment of tithes. And even now, due to changing circumstances, many welfare projects are professionally managed in a much different way than they were previously.[4]

The policies and procedures have changed considerably as the Church, and indeed much of the world, has undergone a transition from an agrarian to a predominantly urban society. But the eternal principle of caring for the needy has not changed. Principles remain steadfast, while policies are modified through continuous revelation.

The Temple

The Lord has cautioned us to "remember that that which cometh from above is sacred, and must be spoken with care, and by constraint of the Spirit" (D&C 63:64). In light of this counsel, we will speak in very general terms about a very sacred area which has undergone some changes during the past century. The holy temple is a very sacred place in which ordinances of eternal significance are performed, including baptism for the dead, the temple endowment, and sealings, or temple marriages, for time and all eternity.

The mode of constructing temples has changed somewhat during the past three decades, but the square footage and the height of a temple spire have little bearing upon the validity of the covenants one enters into in the house of the Lord. Architectural styles may reflect the culture in which the temple is built, but the covenants have not changed, nor will they. Those who would publicly discuss or criticize that which transpires within the temple simply fail to understand the things that matter most.

Temple covenants and promises remain immovable, but it is we who must continually change after making these covenants. The mighty change of heart so frequently mentioned in the Book of Mormon occurs almost overnight with some people, but to others the mighty change is the cumulative result of a lifetime of personal prayer, scripture study, repentance, and sustained service in the kingdom of God.

The Light Never Moves

Our quest to remain steadfast may, if we are not introspective, lead to an undue concern with exactness and the letter of the law. It is well to remind ourselves of Paul's concern that the "letter killeth" as we become more concerned with following the rule than with understanding the purpose of the rule as leading our lives to a higher plane.

On the other hand, when we become too flexible, too open-minded, too creative, and too willing to uncritically accept new ideas, there is always a danger of losing sight of eternal objectives as absolutes. And we are in danger of abandoning absolute values altogether as we begin to consider eternal principles in light of the changing values of the world in which we live.

There is a classic experiment in social psychology which investigates how much the judgments of others influence the way we see things. Professor Muzafer Sherif built a small machine with a bright light in one end and a tiny hole in the other end. A camera-like shutter could control the bursts of light, which could be quickly turned on and off.

As you well know, when we go from a dark room into the bright sunlight, the pupils in our eyes suddenly contract to keep out some of the light, and when we go from the light into a dark room our pupils dilate to let in more light. When one views a pinpoint burst of bright light in a completely darkened room, the sudden contraction of the pupil causes the light to appear to move, even though the machine producing the light is very stable and does not move at all. This is called the autokinetic, or self-movement, effect, and it plays an important role in this experiment.

During the first stage of the experiment one person—let's call him Bill—is led into a dark room and is instructed to judge how far the tiny pinpoints of light move each time he sees a burst of light. His judgment is one inch the first time, two inches the second time, and three inches the third time. After several trials he settles on three inches as his most frequent judgment.

Bill is then excused from the dark room, and Susan is invited to be seated facing the light machine several feet away. She then voices her judgments each time she sees a burst of light. She begins with four inches, then three inches, then two, and she finally begins to repeat estimates of about one inch.

Bill is then invited back into the room with Susan, and both of them are instructed to voice their individual estimates of another series of light bursts. After the first burst Bill says, "Three inches," and Susan says, "One inch." On the next trial Susan says, "One and a half inches," and Bill replies, "Two and a half." After several subsequent trials, they concur that the light moves two and seventeen sixty-fourths of an inch each time.

The interesting conclusion to this experiment may appear, at first, to be trivial, but in many regards it is profound. *The light never moves*. Only our perceptions of the light change. As we associate with others whose opinions differ from our own, their judgments often influence how we view things, and we, in turn, influence their view of the world.

Few of us are ever invited into an experimental laboratory to share our perceptions, but each day of our lives we are required to make important judgments in the laboratory of life. Mormon assures us that "the Spirit of Christ is given to every man that he may know good from evil." The Lord assured us through his prophet that when we are responsive to his Spirit, He will "show unto [us] the way to judge." (Moro. 7:16.) The Savior also referred to himself as "the light of the world: he that followeth me shall not walk in darkness, but shall have the light of life" (John 8:12). This light never moves, and if it appears to move from us, we are the ones who have moved.

Sometimes in the darkened laboratory of everyday life we lose our perspective as familiar landmarks vanish. In such times the light sometimes appears to move and we are torn between our loyalty to eternal principles and our loyalty to those around us whose judgments differ from our own. One of the ways we move from the Light of Christ is by engaging in the game, "Not As Bad As . . ." You know how it goes:

"I may swear a lot, but I never take the Lord's name in vain."

"I don't pay a full tithing, but at least I pay something."

"I go to a few questionable movies, but I never watch X-rated videos."

"Necking is not as bad as petting."

"Sure, I cheat on my income tax, but not as much as most other people."

"I don't consider it gossip when I'm only telling the truth."

"If other people think I dress immodestly, that's their problem."

And so, in the words of our beloved friend Nephi, "thus the devil cheateth their souls, and leadeth them away carefully down to hell" (2 Ne. 28:21).

Although the light never moves, the more often we are in contact with that which is abnormal, degrading, and undesirable, the more normal and desirable it begins to appear. We become less sensitive to the promptings of the still small voice, and our loyalties shift from eternal principles to persons in close proximity. It is the Spirit of Christ which will always help us judge between good and evil. We can acquire this Spirit the same way Lehi did as he was presented a book of scripture in a vision: "And it came to pass that as he read, he was filled with the Spirit of the Lord" (1 Ne. 1:12). The Light of Christ never moves, but stands as a steady and reliable beacon on the shores of an ever-changing sea.[5]

Beware of Poisonous Mushrooms

The story is told of a man on death row who was approached by the warden on the night before his scheduled execution. "What would you like for your last meal?" the warden asked. After a moment's thought, the condemned man replied, "I'd like a big plate of cooked mushrooms. Until now, I haven't dared eat any!"[6]

There are hundreds of species of mushrooms, and many of them are not only edible but delicious. Mushroom hunting is a favorite family activity in many parts of the world, but mushroom hunters must be aware that between seventy and eighty varieties of mushrooms are poisonous. Some of them are fatal. Among the safe mushrooms is the common meadow mushroom, or champignon, found in nearly every neighborhood grocery store. Deep fried, sauteed, served in soups and gravies, or simply topping a pizza, they are not only safe to eat but delicious.

Among the poisonous mushrooms is the *Omphalotus illudens*, or "jack-o'-lantern" mushroom. The body reacts to its poison very quickly with violent nausea and vomiting. Because of this immediate reaction, the "jack-o'-lantern" is not fatal. A much more dangerous mushroom is the *Amanita phalloides*, or "destroying angel." Just one or two in a batch of two dozen can poison an entire family. Because it tastes like an edible mushroom and has no immediate effect, the victim keeps on eating. Then, six to fifteen hours later, when it is digested and its poisons have entered the bloodstream, the victim experiences severe nausea and cramps and unquenchable thirst. Eventually it destroys the liver. There is no known antidote, and the fatality rate is about 90 percent.

Then there are the "doubtfuls" and the "look-alikes." An example of a doubtful mushroom is the *Russula Emetica*. Most of the older mushroom literature classifies it as poisonous, but some of the modern mushroom hunters say it is edible. Whom do you believe? (Clue: *emetica* means "causing vomiting.")

"Look-alikes"—toxic types that resemble edible varieties—are responsible for most cases of mushroom poisoning. For example, the poisonous "jack-o'-lantern" can be mistaken for the "brick cap," a tasty, edible mushroom common in eastern North America. And people who have been poisoned by the deadly "death cup" thought they were picking an edible mushroom that looked very similar.

Mushrooms, Music, Movies, and Magazines

Music, movies, and magazines have a lot in common with mushrooms. For example, they come in countless varieties. Just as some mushrooms are edible and desirable and nutritious, certain kinds of music, movies, and magazines provide nutrition for the soul as they edify, entertain, and uplift.

And just as there are different kinds of poisonous mushrooms, so are there different kinds of music, movies, and magazines that poison the spirits of men and women. Some of these poisons are very much like "jack-o'-lantern" mushrooms because their impact is so repulsive and objectionable that we immediately reject them.

But there are other kinds of music, movies, and magazines that work very much like the "destroying angel"; that is, at first we have no idea that what we are listening to or watching or reading is slowly and surely poisoning our very souls. Often we hear people comment on different entertainments, and we will hear something like, "This tape by the Dirty Gym Sox has ten good songs and only two bad ones." Or, "It was a great movie (or video), with only two or three bad scenes." Or, "Most of the articles in this magazine are very interesting and insightful." But in 1988, only a few toxic mushrooms in a whole dishful put five Oregon people in the hospital on the verge of death.

Telling the Good from the Bad

Mormon tells us that "the Spirit of Christ is given to every man, that he may know good from evil; wherefore, I show unto you the way to judge; for every thing which inviteth to do good, and to persuade to believe in Christ, is sent forth by the power and gift of Christ" (Moro. 7:16).

Just as mushroom hunters develop safety checklists regarding the color, size, and shape of edible and poisonous mushrooms, our loving and protective Heavenly Father has provided us with several checklists to determine whether the things we view, listen to, and read are poisonous or wholesome.

1. The thirteenth article of faith. Just ask yourself: Is this "virtuous, lovely, or of good report or praiseworthy"? If so, "seek after these things."

2. In the Doctrine and Covenants 45:32 the Lord says: "But my disciples shall stand in holy places, and shall not be moved." With the music you play, the videos and TV programs you watch, and the magazines you have lying around, is your home a holy place? Would you feel comfortable if the bishop or stake president were to walk into your family room while you were listening to music or watching TV or a video? Would they feel comfortable in your home?

3. In His Sermon on the Mount, the Savior admonishes us to seek "first the kingdom of God, and his righteousness" (Matt. 6:33). He did not suggest that we just keep the gospel in the "top ten." He lovingly encourages us to make the gospel the top priority in our lives.

4. In the very closing verses of the Book of Mormon, Moroni extends the invitation to "come unto Christ, and be perfected in him, and deny yourselves of all ungodliness" (Moro. 10:32). The real question is not whether heavy metal is worse than hard rock or whether certain TV programs are worse than certain movies. If we wish to avoid being poisoned spiritually, we must ask: Is this music, movie, TV show, or literature ungodly? For example, does it leave me feeling unworthy to approach my Heavenly Father in sincere prayer?

5. The Apostle Paul gave the Thessalonians some great counsel that would protect them, and us, from the poisons of the world. "Prove all things; hold fast that which is good. Abstain from all appearance of evil." (1 Thes. 5:21–22.)

Remember, the same principles that keep mushroom hunters alive will help you stay alive spiritually. Beware of dangerous look-alikes; if it's doubtful, avoid it. (It has been said that there are old mushroom hunters and there are bold mushroom hunters, but there are no old, bold mushroom hunters.) Remember, too, that sometimes the slowest poisons are the most deadly. We can continue to develop our own growing, personalized checklist, and together with the guidance of the Holy Ghost it will help us to judge between the poisonous and the wholesome, and between that which should change in our lives and that which should remain steadfast.[6]

Notes

1. *History of the Church* 7:233, 235.

2. George Q. Cannon, *Gospel Truth*, comp. Jerreld L. Newquist, 2 vols. in 1 (Salt Lake City: Deseret Book Co., 1987), p. 223.

3. Gordon B. Hinckley, "The Scourge of Illicit Drugs," *Ensign* 19 (November 1989): 50.

4. For an excellent presentation of welfare principles, see Dallin H. Oaks, *The Lord's Way* (Salt Lake City: Deseret Book Co., 1991), pp. 102–37.

5. The section called "The Light Never Moves" in this chapter is a revision of the author's article of the same title, which appeared in the *New Era* 13 (August 1983): 50–51.

6. The material beginning with the section "Beware of Poisonous Mushrooms" and continuing to the end of the chapter is a revision of the author's article "Mushrooms, Music, Movies, and Magazines," *New Era* 20 (February 1990): 4–6.

Chapter Eight

INITIATIVE AND OBEDIENCE

During the first sixteen months after the Church was organized on April 6, 1830, the Lord revealed sections 2 through 57 of the Doctrine and Covenants. These revelations included the very specific qualifications and instructions of how the gospel should be preached and very detailed descriptions of the responsibilities of those who hold various offices in the priesthood. Wonderful counsel was given regarding the care of the needy, and numerous admonitions were given concerning obedience to the commandments. Then, in section 58, the Lord revealed the following expectations:

> For behold, it is not meet that I should command in all things; for he that is compelled in all things, the same is a slothful and not a wise servant; wherefore he receiveth no reward.
>
> Verily I say, men should be anxiously engaged in a good cause, and do many things of their own free will, and bring to pass much righteousness;
>
> For the power is in them, wherein they are agents unto themselves. And inasmuch as men do good they shall in nowise lose their reward. (D&C 58:26–28.)

Well-meaning members of the Church write to Church headquarters or to their respective area presidencies asking why it is the Church does not initiate an anti-pornography campaign in their city. Or they wish to know why the Church is not involved in an anti-drug campaign or why the Church does not endorse certain political candidates or does not discourage members from voting for other candidates. Or they wish to know if the Church is going to solicit funds to alleviate suffering in a given area of the world hit by recent earthquakes, floods, or famine. When the Church does sponsor such relief programs, many members are willing to contribute; however, if the Church has not initiated such a program as yet, then many withhold their private contributions.

Often one can determine what is important to people by reading the bumper stickers on their cars. Some people feel very strongly about supporting campaigns to save the whales, save the pandas, save the seals, or save our rain forests, and their intentions are sincere and well founded. At times they are frustrated by the lack of concern demonstrated by their neighbors, but the fact of the matter is: "Men should be anxiously engaged in a good cause, and do many things of their own free will." Individual members using their own initiative can often accomplish much more as private citizens than they can as official representatives of the Church, because invariably there are those who change the focus of attention from the problem to the Church. The Church encourages members to beautify their homes and cities and to work to remove evil elements from the society in which they live, but the specific activities in which they are involved will largely rest with the individual member.

Obedience

The tension between exercising initiative and obediently responding to the admonitions of priesthood leaders is addressed throughout the scriptures. There are those who champion the cause of initiative but who cringe at the thought of obedience. For some people initiative connotes freedom, whereas obedience connotes bondage and submission, but both obedience and initiative involve exercising one's moral agency. Coercion robs one of obedience. Obedience is, and must be, an act involving free will. One must be able to choose to be obedient, and the Lord has revealed that "when we obtain any blessing from God, it is by obedience to that law upon which it is predicated" (D&C 130:21).

Naaman, the Syrian captain of the king's guard, was very willing to take the initiative to make the arrangements to travel to Israel to visit Elisha the prophet to be healed of his leprosy. But when his initiative evoked Elisha's message to "go and wash in Jordan seven times," he resisted following this counsel for at least four reasons:

First, the message was delivered by Elisha's servant rather than by the prophet himself.

Second, he had anticipated that the prophet would resolve his problem in a different way—that is, "He will surely come out to me, and stand, and call on the name of the Lord his God, and strike his hand over the place, and recover the leper" (2 Kgs. 5:11).

Third, the rivers in Damascus were "better than all the waters of Israel" (2 Kgs. 5:12).

Fourth, the prophet's command had been too simple for a mighty man like Naaman. But a courageous and perceptive servant confronted his enraged master by saying: "My father, if the prophet had bid thee to do some great thing, wouldest thou not have done it?" (2 Kgs. 5:13.)

Let it be said to Naaman's credit that he humbled himself, obediently washed himself seven times in the Jordan, and reaped the blessing of obedience as his leprous skin became clean like that of a child (see 2 Kgs. 5:14).

I suspect there may be a little of Naaman in each of us. We can accept counsel better from our bishop than from his emissaries, our home teachers. And we often expect the Lord to answer our prayers with angelic messengers rather than through a concerned neighbor.

Such was the case with Billy and Jimmy, ages five and seven. They lived on a dairy farm not far from a small forest, and one day they asked their mother for permission to play in the woods. She said it would be all right as long as they promised to be home by sundown. But boys will be boys, and these two little fellows got so busy chasing butterflies and squirrels, they completely failed to realize the sun was beginning to set. Suddenly they found themselves in trouble—lost in the middle of the woods. They ran in every direction trying to find the periphery, but to no avail. Finally, Jimmy said, "Billy, let's kneel down and pray for an angel to show us the way home." At the end of the prayer, in boyish faith they looked all around but saw no angel. Jimmy then said, "Billy, you're five, you have fewer sins than I—you pray for an angel." But again the results were negative. As they listened to the scary night sounds of the forest, their feelings went from anxiety to despair. Then suddenly they heard the sound of a cowbell. Old Bossy was in the meadow wending her way home to the barnyard for the evening milking. The boys ran in the direction of the cowbell and followed her home to the farm. They ran into the kitchen, where their anxious mother welcomed them into her outstretched arms.

The two youngsters then told their mother how they had prayed for an angel, but no angel came to deliver them. It had just been a stroke of luck that they heard the cowbell in their moment of desperation. The moral of this little story is this: The Lord will never send an angel to do a job he can get an old cow to do. Or, in more eloquent form, Elder Neal A. Maxwell has observed that, in the Lord's economy, "He will never send a prophet when a priest will do." So often we anticipate flashy answers proclaimed by a thunderous voice, when the Lord's most frequent means of communication is through the still small voice.

Outside of the Salt Lake Valley there are sometimes those who, like Naaman, contend that the rivers of Damascus are "better than all the waters of Israel." This program won't work in Europe or Asia or South America, we are prone to say.

And finally, in our heart of hearts we must sometimes confess that we are more willing to serve as a stake president than as a home teacher, or more ready to be a mission president than to serve as a senior missionary couple in a small remote branch near the end of the earth. Mission presidents and their wives have their pictures published in the *Church News*, but missionary couples serve rather anonymously throughout the world. And a loving Father in Heaven has great blessings in store for them, and grateful mission presidents will praise their names for all the good they do, for their initiative and their obedience.

The atonement of the Savior is the greatest example of obedience, for "though he were a Son, yet learned he obedience by the things which he suffered" (Heb. 5:8), "which suffering caused [him], even God, the greatest of all, to tremble because of pain, and to bleed at every pore" (D&C 19:18). Sister Eliza R. Snow aptly reflected the Savior's obedience in that sacred sacrament hymn "How Great the Wisdom and the Love":

> By strict obedience Jesus won
> The prize with glory rife:
> "Thy will, O God, not mine be done,"
> Adorned his mortal life.[1]

Abraham's willingness to sacrifice his son Isaac was "a similitude of God and his Only Begotten Son" (Jacob 4:5), and demonstrated Abraham's unqualified obedience. Through that experience Abraham gained some insight into the Father's agony during the time His Son bled from every pore in the Garden of Gethsemane and as He hung from the cross on Calvary. And because of the Savior's obedience and because of Abraham's obedience the prophetic blessings of the Abrahamic covenant will continue to come to fruition.

The scriptures are also replete with examples of those who struggled with the proper balance between initiative and obedience. One of the best examples was King Saul. Saul was commanded by the prophet Samuel to smite the Amalekites and to slay all of their animals. But when Saul returned from battle Samuel asked him the probing question: "What meaneth then this bleating of the sheep in mine ears, and the lowing of the oxen which I hear?" Saul explained that his men had "spared the best of the sheep and of the oxen, to sacrifice unto the Lord thy God," whereupon Samuel uttered that immortal phrase: "Behold, to obey is better than sacrifice, and to hearken than the fat of rams." (1 Sam. 15:3–22.)

Saul's initiative in modifying the Lord's command to slay all the animals of the Amalekites was an arrogant act of disobedience, leading Samuel to remind him of the time "when thou wast little in thine own sight" (1 Sam. 15:17).

Initiative

A more successful example of striking the balance between initiative and obedience was Nephi as he sought to obey the Lord's command to return to Jerusalem and obtain the brass plates from Laban. Nephi "was led by the Spirit, not knowing beforehand the things which [he] should do" (I Ne. 4:6).

As Nephi arrived at Laban's house, he found him to be drunk. The Spirit constrained Nephi to slay Laban, but Nephi resisted the prompting. A second time the Spirit said, "The Lord hath delivered him into thy hands." A third time the Spirit admonished Nephi to slay Laban, for "it is better that one man should perish than that a nation should dwindle and perish in unbelief." (1 Ne. 4:10–13.)

Notwithstanding his personal inclination to the contrary, Nephi "did obey the voice of the Spirit" and slew Laban (1 Ne. 4:18). And now he asserted his initiative as he dressed himself in Laban's clothing so that he might gain entry to the treasury where the sacred records were kept. Nephi's creative impersonation of Laban evidently included more than just wearing Laban's clothing, for Nephi tells us that he also impersonated Laban's voice. He was so talented in his impersonation that Laban's servant followed him, and Nephi's brothers, Laman, Lemuel, and Sam were frightened by him. (See 1 Ne. 4:23–28.)

Nephi's obedience and initiative made him an excellent instrument in accomplishing the Lord's purposes.

Notwithstanding the fact that obedience is the first law of heaven, the Lord also expects us to act as agents for ourselves. This involves using our initiative and not being commanded or directed in all things. This is a lesson illustrated in the life of the brother of Jared, Mahonri Moriancumer.[2] He had been directed by the Lord in considerable detail to build eight barges in which the Jaredites would be transported to the promised land. Inasmuch as the barges were designed to be tight "like unto a dish," the brother of Jared asked the Lord how they would be able to breathe. The Lord responded by telling him how to make holes in the top and in the bottom.

The next problem to be solved was the provision of light, for the trip was to eventually last three hundred and forty-four days, an extremely long time to be spent in darkness. But when the brother of Jared presented this problem to the Lord, instead of providing the solution, the Lord asked the question: "What will ye that I should do that ye may have light in your vessels?" (Ether 2:23.) The Lord had assisted Mahonri in solving each of his previous problems, but now He wanted the brother of Jared to exercise some of his own initiative in solving a problem. You will recall how he went to Mount Shelem and "did molten out of a rock sixteen small stones; and they were white and clear, even as transparent glass" (Ether 3:1). He then prayed that the Lord might touch these stones with his finger, and the Lord responded to his request because of his great faith—indeed, "he could not be kept from within the veil; therefore he saw Jesus" (Ether 3:4–20).

While serving as the scribe to Joseph Smith during the translation of the Book of Mormon, Oliver Cowdery asked if he might be able to translate the gold plates. But, to his great disappointment, he was unable to do so. Through Joseph, the Lord told Oliver: "Behold, you have not understood; you have supposed that I would give it unto you, when you took no thought save it was to ask me. But, behold, I say unto you, that you must study it out in your mind; then you must ask me if it be right, and if it is right I will cause that your bosom shall burn within you; therefore, you shall feel that it is right." (D&C 9:7–8.)

Innovative Elders

As a mission president in Austria, I was approached by the mission office staff regarding a very innovative "pilot program" for introducing Christianity to non-Christian investigators. They had met a number of immigrants from various Arab nations who were now living in Vienna. Their "program" would consist of showing their non-Christian friends a video of that great film classic *Ben-Hur*, which portrays segments from the life and crucifixion of the Savior.

I had a very uneasy feeling about this "pilot program" because it represented a considerable departure from the prescribed six proselyting discussions missionaries are instructed to teach. Nevertheless, like Martin Harris, the missionaries prevailed upon me until I finally agreed to try the video "just this one time."

Because of appointed meetings in another city, I was unable to be in the mission home the evening the "pilot program" was to be introduced, so I was very interested to get a report on it upon my return. When I asked for a description of the impact of the *Ben-Hur* video on the investigators, the district leader's face began to glow like a red neon sign as he fumbled for the right words. "Well, President," he said, "we had a lot of office work to do that afternoon, so by the time we got to the video rental store, *Ben-Hur* had already been checked out." I then asked: "Did you just go ahead with the regular first discussion, then?" "No," he said, clearing his throat, "we showed them *The Karate Kid* instead!"

Here was a very clear case in which nineteen-year-old missionaries, left to their own devices, exercised initiative. Needless to say, the "pilot program" died a quiet (and sudden) death, and the missionaries obediently, even cheerfully, began teaching according to the prescribed program. I am pleased to report that some of these excellent investigators did enter the waters of baptism and have remained faithful to the principles of the gospel.

The Balance Between "Must" and "Should"

The balance between initiative and obedience is not so difficult when we view life's tasks in terms of what must be done, what should be done, what would be nice to do, and what should not be done. If we concentrate on the musts and the shoulds we generally remain safely within the confines of obedience, and initiative remains within proper bounds.

It has been an interesting experience during the past several years of living in Europe to receive numerous letters from good members of the Church who have identified the ideal site for building a temple. The fact of the matter is that the selection of countries in which temples will be built and the designation of the specific construction site for a temple are determined by the First Presidency, those whom we sustain as prophets, seers, and revelators. It would be profitable for these well-meaning members to concentrate their efforts on family history and temple work and to leave the selection of temple sites to those whom the Lord has appointed for that purpose. It is well to take initiative within the bounds of our own Church callings while simultaneously following the counsel of those called to preside over us.

Some families strike a balance between initiative and obedience better than others. Some families are governed by a kind of modern law of Moses, consisting of hundreds of household rules to which rewards and punishments are affixed. But in so doing, they, like many of the people living at the time of the Savior, look "beyond the mark" (Jacob 4:14). Their children learn obedience, but initiative is sometimes stifled in the process as children do exactly what is expected, but little more.

As a professor at Brigham Young University for twenty years, I have known students who left home in a state of decision-making paralysis, because their parents had never encouraged or allowed them to take any initiative. One co-ed from California dutifully called her mother each morning to ask which blouse and skirt she should wear to class that day. Another young man was petrified to inform his parents that he intended to change his academic major. His parents had so carefully planned his future as a physician, they would simply not accept his allergic reactions to formaldehyde or his fainting spells while dissecting a cadaver.

When we pursue the more excellent way, involving the pure love of Christ, the balance between obedience and initiative rather naturally falls into place. We do not have to be commanded to contribute to this cause or that, and we do not worry about coming into a Church meeting late because we helped someone change a flat tire on the way. We do not have to wait for the Church to publish a list of approved books to read or videos or movies to be seen or musical groups to be heard or avoided. When we follow the more excellent way we simply ask the question: What would the Savior do in these same circumstances? The tension between initiative and obedience is thus largely resolved.

Innovative Missionary Couples

A missionary couple ready to depart for their field of labor once asked my friend Elder Hans B. Ringger what counsel he would give them about the range of activities they should be engaged in. With typical Swiss wisdom he replied: "If you have to show the bird to the bird dog, you've got the wrong dog. Use your own initiative."

Glen and Emmy Collette from Idaho Falls, Idaho, have served more than one mission together, and we were grateful for the time they served in Austria in the city of Steyr. In order to get to know the people of that city, the Collettes joined the community choir, the stamp-collecting club, and the wood-burning club, and Brother Collette maintained his association with the Lion's Club. They made arrangements with the mayor of Idaho Falls for Steyr to become a sister city to Idaho Falls, and the business leaders of the city held a banquet in honor of the Collettes. They were followed by the Boehmes, who put their carpentry and cooking skills to equally good use in friendshipping those not of our faith.

Floyd and Lucy Mae Glauser blessed the lives of the Austrian Saints by sharing their skills in the Boy Scout program and the Young Women's camp program.

Vernon and Norma Tipton and Paul and Daphne Sharp in Amman, Jordan, exerted great initiative in establishing helpful relationships with the University of Jordan and with various government officials. Bill and Michele Wilson are continuing in this tradition in Jordan.

While William and Barbara Williams served in Croatia, Brother Williams composed a beautiful song about Croatia which endeared him to the visa officials in Zagreb. Sister Williams taught two young girls how to play the electric organ well enough to accompany hymns so that the branch could have adequate accompaniment after the Williamses were released.

Albert and Marge Swensen blessed the Saints with enthusiastic leadership within the Vienna International Branch by providing love and gospel glue which formed a cohesive branch consisting of Filipinos, Africans, Iranians, North Americans, and Europeans.

Dale and Mary Harris taught math and English courses which helped members and investigators improve their employment skills.

Countless other couples continue to perform creative services throughout the world, building bridges of friendship and faith.

A Prisoner of Christ

On at least three different occasions the Apostle Paul refers to himself in his epistles as "a prisoner of Christ." At first blush the use of the label of "prisoner" may denote a sense of indentured servitude and confinement. But when one reads the background of the zealous life of Saul of Tarsus, and then studies the epistles of Paul, one readily concludes that this self-imposed expression describes the obedient willingness of a servant of the Lord who will readily do whatever he is called to do to build the kingdom. In his First Epistle to the Corinthians, Paul explained: "For though I be free from all men, yet have I made myself servant unto all, that I might gain the more" (1 Cor. 9:19).

Heiko Mazurek

The test of true conversion is whether each of us has become a prisoner of Christ and follows His example wherein "the will of the Son [is] swallowed up in the will of the Father" (Mosiah 15:7). A great example of someone striking the balance between obedience and initiative is my friend Heiko Mazurek, a young German who joined the Church while studying music in Vienna. Heiko was walking down the streets of Vienna one day when a Book of Mormon display caught his eye. His Mormon girlfriend had awakened in him some interest in the Church, so he stopped to talk with the missionaries, and they gave him a copy of the Book of Mormon. He began to read it and to accept the missionary discussions, and eventually he was baptized.

Shortly after his baptism he moved back to Germany to accept a position in a symphony orchestra and a position teaching in a music school. As the mission president, I was concerned that a new convert might get lost in the shuffle of moving to a new ward so shortly after baptism. I knew Heiko's stake president since the days when I served as a young missionary, so I called President Ulrich Rueckauer and asked him if he could give Heiko some special attention to assure that he remained active and committed to the kingdom.

A few weeks after Heiko's arrival in Germany, this caring stake president invited him to travel to Stuttgart to a Saturday afternoon stake priesthood leadership meeting to share his conversion story with the brethren. Heiko accepted the invitation with fear and trepidation.

Heiko had never spoken to a large audience before, so the evening before his appointed speech he spent a rather sleepless night tossing and turning. When the alarm clock rang he turned it off and promised himself he would just sleep for a few more minutes and then get up. But he was so exhausted from his fitful night's sleep that he awoke too late to catch the train for Stuttgart in time to arrive at the stake center to give his talk.

This is a situation where obedience requires initiative. Heiko hurriedly dressed and caught a taxi to the very small airport outside of town, and although he was a financially struggling musician, he chartered a small plane to fly him to Stuttgart. Upon landing, he checked out the bus schedule into town, and it was immediately clear that the bus made too many stops along the way for him to arrive at the stake center in time. So, although taxi fare for a twenty-mile trip is exorbitant, he added that expense to the cost of chartering the small plane, and headed for town posthaste.

President Rueckauer called me in Vienna after the meeting and described how Heiko had arrived all out of breath just ten minutes after the meeting had begun. He gave a wonderful and inspiring testimony, and all in attendance were grateful for the sacrifice he had made to attend.

Several weeks later I received a phone call from Heiko. He said he had spoken with his bishop about the possibility of serving a full-time mission, but the bishop had advised him that, because he was engaged to be married and because he was in his mid-twenties, he should go ahead and get married instead of serving a mission. He asked if he might come to Vienna for a month and at least serve a brief mini-mission prior to our departure for home.

We, of course, welcomed him warmly, and we could not resist asking about his experience in giving his first public address at the priesthood leadership meeting in Stuttgart. Heiko rehearsed the details just as President Rueckauer had related them to us. When he concluded, I asked him: "Heiko, why didn't you just call up President Rueckauer and tell him you would not be able to make it to the meeting, and that you would be willing to speak on some other occasion?"

Heiko looked at me almost indignantly as he said: "When the missionaries taught me the gospel, they explained the importance of commitments and of covenants, and they said that when we make a promise to the Lord or one of his servants we are expected to keep our word." Heiko, like the Apostle Paul, had become a willing prisoner of Christ. For the past three years he has served as a counselor in the bishopric of his ward.

Of Mankind and Molecules

Legend has it that Sir Isaac Newton was reading a book one day while propped against the trunk of an apple tree. While deeply engrossed in his book, a ripe, juicy apple descended from an overhanging limb and thumped Sir Isaac a good one on the head. "That's very interesting," Sir Isaac thought, "the ripe apple fell downward as apples generally do. In fact," he continued in thought, "apples always fall down." Newton's "aha" experience led to the formulation of the law of gravity, the discovery of a mysterious, unseen force which causes many of us to adhere to the mattress for several moments after the alarm clock goes off each morning.

Newton also discovered three laws of motion which describe the behavior of molecules. The first of these laws states that *a body at rest remains at rest until acted upon by an external force*. To the extent that we need our spouse, mother, or missionary companion to dislodge us from our mattress when the alarm clock rings, we can be said to be operating at the molecular level of behavior.

Notwithstanding the fact that our bodies are constructed of millions of molecules, the Lord teaches us that "it is not meet that I should command in all things; for he that is compelled in all things, the same is a slothful and not a wise servant. . . . Men should be anxiously engaged in a good cause, and do many things of their own free will." (D&C 58:26–27.) Aha! There's a discovery more important than gravity—moral agency!

Mankind has learned to defy the gravitational pull of the earth through the development of rocketry, but no one has never been able to avoid the consequences of his free agency. We are free to decide between good and evil (see Moses 3:16–17), but we are not free to change the results of our choices. Of course, there is the opportunity for growth and for forgiveness, but these become the results of additional choices.

Sir Isaac's second law of motion states that *the direction of a body in motion is determined by the sum of the forces acting upon it*. To illustrate this principle: When a baseball is thrown at ninety miles an hour and meets the swinging bat of a large and powerful batter, the ball will immediately change direction. The poor ball has no choice but to act at the molecular level, subject to the forces of the pitcher and the batter.

The Apostle James described certain people who live at the molecular level as lacking in faith. Their wavering lifestyles cause them to act "like the wave of the sea driven by the wind and tossed" (James 1:6). Such people lead "lives of quiet desperation," as Thoreau put it, driven by the fashion and fads of the day. They are influenced much more by peer pressure than by the promptings of the Spirit. They are always striving to keep up with the Joneses, seldom realizing the pressure they are exerting upon the Joneses to stay ahead of them! Those who are imprisoned by addictions of any kind operate at the molecular level as their moral agency first becomes impaired and then is completely lost to the overwhelming force of their habits.

The prophet Lehi explained that "there is an opposition in all things" (2 Ne. 2:11). He did not say *to* all things, but *in* all things. Our lives will continue to unfold within an arena of opposing forces, and the natural man lives at the molecular level of behavior, always susceptible to social pressure. But we can rise above this level as we yield "to the enticings of the Holy Spirit" (Mosiah 3:19) and respond to the strivings of the Spirit (see 2 Ne. 26:11) and contend no more against the Holy Ghost (see Alma 34:38) and allow the Spirit to persuade us to do good (see Ether 4:12).

The plan of salvation requires that we be tested (see Abr. 3:24–25), but we are not left alone to face the satanic forces loose in the world. A loving Father not only provided us with the gift of free agency, but also gives us the gift of the Holy Ghost to help us maintain a true and steady sense of celestial direction (see 2 Ne. 32:3–5). Nephi prophesied of the time when Christ will reign "and *because of the righteousness of his people*, Satan has no power" (1 Ne. 22:26, emphasis added). Unlike molecules, we really can determine the direction of our lives, and like an airplane flying through a crosswind, we can make necessary midcourse corrections to return to the divine course leading to exaltation. We can become partakers of the divine nature (see 2 Pet. 1:4–8) and incorporate the fruit of the Spirit (see Gal. 5:22) in our lives. We can undergo a mighty change of heart (see Alma 5:26), a mighty change of direction, and accept the invitation to "come unto Christ and be perfected in him" (Moro. 10:32).

The third law of motion, as formulated by Newton, states that *for every action there is an opposite and equal reaction*. At the human level this law is reflected in certain elements of the Mosaic law such as an "eye for [an] eye, [and a] tooth for [a] tooth" (Ex. 21:24). But the scriptures teach us a more excellent way (see 1 Cor. 12:31; Ether 12:11), and record the Savior's higher law involving admonitions to "turn the other cheek," and to "pray for them who persecute you and despitefully use you" (see Matt. 5:39, 44). As we pursue this more excellent way, our hearts become filled with love, even charity, the pure love of Christ (see Moro. 7:47–48).

Basketballs follow Newton's third law. That is to say, the harder we dribble, the higher they bounce. But husbands and wives, brothers and sisters, missionary companions, and neighbors are free to defy Newton's law. So what if our companion is sometimes brusque or grumpy? We can react with patience, long-suffering, and love. And what if our neighbor's dog is a nuisance? We can negotiate a peace treaty in the spirit of brotherly kindness. Mormon teaches us to "pray unto the Father with all the energy of heart that ye may be filled with this love" (Moro. 7:48).

We often equate purity with chastity and moral cleanliness, all of which is very proper to do. But Mormon speaks of another dimension of purity, and that is charity evidenced by a loving and forgiving heart. A pure heart is free from the impurities of hate, revenge, jealousy, pride, and contention. This kind of purity is not acquired in people whose lives operate at the molecular level in which events and circumstances trigger vengeful thoughts and actions. The pure love of Christ accrues to those who "pray with all the energy of heart that [they] may be filled with this love." Hearts filled with love have little room for anything else, and those who experience this love shall be like the Savior when he appears, for they shall be pure "even as he is pure" (Moro. 7:48).

Notes

1. Eliza R. Snow, "How Great the Wisdom and the Love," *Hymns*, 1985, no. 195.

2. See also Bruce R. McConkie, "Agency or Inspiration?" *New Era* 5 (January 1975): 38–43.

Chapter Nine

PRUNING AND GRAFTING

As His earthly ministry drew to a close, the Savior taught His disciples a wonderful allegory in which He likened himself to the true vine and His Father to the husbandman of the vineyard. He then introduced a very important principle about maintaining vineyards and about improving production: "Every branch in me that beareth not fruit he taketh away: and every branch that beareth fruit, he purgeth it, that it may bring forth more fruit" (John 15:1–2). For those of us who are unschooled in horticulture, it seems perfectly reasonable for the husbandman of the vineyard to prune and take away every branch "that beareth not fruit." What may not seem quite so reasonable is that he purges or prunes every branch that does bear fruit, so "that it may bring forth more fruit." Every fruit grower understands this principle well. If branches are left unpruned, a fruit tree can soon become a giant bush whose weak and flimsy limbs cannot support the large, succulent fruit the tree was intended to produce. Just as branches must be shortened to be strengthened, the fruit itself must often be thinned to allow one blossom to become one large apple instead of permitting four blossoms to produce tiny, insignificant fruit.

The Savior's beautiful allegory is full of meaning as He reminds His disciples and us that He is the vine and we are the branches and that without Him, or detached from Him, "ye can do nothing" (John 15:5). When we think we can "go it alone," it is then that we re-discover the truth of the Savior's statement: without Him we can do nothing. There are many times when we resist the pruning process, but the pruning process is a perpetually important part of the plan of eternal progression wherein we "bring forth more fruit."

The Parable of the Currant Bush

President Hugh B. Brown was a great teacher and orator who eloquently taught the principle of perpetual pruning in his autobiographical parable of the currant bush. As a young man, Brother Brown was pruning the shrubs in his yard one day when he discovered that one of the currant bushes was going too much to wood. Fearing that it would not produce any fruit, he drastically pruned the bush almost to the ground. Afterward the bush seemed to look at him sadly with a tear on every stump. The poor bush seemed to say: "I was nearly half as large as the trees across the fence, and might soon have become like one of them. But now you've cut my branches back."

The young gardener replied with a voice full of kindness: "Do not cry; what I have done to you was necessary that you might be a prize currant bush in my garden. You were not intended to give shade or shelter by your branches. My purpose when I planted you was that you should bear fruit."

The years passed by and Brother Brown was called to serve as an officer in the Royal Canadian Army, where he aspired to become a high-ranking officer. One day an unexpected vacancy entitled him to a promotion. He filled out the appropriate application forms, but the promotion was denied, and across the form someone had written: "This man is a Mormon." Bitterly, he cried to God, "How could you be so cruel to me?"

And then he heard, as it were, a voice echoing from the past: "I'm the gardener here. . . . If I had allowed you to continue . . . you would have failed in the purpose for which I planted you and my plans for you would have been defeated."

Brother Brown humbly replied: "I know you now. *You* are the gardener, and *I* the currant bush. Help me, dear God, to endure the pruning, . . . and ever more to say, 'Thy will not mine be done.' "[1]

The Pruning of the Saints

The history of the restored Church is characterized by the pruning of the Lord's Saints. A profound pruning of personal possessions occurred as the Saints were asked to move from Kirtland to Missouri and from Missouri to Nauvoo. And just as they once again sank their roots and built new houses in Nauvoo, they were pruned from their homes and from the Nauvoo Temple which they loved and they crossed the plains to the Salt Lake Valley. Surely here they would dwell unmolested in peace—or would they?

Many were called to go to Mexico and to southwestern Canada and to three hundred and seventy-seven settlements in between. Many of the Swiss Saints were sent to settle St. George, such a colorful contrast to the lush alpine meadows of their homeland. Many Scandinavian Saints were called to San Pete County, beautiful in its own way, but not like the verdant environs of Copenhagen, Oslo, and Stockholm. Many Welsh and Scots came to southern Idaho—lovely, but not as lush as Cardiff and Glasgow. But through this pruning process they learned obedience through the things which they suffered, and through their sacrifices they became more like their Savior. Their branches became more firmly attached to the True Vine, and their families continue to bear the fruits of the gospel.

Then, after the sagebrush was cleared and homes were constructed and crops were planted and livestock began to thrive, it was time for the family to be pruned of the patriarch of the home for two or three years as he went on a mission to serve the Lord. It was not unusual for a man, like my own grandfather, to leave behind a wife and five young children to care for the farm as best they could in his absence. And through it all, the branches brought forth more fruit, as children learned to identify and love the things that matter most in life.

The Departure of Heber C. Kimball

The departure of Heber C. Kimball on a mission to England is representative of the painful partings of many fathers who were called to leave their families behind in order to preach the gospel. Elder Robert B. Thompson described this poignant pruning process as follows:

> The day appointed for the departure of the Elders to England having arrived, I stepped into the house of Brother Kimball to ascertain when he would start, as I expected to accompany him two or three hundred miles, intending to spend my labors in Canada that season.
>
> The door being partly open, I entered and felt struck with the sight which presented itself to my view. I would have retired, thinking that I was intruding, but I felt riveted to the spot. The father was pouring out his soul to that

> "God who rules on high,
> Who all the earth surveys:
> That rides upon the stormy sky,
> And calms the roaring seas,"

> that he would grant him a prosperous voyage across the mighty ocean, and make him useful wherever his lot should be cast, and that He who "careth for sparrows, and feedeth the young ravens when they cry" would supply the wants of his wife and little ones in his absence. He then, like the patriarchs, and by virtue of his office, laid his hands upon their heads individually, leaving a father's blessing upon them, and commending them to the care and protection of God, while he should be engaged preaching the Gospel in a foreign land. While thus engaged his voice was almost lost in the sobs of those around, who tried in vain to suppress them. The idea of being separated from their protector and father for so long a time was indeed painful. He proceeded, but his heart was too much affected to do so regularly. His emotions were great, and he was obliged to stop at intervals, while the big tears rolled down his cheeks, an index to the feelings which reigned in his bosom. My heart was not stout enough to refrain; in spite of myself I wept, and mingled my tears with theirs. At the same time I felt thankful that I had the privilege of contemplating such a scene. I realized that nothing could induce that man to tear himself from so affectionate a family group, from his partner and children who were so dear to him—nothing but a sense of duty and love to God and attachment to His cause.[2]

Many callings to a position in the Church involve considerable pruning, such as young missionaries who must leave jobs and schooling and friends behind. Pruning can be especially painful for mission presidents and their wives and children as their very means of livelihood are put at risk, often with no secure future in prospect.

The mission president may look forward to returning to his former field of labor, in Korea, Italy, or Peru; however, his wife and children are called upon to weather considerable cultural shock through coming into contact with a foreign language and customs and foods and traditions which are very different from the comfortable confines of home. But through it all, families grow closer and testimonies grow deeper, and love for their new homeland increases, making it very difficult to leave at the end of their mission. As we are pruned of family and friends in one location, we are automatically able to graft into our circle of friends those we learn to love who live in other areas. Such was the case with Heber C. Kimball. Though his parting from his family was very painful when he left for England, leaving England for home was also extremely difficult, as evidenced by his description of his farewell:

> I went and visited the branches in the regions of Clithero and Chatburn, and on the morning when I left Chatburn many were in tears, thinking they should see my face no more. When I left them, my feelings were such as I cannot describe. As I walked down the street I was followed by numbers; the doors were crowded by the inmates of the houses to bid me farewell, who could only give vent to their grief in sobs and broken accents. While contemplating this scene I was constrained to take off my hat, for I felt as if the place was holy ground. The Spirit of the Lord rested down upon me and I was constrained to bless that whole region of country. I was followed by a great number to Clithero, a considerable distance from the villages, who could then hardly separate from me. My heart was like unto theirs, and I thought my head was a fountain of tears, for I wept for several miles after I bid them adieu. I had to leave the road three times to go to streams of water to bathe my eyes.[3]

Releases from Callings

For some members of the Church the most difficult pruning occurs not at the time of the calling but at the time of release. After six years as a bishop, or nine years as a stake president, or four years as a Primary president, or in one case I know, after thirty-five years as a Scoutmaster, one may feel temporarily empty if not somewhat rejected. There is no sin in becoming attached to a calling and to the wonderful people with whom one serves in that calling. But it is well to remember that the offices within the Church are for the perfecting of all the Saints (see Eph. 4:11–14); thus, all the Saints must have opportunities to serve.

There was a time when bishops and stake presidents served for thirty or forty years in their callings, and those who served were greatly blessed for doing so, and they were a blessing to those they served. But during those three decades that one man served as bishop of a ward, perhaps six or eight other brethren were deprived of the blessing of serving in that calling.

It is a great blessing to be called to serve for a limited period as a Seventy among the General Authorities of the Church. But precisely because these callings are blessings, there is wisdom in providing the means whereby several individuals can experience this blessing and several people can be perfected through the pruning process.

Whenever we feel the pangs of the pruning process when released from a Church calling, it may be well to recall the statement of Elder Melvin J. Ballard: "Positions do not exalt, service does."

The Lad with Loaves and Fishes

We can glean a great lesson from the Savior's feeding of the five thousand as recorded in the sixth chapter of John. The Savior surveyed this large congregation and noticed they were in need of nourishment. His Apostle Philip explained that they had insufficient funds to feed such a multitude. Another Apostle, Andrew, came forward and said, "There is a lad here, which hath five barley loaves, and two small fishes: but what are they among so many?" (John 6:5–9.) The Savior then blessed these meager rations, and these were distributed among the masses, leaving twelve baskets full of food after all had eaten.

In this beautiful historical account we recognize the names of Philip and Andrew, for they were Apostles in very prominent positions in the Church. But what of the lad with the loaves and fishes? His name is never mentioned, and his deeds are but a footnote to this great miracle. But the Savior knows his name, and the Savior knows of his generous heart and his desire to serve and literally to give his all. And though, on that particular day, he was pruned of his provisions, this lad left that gathering with a relationship to the Savior which was made possible only by his willingness to accept the pruning process.

There are hundreds and thousands of faithful Latter-day Saint couples who have faithfully paid their tithes and offerings throughout the years. They have sent sons and daughters on missions, and they have wisely conserved their financial resources in order to be self-reliant throughout the golden years of their lives. They have accepted any and all Church callings throughout the years, and now in the autumn of their lives they enjoy relatively good health in comfortable homes, and they experience joy in their posterity as children and grandchildren frequently drop by to visit. Surely there is a crown of righteousness in store for these wonderful Saints. Many of them could be serving on full-time missions, helping the kingdom to grow throughout the world, but some are resistant to the pruning process which would take them from the present comforts of home.

The Perpetual Pruning Process

Daily repentance of our human sins, weaknesses, and mortal frailties involves the repetitive pruning of certain thoughts and actions from our lives. The enslavement of bodies to tobacco, alcohol, coffee, tea, and other drugs of many different kinds often involves great physical discomfort incident to symptoms of withdrawal. Countless are the heartbreaking accounts of individuals who have become so addicted to tobacco, alcohol, or drugs that, though their intentions are strong to quit, they continually lapse into tragic addiction. There are so many good people in the world who would have otherwise joined the Church, or who, but for tobacco or drink, would have received the Melchizedek Priesthood, received their endowments in the temple, and been sealed to their families for time and eternity.

On the other hand, there are myriad encouraging accounts of individuals who did retain their resolve to prune their lives of addictive substances. A recent convert named Harold bore his testimony in a stake conference which Sister Condie and I attended in Germany. This young man of large stature confessed that before meeting the missionaries he had usually smoked three packs of cigarettes a day. After hearing the missionary discussions, he was challenged to quit smoking and to prepare to be baptized.

As he spoke at the pulpit during stake conference, he held up a monthly calendar on which the missionaries had indicated how many cigarettes he would be allowed to smoke that month after he had accepted the invitation to be baptized. The first day he could smoke 45 cigarettes, the second day 40, the third day 35, the fourth day 30, and the fifth day 25. After that he was to reduce his smoking one cigarette a day until the last day of the month when he would quit entirely. He reported that the plan worked very well until midmonth when he had successfully curbed his smoking to 15 cigarettes a day. At that point he reported thinking, "How stupid this is, Harold, to reduce your smoking by one cigarette a day. You know it's wrong. It's bad for your health, and, most important, smoking is against a commandment of God. Why wait another two weeks to quit? Why not quit today?" And so he did!

He then pointed to a heart drawn at the bottom of the calendar by the missionaries. Inside the heart was the following message: "We love you, Harold. We know you can do it." Choking back the tears, this large, very masculine individual said: "And that is what really motivated me to quit."

He had been baptized about three months previously, and it was obvious that this pruning process had brought about the mighty change in his heart and life described so well in the Book of Mormon.

There are others whose lives are afflicted by other addictions not entirely of a physical nature. Some individuals become absolutely addicted to hard rock music, or to watching television, or to watching and reading about athletic contests. Still others are addicted to pornographic television programs, videos, movies, and magazines. To those who may resist pruning pornography from their lives, the Lord has given the stern warning: "And he that looketh upon a woman to lust after her shall deny the faith, and shall not have the Spirit; and if he repents not he shall be cast out" (D&C 42:23; see also D&C 63:16).

A penchant for persistent criticism, complaining, and murmuring is also a habit to be subjected to the pruning process, and each of us knows best which branches need to be cut back so that we might enjoy more fruitful lives.

There is perhaps no more profound description of the pruning process than that proposed by the father of King Lamoni after he had been taught the gospel by Aaron, one of the sons of King Mosiah. This contrite king pleaded with the Lord: "O God, Aaron hath told me that there is a God; and if there is a God, and if thou art God, wilt thou make thyself known unto me, and I will give away all my sins to know thee" (Alma 22:18). And that is precisely what each of us must do if we wish to know God and become like him.

Health

The scriptures teach us that our bodies and spirits, "inseparably connected, receive a fulness of joy; and when separated, man cannot receive a fulness of joy" (D&C 93:33–34). The Word of Wisdom also teaches us the importance of caring for our bodies—temples which house our spirits. But almost universally, notwithstanding our adherence to the Word of Wisdom, the creeping impact of the aging process begins to prune some of our senses and, almost imperceptibly, our general health.

At about age ninety, the venerable President Hugh B. Brown spoke at a devotional assembly at Brigham Young University. Dearly beloved by the membership of the Church for his faithful service in the First Presidency and in the Quorum of the Twelve, this great orator cleared his throat, and in his resonant deep bass voice began his sermon with the following poem:

> My bifocals are real handy,
> My hearing aid's a find,
> I really enjoy my dentures,
> But, oh, how I miss my mind!

We all laughed with him as he made light of his own infirmities, but then it dawned on us that this pruning process often is so gradual as to go unnoticed for several years, until our curiosity overcomes our vanity and we finally agree to have our eyes examined. We are forced to admit that we need reading glasses, and a few years later bifocals and then trifocals, and then, in some cases, surgery to have cataracts removed. And as this great gift of sight begins to dim, we are faced with the matter of having to be very selective in our use of this gift. In the remaining years of our lives, will we have these eyes glued to the television set, or will we search the scriptures and conduct family history research and write personal histories and pay more attention to sunsets and flowers and the radiant faces of children? Will the diminution of sight induce greater preparation to see the face of God? (See D&C 93:1.)

A loss of hearing is another critical component of this lifelong program of purging and purifying. At first it is annoying not to be able to understand everything others say to us, notwithstanding the amusement we may provide them by our disjointed questions and comments unrelated to their conversation. But a loss of hearing can lead to increased isolation as grandchildren find it easier to avoid Grandpa than having to give the same answer three times to his questions.

Like bifocals, hearing aids are helpful, but unfortunately they not only increase the sound of people's voices but also amplify the noise of passing trucks and the hum of the air conditioner. But through it all, the pruning of the acuteness of our physical hearing can and will intensify our sensitivity to the still small voice, which is really felt more than heard.

The pruning of good health is manifest in many other forms, such as the onset of painful arthritis, which can teach us not only patience but also a great appreciation for the Atonement and the pain which the Savior suffered on the cross at Calvary.

Many men and women are pruned of their powers of reproduction and must learn to see themselves and their marriage partners through more spiritual eyes as they learn to express their love in acts of kindness in lieu of physical consummation. Fortunate is the couple who can fully express their physical love to each other. Even more fortunate is the elderly couple whose love continues to grow even more without the physical manifestation of love.

Wealth

Many a sermon has been based on the statement in Paul's letter to Timothy that "the love of money is the root of all evil" (1 Tim. 6:10). The point is generally made that it is not money which is the root of evil, but the love of money. Few of us ever really know how much we do love money unless and until we have lost large sums of it or have become completely destitute. It is then that we must learn, sometimes the hard way, whether our happiness is dependent upon the things money can buy, or whether we find greater joy in those things of eternal worth which cannot be purchased by silver or gold.

A poet unknown to me has penned the following verse which describes so well the importance of maintaining a proper perspective in our quest for the wealth of this world:

> He spent his health to gain his wealth,
> And then he tried in vain
> To spend his wealth to gain his health
> Back again.

The law of tithing, the law of fast offerings, and general admonitions to be generous with our means in helping others are all part of the Lord's pruning process to provide a means of demonstrating to Him whether we love Him more than the wealth of this world.

In the Book of Mormon the prophet Jacob very pointedly chastened the Nephites for their pride, their unchastity, and their love of riches. Regarding the latter, he said:

> Think of your brethren like unto yourselves, and be familiar with all and free with your substance, that they may be rich like unto you.
>
> But before ye seek for riches, seek ye for the kingdom of God.
>
> And after ye have obtained a hope in Christ ye shall obtain riches, if ye seek them: and ye will seek them for the intent to do good—to clothe the naked, and to feed the hungry, and to liberate the captive, and administer relief to the sick and the afflicted. (Jacob 2:17–19.)

There are many dedicated Latter-day Saints who have acquired considerable wealth and have consecrated their wealth for the blessing of the lives of others, to help the work of the kingdom roll forth in missionary work and the building of temples. One such married couple I know have worked very hard in honorable, honest labor to acquire their fortune, and they consider themselves to be stewards over wealth which ultimately, in an eternal sense, does not belong to them. Because of their commitment to the Church, they willingly prune themselves of their wealth in bequeathing generous, anonymous contributions to the building of the kingdom. For them, the pruning process is not a painful procedure, but rather a blessing providing them with joy compounded daily.

Elder Lionel Kendrick related an account of another kind of self-pruning at the other end of the socio-economic continuum. In the Philippines there is a good and faithful member of the Church who is a fisherman. Each day he makes his catch and then brings the fish to the open fish market for sale. His prices are invariably much, much lower than his competitors', and when asked why he does not raise his prices to be in line with those of the other fishermen, he humbly replied: "The members of the Church and my neighbors all buy their fish from me. If I raised my prices to match the other fishermen's, many of them could not afford to eat fish." And then he added with a twinkle in his eye, "I have an agreement with the Lord: I help take care of his poor, and he provides me with fish. There are days when the other fishermen come back with their boats empty, but the Lord makes sure I always return with a good catch!"

I recently spoke with a wonderful married couple who are

faithful Saints who have served long and well in various callings in the kingdom. They had recently owned a very large, expensive home located in an area of California afflicted by brushfires. Their beautiful home and virtually all of their physical possessions, including family photos and historical documents, were destroyed by a fire which very suddenly swept down the hills fanned by gusts of wind. And are they bitter? Disappointed, yes, but not bitter. They explained that losing everything of material value had helped them realize how cluttered their lives had become with things and how much of their time and energy had been devoted to worldly possessions.

In a very real sense, being pruned of their possessions had become a spiritually cleansing process allowing them to re-prioritize their values in life. For them, a call to serve a mission did not involve the usually painful process of packing the belongings they would take with them and arranging for storage for the things left behind. Nor did they have concerns about arranging to have someone care for their home in their absence. They literally came on their mission with all of their earthly belongings in a few suitcases. The fire had taught them the tentative nature of mortal life and had engendered greater faith in the things of eternity.

Shortly before entering the Garden of Gethsemane, the Savior asked his disciples: "When I sent you without purse, and scrip, and shoes, lacked ye any thing? And they said, Nothing." (Luke 22:35.)

In the final verses of the Book of Mormon, Moroni extends an eloquent invitation to "come unto Christ, and be perfected in him." Then, alluding to the pruning process, he continues: "And deny yourselves of all ungodliness." (Moro. 10:32.) Even though we may carry a current temple recommend attesting to our general worthiness, each of us can still prune unkind and uncharitable thoughts and actions from our lives. And we can prune pride and criticism and impatience and intolerance and procrastination and irreverence and gossip and all other forms of ungodliness from our lives, that we may bring forth more fruit and remain eternally attached to the True Vine.

Grafting

The great British poet William Wordsworth, though he died in 1850, described so well the world in which we live today as he penned the lines:

> The world is too much with us; late and soon,
> Getting and spending, we lay waste our powers:
> Little we see in Nature that is ours;
> We have given our hearts away, a sordid boon!
> The sea that bares her bosom to the moon;
> The winds that will be howling at all hours,
> And are up-gathered now like sleeping flowers;
> For this, for everything, we are out of tune.[4]

Implicit in Wordsworth's lines is the notion that our lives consist of only so much time and energy, and that time and energy invested in the fleeting things of this world rob us of opportunities to become in tune with nature and with the God of the universe. Thus, the pruning process is so necessary in order to allow time and place for the grafting process to occur. Among many other things, the grafting process involves seeking after "anything virtuous, lovely, or of good report or praiseworthy" (Articles of Faith 1:13) and making them an integral part of our lives and thereby blessing the lives of others.

Benjamin Franklin observed that "time is the stuff that life is made of," and in the Doctrine and Covenants the Lord has said that "he who is faithful and wise in time is accounted worthy to inherit the mansions prepared for him of my Father" (D&C 72:4).

Our time, indeed our very life, is not only characterized by perpetual pruning, but also by the constant accumulation of experiences, thoughts, and knowledge conducive to the formation of celestial character. Just as the Savior spoke of the necessity of pruning the branches of the true vine, the prophet Zenos's allegory of the tame olive tree alludes to the need of grafting branches from wild olive trees into the tame tree to save its very life. This allegory depicts the scattering and gathering of Israel and the grafting of the wild branches of the Gentiles into the tame olive tree of the house of Israel.

Just as the olive tree was saved through grafting, there are many things which must be grafted into our lives to sustain us physically, spiritually, intellectually, and emotionally. Capturing the essence of both pruning and grafting in the same verse, the Apostle James admonishes us to prune or "lay apart all filthiness and superfluity of naughtiness, and receive with meekness the engrafted word, which is able to save your souls" (James 1:21).

Grafting Recipes of Righteousness

Individual and family scripture study, seminary, institute, and Sunday School classes, priesthood quorums, Relief Society classes, family home evenings, and firesides all provide us with excellent opportunities to receive the word and to engraft it into our souls. In the next verse James continues to exhort us to be "doers of the word, and not hearers only" (James 1:22). We must do more than just study, read, or hear the word of God; it must become part of us, and as it becomes part of us we then act according to the word.

Nephi understood the importance of the engrafted word. His closing counsel focuses upon the admonition to "feast upon the words of Christ; for behold, the words of Christ will tell you all things what ye should do" (2 Ne. 32:3).

The Savior himself underscored the importance of literally making His word a part of us as He instructed His disciples, "If ye abide in me, and my words abide in you, ye shall ask what ye will, and it shall be done unto you" (John 15:7). The word *abide* refers to residing or staying firmly in the same place. When young branches are grafted into an older tree, the new branches literally become part of the old tree. By the same token, when branches are pruned from the parent tree, unless they are grafted back into another tree they will die. Such is the case with our persistent temptations and the sins that follow. If we prune them from our lives and then refuse to re-graft them into the tree, they will die from lack of attention. The pruning of the excessive baggage of sin must be just as permanent as the grafting of the word of God. (See Alma 7:15.)

His word must not just pass through our minds on occasion but be written in the "fleshy tables of the heart" (2 Cor. 3:3). When this occurs, and when we become "doers of the word, and not hearers only," then the grafting of godly attributes will follow as a natural consequence.

Mormon understood the necessity of not only reading the scriptures but also engrafting them into our lives, for he exhorts us to "*lay hold* upon the word of God" (Hel. 3:29, emphasis added). The expression "lay hold" appears in great literature about the sea as the captain shouts in the middle of the storm: "Lay hold o' the rail, mates." As the ship is tossed and turned by turbulent waves, safety is only assured to those who lay hold of the rail on the deck of the ship. Casual observers will surely be cast overboard. Only those hanging on to the word of God for dear life will be saved from the tempests of this mortal existence.

The Lord commanded the Saints to teach and to learn "of things both in heaven and in the earth, and under the earth; things which have been, things which are, things which must shortly come to pass; things which are at home, things which are abroad; the wars and the perplexities of the nations, and the judgments which are on the land; and a knowledge also of countries and of kingdoms" (D&C 88:79). The Lord further admonished the Saints to "teach one another words of wisdom; yea, seek ye out of the best books words of wisdom; seek learning, even by study and also by faith" (D&C 88:118).

That which is virtuous, lovely, of good report, or praiseworthy should be engrafted into our lives, and this includes great literature, great music, and the other fine arts in their most inspiring and lofty forms.

The Apostle Peter admonishes us to become "partakers of the divine nature" and exhorts us to diligently "add to [our] faith virtue; and to virtue knowledge; and to knowledge temperance; and to temperance patience; and to patience godliness; and to godliness brotherly kindness; and to brotherly kindness charity." (2 Pet. 1:4–7.)

As with many other blessings we receive, the Lord does not inoculate us against impatience in order that we may suddenly become patient and kind and tolerant and loving. Instead He permits conditions within the laboratory of earth life in which these godly traits will be learned and practiced. For example, He may bless us with a lively four-year-old whose favorite sport is jumping off the piano. We may be blessed with teenagers who interrupt the solitude and sanctity of our homes with so-called music composed in another age by performance groups from another planet. Or, we may have roommates who seem to feel that their free agency always gives them the right-of-way. Or, we may be blessed with demanding teachers who make us rewrite our papers until they not only are readable but sometimes even border on eloquence. Or, we may be blessed by an exacting employer who tests the very core of our souls while teaching us how to pursue excellence, orderliness, and punctuality, and in the process we gain self-confidence as well as patience. Or, we may live next door to fastidious neighbors whose lawn is always free from dandelions and crab grass and whose driveway has never tasted a drop of oil but who complain when our autumn leaves fall across their property line. And through it all (if we survive), we indeed learn to be more tolerant, patient, and charitable—and maybe even more tidy.

It is through our interactions with others that many of our bad habits are pruned as true friends approach us "speaking the truth in love" (Eph. 4:15). Our friends and roommates and brothers and sisters and parents and spouses are all helpful in pruning our penchant for criticism and chronic crotchetiness, stifling our intemperate remarks, smothering our intolerant attitudes, and boldly encouraging us to overcome our emotional immaturity. These same friends help us to engraft the traits of godliness into our lives, and it is sometimes only after a loved one has passed on that we realize that his or her stern demeanor was much like a sugar cube—hard, but sweet.

The Okavango River

In the mile-high central highlands of Angola, the Kubango River begins to flow southeasterly toward Botswana, where it becomes known as the Okavango River. The stream starts in an area in which there is an annual rainfall of up to fifty-two inches. Given such a great volume of rain at the headwaters, one could easily assume that this river would continue to increase in size and volume as tributary streams flowed into the mainstream. But such is not the case, and this makes the Okavango River very unusual. Whereas most large rivers continue to pass through a network of drainage systems which cause them to increase in size and depth until they eventually reach the ocean or a large sea, the destination of the Okavango is much different.[5]

At certain points along the first 230 miles of the river it becomes as wide as nine hundred feet, but as it pursues its thousand-mile course, unlike most other rivers it accumulates no additional fresh water from tributaries. Thus, as it proceeds along its course it becomes more shallow and sluggish, flowing into a triangular swamp tract in Botswana. In these lowlands the river increases from one mile wide to about seven miles wide until it flows into a swampy delta about one hundred and fifty miles wide where it eventually just disappears into the desert sand. What a pitiful ending for the fourth largest river in southwestern Africa! And what a tragedy that this precious water could not be put to use to rejuvenate this parched land!

Some individuals are a little like the Okavango River. Their lives begin in a very supportive, nurturing environment with a rich supply of the living water of the gospel. The first part of their life's course exhibits all of the evidence of a highly adequate supply of fresh water. But unless they continue to replenish this water supply with tributaries of gospel study, prayer, fasting, faithful tithes and offerings, regular participation in Church meetings, obedience to the commandments, and continual service in the kingdom, what once was a mighty testimony of the gospel can wither and become lost in the sand, as it were.

Our lives, like large rivers whose destination is the open sea, must continually accumulate new knowledge, new experiences, new sacrifices, new challenges, new thoughts, and new righteous desires, and the traits of godliness if we are to reach our celestial destination.

Another lesson may be drawn from the Okavango River. At the headwaters the channel is focused, swift, and relatively narrow, but as it continues along its course it becomes broader and slower. It covers much more ground, but it loses its depth and direction and focus until its volume and strength are dissipated over a large area of sand, where it simply disappears. Hence, the need to listen to the Lord's timely, yet timeless, counsel to focus our lives in the strait and narrow channel and to keep "an eye single to the glory of God" (D&C 4:5).

The Golden Years

It has become common among many retired people to say, "I'm so busy now, I don't know how I used to have time to go to work." We sometimes smile that all-knowing smile, revealing our thoughts that the reason why they are so busy during retirement is that it takes them so long to prepare meals and wash the dishes and tie their shoes and take catnaps during the day that there is less time for other things.

But such is not necessarily the case. In the lives of many senior citizens, now that the tasks of rearing a family and making a living have been accomplished, there are boundless opportunities to catch up on all the interesting and inspiring aspects of life they may have missed earlier in life. There is now time to serve a mission or two or to work in the temple a few days each week. There is uninterrupted time to do more family history and to visit the grandchildren and to write letters and read good literature and attend concerts and, in the sunset years, to prune away the superficial things of life and to graft into their lives the things that matter most. They learn that as lives become pruned of temporal concerns and the things of this world, there is more time and room for engrafting the things of eternity. In so doing, they learn the secret of the Savior's statement: "I am come that they might have life, and that they might have it more abundantly" (John 10:10).

Notes

1. See Hugh B. Brown, *Eternal Quest* (Salt Lake City: Bookcraft, 1956), pp. 243–45.

2. Cited in Orson F. Whitney, *Life of Heber C. Kimball* (1888; reprint, Salt Lake City: Bookcraft, 1992), pp. 108–9.

3. Cited in Whitney, *Life of Heber C. Kimball*, pp. 187–88.

4. Excerpted from William Wordsworth, "The World Is Too Much With Us," in Stanley B. Greenfield and A. Kingsley Weatherhead, eds., *The Poem: An Anthology* (New York: Appleton-Century-Crofts, 1968), pp. 161–62.

5. See *Encyclopaedia Britannica*, 15th ed., Macropaedia, s.v. "Okavango River."

Chapter Ten

REPROOF AND RECONCILIATION

In the very first chapter of the Book of Mormon, we read of a marvelous vision given to Father Lehi in which he was given a book to read, and "as he read, he was filled with the Spirit of the Lord" (1 Ne. 1:12). That experience can be replicated by each of us. As we follow the example of the sons of Mosiah and search the scriptures diligently and fast and pray about what we have studied, then we, like they, can be blessed with "the spirit of prophecy, and the spirit of revelation" (Alma 17:2–3).

Nephi explained that even passages of scripture which are difficult to understand "are plain unto all those that are filled with the spirit of prophecy" (2 Ne. 25:4). He also admonished us to "feast upon the words of Christ," with the wonderful promise that "the words of Christ will tell you all things what ye should do" (2 Ne. 32:3).

As we continue to search the scriptures we are struck with the truth of Nephi's promise: the words of Christ *will* tell us all things that we should do. There are certain passages of scripture which comfort, inspire, and edify us, and give us hope. Other passages enlighten our minds with an understanding of the doctrines of the kingdom. Still other passages, termed "wintry verses" by Elder Neal A. Maxwell, clearly point out our sins and shortcomings and impel us to undergo a mighty change of heart and improve our lives.

Lessons from Liberty Jail

Some of the most eloquent and moving passages in all of holy writ are found in section 121 of the Doctrine and Covenants. A brief review of the historical context in which this revelation was given will perhaps help us more fully to appreciate the content of the Lord's profound instructions.

This revelation is dated 20 March 1839, a time of great trial for the Saints as their prophet languished in Liberty Jail. The previous year had been characterized by tremendous turmoil and had been filled with bitter disappointments. Just eleven months earlier Oliver Cowdery and David Whitmer, two of the special witnesses of the Book of Mormon, had both been excommunicated from the Church. George Q. Cannon wrote of this event: "It was a sorrowful day for Joseph when he lost the companionship of these men who had been with him during many trials and who had participated with him in the glorious understanding of heavenly things."[1]

About this same time several members of the Quorum of the Twelve—William E. McLellin, Luke S. Johnson, John F. Boynton, and Lyman E. Johnson—were also excommunicated from the Church, and some of them became vindictive opponents actively involved in fomenting the animosity of enemies who were bent on the destruction of the Church. By August of 1838 mobs in Missouri had begun a concerted effort either to eradicate the Saints or to drive them into exile.

On October 25 the first apostolic martyr of this dispensation, Elder David W. Patten, was mortally wounded by a hostile mob in the Battle of Crooked River. Of Elder Patten, the Prophet Joseph said: "Brother David Patten was a very worthy man, beloved by all good men who knew him. He was one of the Twelve Apostles, and died as he had lived, a man of God, and strong in the faith of a glorious resurrection, in a world where mobs will have no power or place. One of his last expressions to his wife was—'Whatever you do else, O! do not deny the faith.'"[2]

A few days later, on October 30, a demonic mob of about 240 men mercilessly attacked several families of Saints who were gathered at Haun's Mill. Seventeen lost their lives, including two children, and twelve other individuals were wounded.[3] Some of the bodies of the deceased were mutilated by the fiendish mob before they left the scene of carnage.

On October 31, the Prophet and a few others were arrested on false charges near Far West. Two days later, before leaving for Independence under guard, they asked for the privilege of bidding farewell to their families. Joseph recorded:

I found my wife and children in tears, who feared we had been shot by those who had sworn to take our lives, and that they would see me no more. When I entered my house, they clung to my garments, their eyes streaming with tears, while mingled emotions of joy and sorrow were manifested in their countenances. I requested to have a private interview with them a few minutes, but this privilege was denied me by the guard. I was then obliged to take my departure. Who can realize the feelings which I experienced at that time, to be thus torn from my companion, and leave her surrounded with monsters in the shape of men, and my children, too, not knowing how their wants would be supplied.[4]

After being imprisoned for four days in Independence, Missouri, the Prophet and six other brethren were then taken to a crudely fashioned prison in Richmond, where on November 9 all seven prisoners were chained together and left to lie on a cold, bare floor where they were guarded around the clock.

One of Joseph's fellow prisoners was Parley P. Pratt, who described their imprisonment as follows:

In one of those tedious nights we had lain as if in sleep, till the hour of midnight had passed, and our ears and hearts had been pained, while we had listened for hours to the obscene jests, the horrid oaths, the dreadful blasphemies and filthy language of our guards, Colonel Price at their head, as they recounted to each other their deeds of rapine, murder, robbery, etc., which they had committed among the "*Mormons*" while at Far West and vicinity. They even boasted of defiling by force wives, daughters and virgins, and of shooting or dashing out the brains of men, women and children.

I had listened till I became so disgusted, shocked, horrified, and so filled with the spirit of indignant justice, that I could scarcely refrain from rising upon my feet and rebuking the guards; but had said nothing to Joseph or anyone else, although I lay next to him, and knew he was awake. On a sudden he arose to his feet and spoke in a voice of thunder, or as the roaring lion, uttering, as near as I can recollect, the following words:

"*SILENCE, ye fiends of the infernal pit. In the name of Jesus Christ I rebuke you, and command you to be still; I will not live another minute and bear such language. Cease such talk, or you or I die THIS INSTANT!*"

He ceased to speak. He stood erect in terrible majesty. Chained, and without a weapon; calm, unruffled and dignified as an angel, he looked upon the quailing guards, whose weapons were lowered or dropped to the ground; whose knees smote together, and who,

> shrinking into a corner, or crouching at his feet, begged his pardon, and remained quiet till a change of guards.
>
> I have seen ministers of justice, clothed in magisterial robes, and criminals arraigned before them, while life was suspended upon a breath in the Courts of England; I have witnessed a Congress in solemn session to give laws to nations; I have tried to conceive of kings, of royal courts, of thrones and crowns; and of emperors assembled to decide the fate of kingdoms; but dignity and majesty have I seen but *once*, as it stood in chains, at midnight, in a dungeon in an obscure village of Missouri.[5]

The end of November, Joseph and his companions in irons were taken to yet another prison in the little town of Liberty, Missouri. There they would spend the next four cold, damp, and dreary wintery months in Liberty Jail. How ironic the name: "*Liberty* Jail." At first the brethren were allowed no correspondence or visitors, but gradually their jailors relented. While it was a blessing to receive occasional visitors, it was also a time of great tribulation to receive occasional reports of the heartless persecution of the Saints and of their many privations. Finally, on or about March 20, the Prophet offered the following prayer in eloquent desperation: "O God, where art thou? And where is the pavilion that covereth thy hiding place? How long shall thy hand be stayed, and thine eye, yea thy pure eye, behold from the eternal heavens the wrongs of thy people and of thy servants, and thine ear be penetrated with their cries?" (D&C 121:1–2.)

And sweetly and serenely the divine answer was given: "My son, peace be unto thy soul; thine adversity and thine afflictions shall be but a small moment; and then, if thou endure it well, God shall exalt thee on high; thou shalt triumph over all thy foes" (D&C 121:7–8).

Among many other comforting and inspiring instructions, within this historical context of vile hatred and persecution of the Saints, the Lord then gave the Prophet Joseph Smith some of the most exquisite and sublime counsel found anywhere in the scriptures:

> No power or influence can or ought to be maintained by virtue of the priesthood, only by persuasion, by long-suffering, by gentleness and meekness, and by love unfeigned;
>
> By kindness, and pure knowledge, which shall greatly enlarge the soul without hypocrisy, and without guile—
>
> Reproving betimes with sharpness, when moved upon by the Holy Ghost; and then showing forth afterwards an increase of love toward

> him whom thou hast reproved, lest he esteem thee to be his enemy;
>
> That he may know that thy faithfulness is stronger than the cords of death (D&C 121:41–44).

This revelation did, in fact, ironically make of a dungeon a jail of liberty, for thereafter the Prophet gained his liberty, if you will, his freedom from despair, freedom from feelings of isolation and abandonment, freedom from feelings of hopelessness. Feelings of revenge were subdued and replaced by the supernal and certain knowledge that a loving Father in Heaven and His divine Son had not forgotten him in his trials as the Lord assured him: "Know thou, my son, that all these things shall give thee experience, and shall be for thy good. The Son of Man hath descended below them all. Art thou greater than he? Therefore, hold on thy way, and the priesthood shall remain with thee. . . . Fear not what man can do, for God shall be with you forever and ever." (D&C 122:7–9.)

The Major and the Corporal

A few years ago I received the assignment to reorganize the stake presidency in a city surrounded by a very large military base. After interviewing almost three dozen very fine, dedicated men, the Lord's Spirit manifested itself in the calling of a man who was the father of nine children and who served as a major in the U.S. Air Force.

Several months after his call, this new stake president related an interesting incident which had occurred in the course of his military duties. He had received a visit from a sergeant who complained to him that a young corporal was causing a great deal of disturbance and concern among many of the enlisted men. The corporal was lazy and rather slow to observe commands and often exhibited rebellion in the ranks. The sergeant implored the major/stake president to have a frank talk with the young corporal to "straighten him out" once and for all.

The major invited the sergeant to bring this young corporal into his office. When they arrived, this ordinarily soft-spoken stake president, in his role as air force major, raised his voice, shook his fist, pounded the table at the appropriate times, and told the young corporal that he needed to grow up, act like a man, accept responsibility, and learn to follow the rules or he would never amount to anything in life. After this rather emotional experience the corporal was dismissed, visibly shaken from this scolding in the major's office.

Two days later the stake president was walking across the military compound when he spotted the young corporal, who, upon sighting the major, hurriedly crossed the street to avoid another stressful encounter. The wise major maneuvered himself into the path of the young man, requiring a begrudging salute and greeting. To the corporal's surprise, the major put his arm around the shoulder of his young friend and said, "You know, son, I really am sorry that our confrontation a few days ago was necessary, but I sincerely wanted to help you change the direction your life was taking. It is precisely because I care about you that I talked to you the way I did."

The major then gave the corporal a manly one-armed hug and told him his door was always open whenever he had a problem or whenever he wanted someone to talk to. The young corporal heaved a great sigh of relief and walked away with a broad smile on his face.

As the major entered his office headquarters he was suddenly confronted by his friend, the sergeant, who told him that he had been watching the drama of reconciliation out of his own office window. "Pardon my boldness, Major, but I just don't get it. Two days ago you were shaking your fist in his face, and today you put your arm around him. What gives?"

The major replied: "That's section 121 in action, Sergeant."

A short time later the major was walking past a classroom where the sergeant was instructing his colleagues in the fine art of military leadership principles. To the major's surprise, he heard the sergeant say, "And most important of all, remember section 121: you chew 'em out first, and then you pat 'em on the back."

Someone in the class asked, "Where is that principle found?" The sergeant replied, "It's section 121. I've looked in several military manuals, and I haven't found which it is yet, but when I do I'll give you the reference. Just remember section 121."

The Details

For the benefit of the sergeant and any others who are interested in learning more of section 121, let us examine the key elements of the Lord's instruction:

Persuasion. The historical context within which section 121 was revealed cries out for the redressing of injustices, but the Lord spoke of persuasion rather than revenge.

There is a time-worn adage that "one convinced against his will is of the same opinion still." Persuasion takes more time than coercion or intimidation, but the results are much longer lasting and relationships are strengthened rather than alienated.

A grand old hymn describes so well the place of persuasion within the Lord's plan of perfecting his children:

> Know this, that every soul is free
> To choose his life and what he'll be;
> For this eternal truth is given:
> That God will force no man to heav'n.
>
> He'll call, persuade, direct aright,
> And bless with wisdom, love, and light,
> In nameless ways be good and kind,
> But never force the human mind.[6]

Long-suffering. Seen through temporal eyes, how ironic it is that the Prophet Joseph had asked the Lord, "How long shall thy hand be stayed?" and the Lord spoke to him of long-suffering. Long-suffering refers to exercising patience, tolerance, compassion, and goodwill in seeking to influence the attitudes and behavior of others. For the mother of a headstrong three-year-old who is not particularly fond of eating vegetables, long-suffering may be measured in a matter of minutes. Parents of teenagers may measure long-suffering in months, and the wife of a less-active prospective elder who is struggling with the Word of Wisdom may measure long-suffering in years.

Gentleness. Again we are struck by the contrast between the historical context and the content of section 121. The Prophet implored the Lord to "behold from the eternal heavens the wrongs of thy people and of thy servants," and the Lord spoke to him of gentleness rather than vengeance.

As a new mission president who was anxious to move the work forward posthaste, I found myself nipping at the heels of some of the young elders who, in their immaturity, were not very responsive to counsel. Then one day a wise assistant, a missionary several years older than the others, told me candidly: "President, sometimes young lions respond better to a pound of fresh meat than to the whip." I saw his point immediately, and I will ever be grateful to him for his courage and his candor. Gentleness is always necessary in our relationships with spiritually sensitive and tender-hearted women, but gentleness is also appreciated when dealing with gentlemen.

Meekness. Perhaps there is no greater example of meekness than that exemplified by the Savior on the cross. The Savior had the power to call down legions of angels in retribution for the humiliation He had suffered at the hands of unjust judgmental councils and the pain inflicted upon Him by the Roman soldiers who had carried out the mandate of a frenzied crowd and a timid magistrate. But instead of calling down revenge from heaven, He prayed for the Roman soldiers: "Father, forgive them; for they know not what they do" (Luke 23:34).

Love Unfeigned. Dale Carnegie's classic best-seller *How to Win Friends and Influence People* and many other books of the same genre have had a very positive influence upon millions of readers. Managers and executives who may resist incorporating biblical teachings in their lives will, nevertheless, occasionally give the Golden Rule a try if it is couched in managerial jargon. The general recipe found in many books on leadership is "call 'em by their first name, slap 'em on the back, and tell 'em you love 'em." The implications are that the employees will then work more productively when they feel they are appreciated. While this approach is far superior to an autocratic leadership style, it is not exactly what the Lord describes in section 121.

Unfeigned love is rooted in charity, the "pure love of Christ" (Moro. 7:47). This kind of love is more concerned with eternal consequences that immediate results. Elder Dallin H. Oaks has analyzed why it is we are motivated to serve others, and he proposes six different levels of motivation: (1) Hope for an earthly reward, (2) a desire for social companionship, (3) fear of punishment, (4) a sense of duty, (5) a hope for a heavenly reward, and (6) charity, the pure love of Christ.[7]

Kindness. To have the Lord speak of kindness amid a background of evil persecution once again illustrates the eternal lovingkindness of the Savior. One of the kindred attributes of kindness is the ability to suspend judgment. A wise friend once observed that even the Lord himself waits until a man has passed on until He judges him.

Pure Knowledge. This is one of the most crucial elements of the Lord's formula for influencing others for good. Pure knowledge is much more than a passing observation, a hunch, or hearsay evidence.

Among other things, the Lord revealed that pure knowledge "shall greatly enlarge the soul without hypocrisy, and without guile." Before launching into the next step of the Lord's method for bringing about desired change, it is well to emphasize the need and the importance of pure knowledge of the circumstances and pure knowledge of the intent of the heart of the person or persons who have become the focus of our attention.

It was precisely due to a lack of pure knowledge that the Savior was crucified and that the Prophet Joseph Smith was martyred. It would behoove each of us to get all the facts straight before disciplinary action is taken or chastening words are spoken.

Reproving Betimes with Sharpness. If one were asked to define the words *reproof* and *reproving*, the definitions given would likely reflect the personality, disposition, and inclinations of the definer. Those who are kind and gentle would speak in terms of correction or improving, while those who are more assertive and bold may define *reproof* in terms of "a good chewing out."

In an earlier revelation the Lord assured Joseph that "whom I love I also chasten" (D&C 95:1). Chastening, like reproving, often carries the connotation of receiving the wrath of God or of another mortal, but a closer inspection of the root *chaste* may help enlighten us and soften our interpretation of the chastening process. *Chaste* refers to purity, and *chasten* refers, among other alternative definitions, to purifying or making pure. It is in this sense that the Lord revealed that "all those who will not endure chastening, but deny me, cannot be sanctified" (D&C 101:5). In this context, the object of chastening or reproving is more to purify than to punish. The goal of reproving betimes with sharpness should be the removal of undesirable elements from a relationship, or the changing of improper conduct or attitudes of an individual or group.

If one were to ask a group to define the word *betimes*, an obsolete and archaic English word from the Shakespearean era, some would say that betimes meant "often" or "frequently," while others would define it as "occasionally." As a matter of fact, it means "before it is too late." Any correction, to be of real value, must occur before it is too late. Elder LeGrand R. Curtis, an orthodontist, tells me that it is much easier to straighten the crooked teeth of a thirteen-year-old than those of a thirty-year-old.

Sharpness, like *reproof* and *betimes*, is also interpreted in many different ways. In the Spanish translation of the Doctrine and

Covenants, for example, the translator uses the word *severidad*—in English, *severity*—to capture the meaning of *sharpness*. In the German translation of the same word, the translator uses the word *deutlichkeit*, or in English, *clarity*. I would favor the latter version over the former. It would be my personal interpretation that the use of the word *sharpness* in this verse is akin to describing a series of photographs, some of which are a little fuzzy or unclear or out of focus, and others of which are very clear, in focus, and sharp.

Mormon explained to his son the challenge of reproving with sharpness as he wrote: "I am laboring with them continually; and when I speak the word of God with sharpness they tremble and anger against me; and when I use no sharpness they harden their hearts against it" (Moro. 9:4).

Sharpness would tend to indicate that one concentrates on a single problem at hand without straying too far from the agenda. If I need to be chastened for my lack of punctuality, perhaps now is not the time to make mention of my baggy trousers and my unshined shoes. Reproving with sharpness would exclude expressions such as "and another thing I don't like" and "you always do that" or "you never do this." Sharpness, in the sense of focus and clarity, means we strive to resolve a specific problem without any overkill or reference to history.

When Moved Upon by the Holy Ghost. The companionship of the Holy Ghost transcends all of the other component parts of the Lord's righteous recipe for reproving betimes with sharpness. Of course, gentleness and kindness and all of the other attributes invite the Spirit of the Holy Ghost into a relationship, and "when a man speaketh by the power of the Holy Ghost the power of the Holy Ghost carrieth it unto the hearts of the children of men" (2 Ne. 33:1).

It is never an easy task to reprove another person, and it should certainly never be seen as an enjoyable task. But when reproof is to be given, it should be given before it is too late. As a bishop I became aware of a husband in the ward who had begun to show undue attention to a sister in the ward, causing his wife to become very jealous. It was very difficult to reprove this good man regarding his improprieties, but, great soul that he is, he changed his behavior, a marriage was strengthened, covenants were kept, and all parties concerned were the better for it.

The question is frequently asked: How can I tell if I am being moved upon by the Holy Ghost to reprove another person? May I humbly suggest a few indicators that the Holy Ghost is moving us to action:[8]

1. We are not filled with feelings of anger or contention. It may be necessary to reprove someone, but when we have feelings of enmity toward that person, we are more likely to injure than to edify.

2. We do not use unkind language in our reproof. The Holy Ghost will withdraw when unkind words are spoken. We can address the behavior without attacking the person.

3. We do not seek to threaten the self-esteem of the other person. The goal of the reproof should be to help a good person become better, not to tear him or her down. The objective should be a "mid-course correction," not a "scorched earth" policy.

4. We stick to the essentials and focus upon the specific problem as discussed above. There should be no overkill of the problem.

5. We are not overly anxious to engage in the reproof. Ofttimes the reproof is as painful for the reprover as for the reprovee.

6. After the reproof we are at peace with ourselves, knowing that the Lord's will has been done and that our actions have, indeed, been confirmed by the Spirit.

7. We have no feelings of "that serves him right." When we are moved upon by the Spirit to reprove someone, the reproof is not a vindictive act of retribution but a redemptive act of sincere concern.

8. The reproof is based upon pure knowledge, not hearsay, or gossip, or unfounded rumors. With pure knowledge as the basis of reproof we correct in the spirit of the Lord's revelation that "whom I love I also chasten" (D&C 95:1).

9. We have the door wide open for reconciliation. We show an "increase of love" and make it easy for him or her who was reproved to love us in return.

What Reproof Is Not

In the scriptural sense of section 121, reproving betimes with sharpness does not include persistent criticism and crotchety behavior. Nor does reproof include behavior described by behavioral scientists as displaced aggression. Sometimes we may become frustrated in the pursuit of a given goal and take out those frustrations on other nearby persons who have had nothing to do with our frustrations. This is clearly not the reproof of which the Lord has spoken. This is merely immature behavior on our part.

Reconciliation

Showing Forth Afterwards an Increase of Love. The prophet Brigham Young admonished the Saints never to inflict a wound larger than the balm they have to bind it back up again. This is the spirit of the Lord's injunction about "showing forth afterwards an increase of love toward him whom thou hast reproved lest he esteem thee to be his enemy; that he may know that thy faithfulness is stronger than the cords of death" (D&C 121:43–44).

While the person who initiates the reproof has an obligation to show forth an increase of love after the reproof, the person being reproved also has an obligation to assist in the reconciliation process. When we are reproved by another person—a parent or priesthood leader, for example—we should first be humble and meek enough to accept the reproof. President Benson observed that pride is concerned with who is right while humility is concerned with what is right.

The greatness of the Apostle Peter's heart can be found in his ready acceptance of the Savior's rather frequent correction of his behavior.

And notwithstanding the numerous corrections which the Savior made in Peter's life, the Savior never released Peter from his responsibilities, but rather strengthened him. To Peter's credit, let it be said that he listened, he accepted the reproof, he learned, and he changed. The Lord has said that "the power of my Spirit quickeneth all things" (D&C 33:16), and this is certainly true with regard to "reproving betimes with sharpness." When done correctly with the Spirit of the Holy Ghost, reproving can accelerate learning and changes in attitudes and behavior which otherwise might have taken years or might never have occurred at all.

When reproving is accompanied by unconditional, Christlike love and sincere concern for him who has been reproved, then our relationship will become even stronger than before. This is even possible when the person doing the reproving did so with a little "overspray" on the problem or when he or she may not have chastened us as diplomatically and tactfully as we would have desired. In such instances we should accept the reproof in the spirit in which it *should* have been given.

Pahoran: A Master at Reconciliation

There are few better examples of mature reconciliation than the response of the chief judge Pahoran to Captain Moroni's impassioned plea for military assistance which was followed by unfounded aspersions to possible treason. Pahoran realized that Moroni had written his letter in the heat of battle and while in desperate straits. Taking the context into consideration, Pahoran responded in the following conciliatory manner to Moroni: "I do not joy in your great afflictions, yea, it grieves my soul. . . . And now, in your epistle you have censured me, but it mattereth not; I am not angry, but do rejoice in the greatness of your heart. . . . And now, Moroni, I do joy in receiving your epistle, for I was somewhat worried concerning what we should do, whether it should be just in us to go against our brethren." (Alma 61:2, 9, 19.)

Pahoran was not concerned with who was right, but rather with what was right. At this time in Nephite history it was right for Moroni and Pahoran to unite in a common cause, and Moroni and Pahoran, thus reconciled, combined forces to establish peace once again in the land.[9]

Disciplinary Councils

The conducting of disciplinary councils is a formalized, organizational form of reproving before it is too late. And the decisions of these councils are made prayerfully as those who make up the councils are moved upon by the Holy Ghost.[10] Disciplinary councils can and should be a sweet, sanctifying experience for all concerned when all parties involved are meek and lowly of heart and when decisions are based upon pure knowledge. Elder Robert L. Simpson referred to such councils as "courts of love." But, even under the best of circumstances, it is difficult for a bishop or stake president to hold a disciplinary council, especially if it involves an individual with whom one has had a long and lasting friendship.

Such was the case in a small town in a remote stake of Zion in which nearly all of the members were cattle and sheep ranchers and men of the soil. Two neighbors, who were also relatives, had grown up together and had shared farming equipment with each other throughout the years. They could scarcely have been closer had they been born into the same family.

Eventually, one of these two men was called to be the stake president, and he served the members of his stake righteously and in dignity. And then came one of the greatest trials in his entire tenure as stake president. Rumors began to circulate that his long-standing neighbor had begun to have an extramarital affair with a woman in the community. Moved upon by the Holy Ghost, the stake president confronted his neighbor, who did not deny the rumors.

The stake president lost many a sleepless night pacing the floor wondering what the Lord would have him do. Did his lifelong friend really have to experience a disciplinary council? Perhaps he could postpone the whole matter until he was released as stake president, then the new stake president could resolve the matter. But if he waited too long to take some course of corrective action the sins would only be compounded and families would be broken and lives destroyed. The Spirit prompted him to act now, before it was too late.

The disciplinary council was convened and went late into the night as the members of the high council, all of whom had known and loved their wayward friend long and well, carefully and mercifully weighed the evidence. After prayerful consideration the decision was rendered and confirmed by the Spirit: this adulterous man was to be excommunicated in order that he might truly undergo a mighty change of heart and eventually experience the refreshing, cleansing waters of re-baptism. This spiritual surgery would save a soul and a family.

The stake president returned home from the stake center that night feeling as though his best friend had died. But the next morning, to his surprise, as he looked out the window, his eyes beheld a sheep hanging from a tree. It had been killed the night before and had been carefully skinned and cleaned. This was a present from his neighbor who had been excommunicated the night before. This neighbor sensed how heavily his sins weighed upon the stake president. In order to show his love and gratitude for this concerned shepherd, as soon as he returned home from the disciplinary council, he sought out a prize sheep, which he killed and dressed and presented to his spiritual leader as a sign of reconciliation.

Our loving Savior is ever anxious for each of us to become reconciled with Him through His at-one-ment. Indeed, He has assured us: "Behold, I stand at the door, and knock: if any man hear my voice, and open the door, I will come in to him, and will sup with him, and he with me" (Rev. 3:20).

Notes

1. George Q. Cannon, *Life of Joseph Smith the Prophet* (Salt Lake City: Deseret Book Co., 1986), p. 238.

2. *History of the Church* 3:171; hereafter cited as *HC*.

3. See *HC* 3:326.

4. *HC* 3:193.

5. Parley P. Pratt, *Autobiography of Parley P. Pratt,* ed. Parley P. Pratt, Jr. (1874; reprint, Salt Lake City: Deseret Book Co., 1985), pp. 179–80.

6. "Know This, That Every Soul Is Free," *Hymns*, 1985, no. 240.

7. See Dallin H. Oaks, *Pure in Heart* (Salt Lake City: Bookcraft, 1988), pp. 37–49.

8. The material presented here is a modification of the author's article "Reproving with Love," *Ensign* 9 (August 1979): 18–19.

9. See Spencer J. Condie, "Righteous Oaths, Reproof, and Reconciliation," in Kent P. Jackson, ed., *Alma 30 to Moroni*, vol. 8 of *Studies in Scripture* (Salt Lake City: Deseret Book Co., 1988), pp. 80–91.

10. See M. Russell Ballard, "A Chance to Start Over: Church Disciplinary Councils and the Restoration of Blessings," *Ensign* 20 (September 1990): 12–19.

Chapter Eleven

GOOD CHEER AND SOLEMNITY

Two of the major messages of the Book of Mormon are that "men are, that they might have joy" (2 Ne. 2:25), and that "wickedness never was happiness" (Alma 41:10). The Prophet Joseph further taught that "happiness is the object and design of our existence; and will be the end thereof, if we pursue the path that leads to it; and this path is virtue, uprightness, faithfulness, holiness, and keeping all the commandments of God."[1]

The context in which the Prophet made this statement in August of 1842 makes his teaching all the more profound. Here was a man who had been subjected to tar-and-feathering in Ohio, imprisonment in Richmond, Missouri, and an extended incarceration in Liberty Jail. Furthermore, he and his lovely Emma had buried four of their own infants—Alvin, the twins Thaddeus and Louisa shortly after birth, and little Don Carlos at age fourteen months—as well as an adopted son, Joseph Murdock Smith, who died at eleven months. Yet the Prophet asserts that "happiness is the object and design of our existence."

Several times throughout the scriptures we are admonished, indeed commanded, to "be of good cheer." Sometimes this commandment is given at a time when things look very bleak, indeed. Such was the case with Nephi, the great-great-grandson of Alma the Younger. It had been about five years since Samuel the Lamanite had prophesied the marvelous signs of the Savior's birth, and now many of the people were beginning to say: "Behold the time is past, and the words of Samuel are not fulfilled," and a day was determined at which time those who believed in Samuel's words would "be put to death except the sign should come to pass" (3 Ne. 1:6, 9).

As Nephi beheld the wicked designs of many of the people, "his heart was exceedingly sorrowful," and he "cried mightily to his God in behalf of his people" (3 Ne. 1:10–11). It was then that he heard the command and the promise: "Lift up your head and be of good cheer; for behold, the time is at hand, and on this night shall the sign be given, and on the morrow come I into the world" (3 Ne. 1:13). Man is that he might have joy, but sometimes that joy, like the Prophet Joseph's glorious first vision, can only be ours after we have wrestled with the powers of darkness and discouragement.

Be of Good Cheer, Little Children

The time was August of 1831, and persecution was beginning to mount against the struggling band of Saints who received the Savior's comforting counsel: "Be of good cheer, little children; for I am in your midst, and I have not forsaken you" (D&C 61:36). Three months later the Lord reiterated the command to "be of good cheer, and do not fear, for I the Lord am with you and will stand by you; and ye shall bear record of me, even Jesus Christ, that I am the Son of the living God, that I was, that I am, and that I am to come" (D&C 68:6).

Another three months later, on the evening of March 24, 1832, the Prophet and his wife Emma were to suffer one of the most traumatic events of their lives. Eleven months earlier Emma had given birth to twins—a boy and a girl—on April 30, 1831, but, alas, they lived only three hours. Coincidentally on the same date Brother and Sister John Murdock became the proud parents of twins, Joseph and Julia, but their mother tragically died after childbirth. Thus, nine days later Emma began to rear these little Murdock twins in her own home to fill the void of her own lost twins. Now, almost a year later, the little twins lay in bed sick with the measles, when a mob burst through the door and dragged Joseph out of the house where he was beaten and his face was severely scratched and disfigured, and he was then subjected to the humiliating ritual of being tarred and feathered.

After spending the evening removing the tar and feathers, the Prophet prepared himself for the Sabbath when he "preached to the congregation as usual, and in the afternoon of the same day baptized three individuals."[2] The following Friday little Joseph Murdock died from exposure to the cold from the evening the mob dragged the Prophet from the house.

Cheerful Redressing of Wrongs

It is very significant that seven years later, in March of 1839, while the Prophet was still languishing in Liberty Jail in Missouri he wrote a letter to the Saints suggesting they gather up "a knowledge of all the facts, and sufferings and abuses put upon them by the people of this State" (D&C 123:1). After a rather detailed outline of the steps which should be taken to gain redress from the wrongs committed against them, Joseph Smith concluded: "Let us cheerfully do all things that lie in our power" (D&C 123:17).

The loss of life and property had been great, and as citizens of the state of Missouri and as American citizens, the Saints should have been protected by the laws of the land. But they had received no such protection and had, on the contrary, been the victims of heartless marauders. Thus, it was entirely proper to seek redress from the government of the state of Missouri. But the Prophet admonished the Saints to do so cheerfully.

So much energy is wasted in feelings of hatred and revenge, but when we can seek to set things right cheerfully, "we stand still, with the utmost assurance, to see the salvation of God, and for his arm to be revealed" (D&C 123:17). When we harbor mean-spirited feelings of retribution, we are on the devil's turf; but when we seek redress cheerfully, the Lord is on our side.

André and Yvette

"Why is it you always seem to be so very happy?" I asked André, a seventy-year-old bearded immigrant from the French-speaking region of Switzerland. "Well, you see my father was a verree 'appy man. Each night we children would look out the window to see when our father would return from his work. As soon as we see him coming down the road we would run to meet him. He would carry one child on his shoulders and another in his arms and we would sing our way back to our house." Then, pausing briefly once again to reflect upon the question, he mused, "I guess I am always a verree 'appy man because I never knew we were *not* supposed to be 'appy."

During his lengthy apprenticeship as a master furniture maker in Switzerland, André met and fell in love with the very lovely and radiant Yvette. After a three-year engagement he finally received her father's approval and blessing to marry.

As young converts to the Church, a marriage "until death do you part" did not satisfy André and Yvette, so in 1949, with sixty-six dollars in their pockets, they set sail for Logan, Utah, under the sponsorship of a greatly beloved missionary, Serge Ballif. In the Logan Temple they would be sealed for time and for all eternity.

As they left Switzerland for America, Yvette was already six months pregnant, and shortly after their arrival she gave birth to twin baby boys. Sharing a sorrow experienced by Joseph Smith and Emma, tragically their joy was very short-lived as the premature little ones died not long after birth.

André was self-employed for those first two and a half years in Logan, and business was very slow, so they decided to seek their fortune in California. Without steady employment, and almost destitute, they celebrated their first Thanksgiving Day in California with one hot dog each.

Never one to allow external circumstances to control his life, André volunteered to assist the contractor in charge of the construction of an LDS chapel in Westwood. After the contractor observed his skill and dedication for several days, André was hired as a carpenter. After working on the chapel by day, André repaired furniture by night in a small shop which he had rented.

Yvette was expecting again, and soon they were blessed with a lovely little daughter. André worked seventeen hours nonstop to construct a specially designed cradle for this precious little child, and the cradle has become a family heirloom used by their grandchildren.

Soon thereafter, Yvette's parents visited them in California and assisted them in the purchase of a building in West Hollywood for the enormous sum of thirty thousand dollars. They also assumed a loan to expand and remodel the building. Yvette would become a dealer of antique furniture, and André would build custom-made fine furniture. But in spite of her very sensitive artistic tastes and his excellent talents as a master craftsman, somehow the business was always struggling. Then one day a member of the bishopric, an accountant, sat down with André for a heart-to-heart talk. He asked André how he determined the price for the lovely furniture he built. "Well," said André, "if a piece of wood costs me ten dollars and I use half of it, I charge the customer five dollars. If a quart of stain costs two dollars and I use half of it, I charge the customer one dollar."

The accountant explained to André some basic business principles and the need to assure a profit which could then be reinvested in more materials. He carefully explained that André must charge a little extra not only for the wood and stain but also for the cost of the building, the insurance, the lights, and the future replacement of equipment.

André and Yvette may have been naive with regard to business in the big city, but they were very astute in assessing quality antiques which they purchased for resale. Their Swiss pride and work ethic involving sixteen-hour workdays also assured the quality of their custom-made furniture. The combination of French artistry and Swiss precision guaranteed that each piece of fine furniture was a masterpiece.

With some of their profits they began to remodel the business until it assumed a sixteenth-century European charm, complete with an Old World roof and small, diamond-shaped windows welded together in sections. The interior also exuded European warmth, with beautiful terra-cotta floors and oak plank paneling on the walls.

Yvette and André expanded not only their business but also their family. With the passage of time, their daughter, Rachelle, and her husband, Roger, have blessed the Liardets with five handsome grandchildren who live just five minutes from their doting grandparents.

Over the years, the Liardets' establishment in West Hollywood became the scene of numerous movies whenever the script called for a sixteenth-century European business establishment. It also served as the decor for Santa's workshop in various TV Christmas commercials. The Liardets developed a warm and lasting eighteen-year friendship with the Bill Cosby family, and this was the beginning of the snowball effect, as the reputation of Liardet furniture began to spread throughout the entire United States.

Several years ago the bishop of their ward approached the Liardets about going on a mission. Before entering the Missionary Training Center in Provo, André and Yvette engaged the services of an accountant and lawyer to arrange for the sale of their business. While making an inventory of their assets, the lawyer said, "André and Yvette, I didn't realize that you were millionaires." "We are?" they responded in innocent surprise. "Yes, this building is worth one and a half million dollars." "It is?" André reacted enthusiastically. An inventory was made of the antique furniture, and, again, the sum was very substantial. When the cost of equipment and other assets were all included, the fact was confirmed: the Liardets were multi-millionaires without ever really realizing it.

"It was very surprising to learn we were millionaires," André explains with childlike glee. "All we did was charge a little profit on everything we sold, just like the member of the bishopric told us to do. We just kept working hard all these years with love for the art and just sold more and more, until heerre we arrre—millionaires!" André then hastens to add: "But not in the bank. After paying our tithing, repaying our bank loan, income tax, and the real estate commission, the money go fast out."

Austria Bound

When the Liardets arrived at the airport in Vienna, Austria, in October of 1984, we knew the Lord had blessed our mission with some very special Saints. But how does one find adequate housing for multi-millionaire missionaries who are urgently needed to assist a struggling branch whose members live as many as seventy-five miles from each other? After several days of looking, it became apparent that the best option in the entire city of Leoben was a two-room apartment above the butcher shop. The smell of sausage and raw meat wafted up the stairwell and would be offensive even to meat lovers, but the Liardets are vegetarians. Nevertheless, they cheerfully endured.

When we first visited them in their apartment, my heart sank. The half-size bathtub was in the kitchen, only a few paces from the stove! "I am so sorry we couldn't find anything better," I said apologetically. With his typical *savoir-faire* and enthusiasm, Brother Liardet replied, "Do not worree, Bruder Condie, I can sit in the tub and take a hot bath while Yvette hands me my bowl of soup. I cannot even eat soup in the tub at home. It is very convenient for us."

These wonderful missionaries were assigned to visit inactive members and part-member families and to contact referrals in remote places. The Liardets had the perfect personalities to win their way into the chilly hearts of inactive members. After visiting one prospective elder's family, it became apparent that not only was *he* cool, but his *apartment* was also very cold due to an obvious lack of fuel.

A few days later the Liardets appeared on the doorstep with two large sacks filled with coal briquets. As the man gingerly opened the door, Brother Liardet enthusiastically announced: "Here are two sacks of coal." "But I can't accept this gift from you," the man replied defensively. "We don't even know each other that well." With an ever-broadening smile, André rejoined: "But the coal is not for *you*, it is for your *oven!*" Completely disarmed, the inactive member accepted their gift in behalf of his oven and invited them in, and they began to develop a warm relationship.

Not only were their great fellowshipping skills an indispensable asset, but the Liardets also put their artistic skills to good use. Many of our missionaries found street displays to be a productive means of contacting and finding people to teach. Unfortunately some of the street displays had, well, what shall we say, a bit of a "homemade" look about them. The Liardets taught the young missionaries to take pride in the Church and in their representation of the Church. André became friends with a furniture maker and together they produced some very attractive folding stands for the displays. Each display not only had a beautiful message but also was a piece of attractive furniture.

Sometimes the young missionaries were a bit timid in approaching people on the streets, but they always took courage when André was there. André would smile broadly at each passerby and hold out a book, saying, "Ein Buch Mormon für Sie" ("A Book of Mormon for you"), with such enthusiasm that few could refuse.

Boundless Creativity

André and Yvette were never ones to worry about how old they were before starting new projects. Several years ago, with that same adventurous spirit which brought them to America, André had the urge to learn to play the cello. There are some who might say, "If you don't start playing a stringed instrument before you are fifteen, then forget it." But that kind of rhetoric did not faze André, and so rather late in life he bought a cello and began taking lessons.

He did not bring his cello with him to Austria on the plane, but he did buy a nice one upon his arrival, and this cello became a great entree in doing missionary work. His music opened a number of the doors of musicians and music lovers in the melodic land of Austria. His organization of and participation in chamber concerts in various chapels and private homes became an ice-breaking method for timid

Austrian Saints to introduce their friends to other Church members and ultimately to the gospel.

Looking back on the lives of the Liardets, it is clear that they understood Lehi's observation that "it must needs be, that there is an opposition in all things" (2 Ne. 2:11), for they have known opposition firsthand. But they also know that "men are, that they might have joy" (2 Ne. 2:25). Or, as André would put it: "I never knew that we were *not* supposed to be 'appy." As this manuscript was in preparation, while returning to their home in California following their attendance at general conference, Yvette and André were involved in a tragic automobile accident in which Yvette was killed. With a firm testimony of the resurrection and of eternal marriage, Brother Liardet continues to maintain his cheerful, sweet spirit, notwithstanding the loneliness he feels without his sweet Yvette.

Light-Mindedness

Although the Lord has admonished us to be of good cheer, he also warns us to "cease from all [our] light speeches, . . . and light-mindedness" (D&C 88:121). Mark Twain once contended that the Lord himself has a sense of humor as proven by observing some of His creations. Twain alluded, of course, to some of his fellow beings of the human species, but when one strolls through a large zoo and observes a hippopotamus or a whooping crane, a camel, a giraffe, or a monkey, one is led to believe that our loving Heavenly Father does indeed possess a wonderful sense of humor. In fact the Lord has revealed to us that He has created all things "to please the eye and to gladden the heart" (D&C 59:18). So where lies the difference between good cheer, which is desirable, a sense of humor, which is sometimes indispensable for survival, and light-mindedness, which is divinely discouraged?

The subject matter and how it is treated is largely the determining factor in discerning between acceptable light-heartedness and good humor, and questionable light-mindedness. When the Father and the Son appeared to Joseph in the Sacred Grove, the Savior spoke of some professors of religion "having a form of godliness, but [who] deny the power thereof" (JS–H 1:19). The form and the power, or the form and the content, should be compatible.

That great British musical team of William Gilbert and Arthur

Sullivan brought great entertainment to the world through their mirthful and whimsical operettas such as *Trial by Jury*, *H.M.S. Pinafore*, *The Mikado*, and *The Pirates of Penzance*. The lyrics are flippant, often with doggerel verse, which make them all the more delightful, and the plots are generally uncomplicated satires on the pomposity of certain segments of society. A Gilbert and Sullivan operetta always provides delightful entertainment, and that is its only goal.

The lifting operetta music is an appropriate vehicle for the humorous lyrics. But when Arthur Sullivan wrote the music to that great anthem "Onward, Christian Soldiers," instead of a lilting operatic melody he used a more solemn, majestic accompaniment which matched the content of that hymn. But to have used the words of "Poor Little Buttercup" with the majestic melody of "Onward, Christian Soldiers" would have robbed the entertainment value from the first song, and to have used a light, carefree melody with the latter hymn would have deprived it of its inspirational value.

Such is the case with humor and light-mindedness. The subject matter of humorous stories, jokes, puns, and tall tales is almost boundless. We can joke about a lot of things, but two considerations are paramount: First, the Lord has said in our day, "Remember that that which cometh from above is sacred, and must be spoken with care, and by constraint of the Spirit" (D&C 63:64). This would preclude making light of sacred ordinances, or prayer, or the scriptures, or of prophets, living or dead. A second caution in the use of humor is that it should neither hurt nor harm any individual or group of individuals. Ethnic jokes are generally very funny to everyone except to him who is the butt of the joke.

Solemnity

As with other principles in tension, problems occur when solemnity is carried to the extreme. No one enjoys being around a crotchety old pessimistic person whose lifelong habit of criticizing and complaining is reflected in his sour old puss. But on the other hand, there is the occasional man of good cheer, the hail-fellow-well-met who has concentrated so much of his life's energy on being the life of the party that he sometimes glosses over the things that matter most when the party's over.

In 1831, only ten months after the organization of the Church, the Lord declared: "Hearken ye to these words. Behold, I am Jesus Christ, the Savior of the world. Treasure these things up in your hearts, and let the solemnities of eternity rest upon your minds." (D&C 43:34.)

Notwithstanding perpetual persecutions, this was a season of rejoicing. The Book of Mormon had been printed, the Church had been organized, and revelations flowed freely from the Lord to his young prophet on earth. This was a time of great joy. And amid this joy, the Savior reminded the Saints to "let the solemnities of eternity rest upon your minds."

Four years after this revelation was received, the Quorum of the Twelve Apostles was organized on February 14, 1835. They were ordained and set apart the following day and then given an apostolic charge by Oliver Cowdery to "cultivate great humility," for, said Oliver, "I know the pride of the human heart." He admonished them further: "God does not love you better or more than others. . . . Be not lifted up when ye are called good men."[3]

Oliver Cowdery's counsel was particularly timely when one considers the respective ages of those newly called Twelve Apostles at the time of their call: Thomas B. Marsh, 35; David W. Patten, 35; Brigham Young, 33; Heber C. Kimball, 33; Orson Hyde, 30; William E. McLellin, 29; Parley P. Pratt, 27; Luke S. Johnson, 27; William Smith, 23; Orson Pratt, 23; John F. Boynton, 23; and Lyman E. Johnson, 23. Each was given a sweet and powerful blessing under the hands of the Three Witnesses, and now their ministry could begin in solemnity.

A month later, on March 15, having recognized their having taken their sacred callings too lightly, the clerks for the Twelve, Orson Hyde and William E. McLellin, recorded:

> The Twelve met in council, and had a time of general confession. On reviewing our past course we are satisfied, and feel to confess also, that we have not realized the importance of our calling to that degree that we ought; we have been light-minded and vain, and in many things have done wrong. For all these things we have asked the forgiveness of our heavenly Father; and wherein we have grieved or wounded the feelings of the Presidency, we ask their forgiveness. . . . We have unitedly asked God our heavenly Father to grant unto us through His Seer, a revelation of His mind and will concerning our duty the coming season, even a great revelation, that will enlarge our hearts, comfort us in adversity, and brighten our hopes amidst the powers of darkness.[4]

In response to their request, the Prophet Joseph received section 107 of the Doctrine and Covenants, which meticulously outlines the duties of the various priesthood offices.

Mormon: A Sober Young Man

That great prophet for whom the Book of Mormon was named was described at the age of ten as being "a sober child" and "quick to observe" (Morm. 1:2). It is my personal view that solemnity and teachability are purposely mentioned in close proximity. The Lord set forth as one of the requirements for successful missionary labors "an eye single to the glory of God" (D&C 4:5). When we are light-minded, we are easily distracted from the things of the Spirit and from the things of eternal worth. But when we let the "solemnities of eternity" rest upon our minds, then the power of His Spirit will "quicken all things" (D&C 33:16).

This was certainly true in Mormon's life. At age fifteen, "being somewhat of a sober mind," he was "visited of the Lord, and tasted and knew of the goodness of Jesus" (Morm. 1:15). At age sixteen he became the leader of the Nephite army, and at about age twenty-four he retrieved the gold plates spoken of by Ammaron and began to add to Nephi's plates the record of his own people (see Morm. 1:3; 2:17–18). From Mormon's life we observe that solemnity is conducive to singleness of purpose.

Good Cheer and Solemnity in Tension

When people ask, "What is the difference between your church and my own?" we are prone to speak of living prophets and Apostles, of priesthood authority, of the gift of the Holy Ghost, of the Word of Wisdom, of the Book of Mormon, and of a host of other teachings. The intent of our instruction is often to show them that our church is the restored Church of Jesus Christ and, therefore, the only true church on the face of the earth. To some people this sounds a bit arrogant, as if we are trying to put them down. But there is one area in our church wherein we can learn a great lesson from the members of other churches, and that is reverence. It is in our meetings that the godly traits of good cheer and solemnity meet on a collision course.

Latter-day Saints treasure their families, and many of them have large families, and little children make disturbing noises in meetings, teenagers have urgent thoughts that cannot wait to be shared until later, impatient parents feel a need to maintain a minimal decorum in the seventh row of the chapel, and before long, thoughts no longer focus upon the things of eternity.

Several years ago one of the good bishops in our stake, a convert from another church, returned from a funeral of one of his close relatives. He gave a brief report to the stake presidency and high council about his feelings of returning to his previous church. He said: "You know, everyone was so reverent, so attentive to the beautiful prelude music, so engrossed by the sermon delivered by a highly educated pastor who was a very polished speaker. I thought how wonderful it would be if we could have this kind of reverence in the ward in which I preside as bishop." He then paused, and reflected, and then his face broke into a broad smile as he said: "But it's so good to be back in my home ward where all the members are so warm and friendly, and are so glad to see one another!"

How unfortunate it is that a choice must be made between sociability and reverence. Within the holy temple, where young children are present only under special circumstances, there is a greater aura of reverence than is the case in sacrament meetings of a garden-variety ward. It is a continual challenge when a people who truly accept the Lord's counsel to be of good cheer must suddenly shift into a solemnity mode. But if we and our children fail to show appropriate reverence in our meetings, eventually our church services are no longer worship services, but social gatherings.

Family home evening is a wonderful forum to discuss a communal strategy for maintaining greater reverence in Church meetings. Home teachers can be helpful in committing family members, individually and collectively, to becoming more reverent. And bishoprics can do much to plan meetings which assure maximum reverence. Ward organists have a wonderful opportunity to edify and to inspire the members of the ward to become more reverent as they arrive early to the sacrament meeting, with carefully selected prelude music which invites the Spirit of the Lord. A bishopric who have planned the last detail of the meeting far in advance and who are seated quietly on the stand can provide an excellent example for others to follow. A dignified greeter at each door can quietly welcome everyone and simultaneously set the tone for conduct in the chapel. Speakers who have been given a suggested topic several weeks in advance and who give well-prepared talks also contribute to the spiritual milieu of a meeting, and when inspirational talks are complemented by inspiring hymns and a special, appropriate musical number, sacrament meeting can become a sublime experience capped by the renewal of sacred covenants during the administration of the sacrament.

A reminder at the conclusion of the meeting to conduct visiting in the foyer can also do much to assure reverence in the chapel. There must be a balance between solemnity and good cheer, and both can be experienced in different areas of the Church building.

Sociability vs. Solitude

Related to the issues of cheerfulness and solemnity are the needs for sociability and solitude. The Savior's perfect life demonstrated a need for both. Before he began his ministry he spent forty days in the desert, fasting and communing with his Father. Later, after teaching the multitudes, "he departed thence by ship into a desert place apart. . . . And when he had sent the multitudes away, he went up into a mountain apart to pray: and when the evening was come, he was there alone." (Matt. 14:13, 23.)

Today's busy bishops and stake presidents and mission presidents often find themselves in a situation in which solitude seems virtually impossible. After working hours, when they are not conducting interviews or holding meetings, they are at home alone with their families—and the telephone which rings incessantly. But, following the Savior's example, there are occasional times when one should, indeed must, find some moments alone to meditate and regroup one's emotional and spiritual and physical resources to face the recurring challenges which never seem to subside. A brisk walk through the woods, a drive through the canyon, or a temple session with adequate time for prayerful meditation are all helpful ways to restore our resilience so that with recharged spiritual batteries we can face the multitudes.

When one becomes a committed Latter-day Saint, sociability is almost guaranteed, given the assignments of home teaching and visiting teaching, the meetings we are asked to attend, and the service projects we are engaged in. Sociability guarantees true friendship and brotherhood and sisterhood, and so, through all the meetings, there must still be other opportunities for building in-depth social relations over and above the organizational ties that bind.

Research into the factors which assure the retention of new converts to the Church indicates two major challenges: First, the new convert must obtain and retain and nourish a testimony of the gospel. Second, new converts must make a social transition from a group of friends who may enjoy smoking, and drinking tea, coffee, or martinis together, and who may take weekend vacations in lieu of attending church services. When some of these individuals join the Church they must secure a new group of friends with values and behavior compatible with the teachings of the gospel. When new converts are left alone in social isolation, their quest to remain active in the Church becomes most difficult. This is where good cheer is especially needed in our social relationships.

Good Cheer and Solemnity in Balance

Every season of the year holds its own charm and beauty. The blossoms of spring and the returning song of the birds is, indeed, a joyful time of year. The days grow increasingly longer as the sun begins to warm the earth after the chill of winter. Then come the lazy days of summer and fun and the excitement of vacations and family reunions and no more school. And when the autumn leaves begin to turn, one is struck again by the ever-changing beauty of this world in which "all things are created and made to bear record" of a loving Father in Heaven (see Moses 6:63). Then come the cold days of winter, and this is the season which divides people into two groups: happy skiers and long-suffering non-skiers. But many will agree that there is never a more beautiful time of year than Christmastime.

Christmas music is played on the radio and in the department stores, professional offices, and business establishments, and the sounds of carols and carolers is heard everywhere wafting on the cold December air. These songs of Christmas create a cheerful mood in even the most sober of souls. But there is a concern with the celebration of Christmas in America which has become more apparent to me from living abroad. American Christmas festivities are largely a mixture of the contributions of the countless Europeans who emigrated to America and brought with them some of the traditions of England,

Holland, Germany, Scandinavia, Austria, France, and many other countries.

The Germans contributed the Christmas tree and "Silent Night" and Martin Luther's "Away in a Manger." The Dutch and Danes contributed legends of a saint named Nikolaus who went around giving people gifts and doing good to others. The French gave us "O Holy Night" and Santon de Provence crèche scenes depicting the Savior's birth in a manger surrounded by peasant shepherds in southern France. All of these traditions, and many more, have helped to make Christmas a time of fellowship and goodwill.

To these European traditions and Christmas carols have been added the uniquely American contributions of *'Twas the Night before Christmas*, "Rudolph the Red-Nosed Reindeer," "Santa Claus Is Coming to Town," and "Frosty the Snow Man." These cheerful stories and songs are supplemented by "I'm Dreaming of a White Christmas," "Silver Bells," and "Jingle Bell Rock," all of which are appropriate in their place. All of this music and the story of *How the Grinch Stole Christmas* make us happy and entertain us. But if we are not careful, slowly but surely the solemn, sacred purpose for celebrating Christmas will be lost.

I know several Europeans who speak English, and so I wanted to send these families with young children an illustrated copy of a storybook about the first Christmas in Bethlehem. I was amazed at the number of children's books about Rudolph and Frosty and the Grinch and Santa Claus, but in most bookstores a religious version of Christmas was nowhere to be found.

It would be well for each and every family during the Christmas season to read Luke, chapter 2, and Matthew, chapter 2, and to reflect not only upon the "good tidings of great joy," but also upon the Savior's atonement for us. It would also be well to foster family programs of assisting those in need at this time of year, and then to express prayers of gratitude for our own blessings. Christmas is, indeed, a time of "good tidings of great joy," but it is also a time to "let the solemnities of eternity rest upon [our] minds" (D&C 43:34).

Notes

1. Joseph Smith, *Teachings of the Prophet Joseph Smith*, sel. Joseph Fielding Smith (Salt Lake City: Deseret Book Co., 1938), pp. 255–56.

2. *History of the Church* 1:260–64; hereafter cited as HC.

3. HC 2:194–97.

4. HC 2:209, 210.

Chapter Twelve

BOLDNESS AND MEEKNESS

If ever there was a common characteristic among successful missionaries it is the trait of boldness, the courage to follow the Lord's oft-repeated admonition to "open your mouths" (see D&C 24:12; 28:16; 30:5,11; 33:8–10; 60:2).

After the resurrection and ascension of the Savior, the Apostle Peter boldly testified of "Jesus of Nazareth, a man approved of God." His testimony stirred the hearts of three thousand souls who "received his word and were baptized." (Acts 2:22–41.) Later, Peter and John went to the temple where they beheld a lame man begging for alms near the temple gate. Peter looked at the man and said, "Silver and gold have I none; but such as I have give I thee: In the name of Jesus Christ of Nazareth rise up and walk" (Acts 3:6). Peter then lifted him up and the man began to walk and leap in ecstasy. When the Sadducees heard of this event, they called Peter and John to appear before a council to be cross-examined. "Now when they saw the boldness of Peter and John, and perceived that they were unlearned and ignorant men, they marvelled; and they took knowledge of them, that they had been with Jesus. And beholding the man which was healed standing with them, they could say nothing against it." (Acts 4:13–14.)

Two other great missionaries, Paul and Barnabus, "waxed bold" as they proclaimed the gospel in Antioch, and when they were expelled from that place they went to Iconium where they courageously continued "speaking boldly in the Lord" (Acts 13–14).

Apollos was yet another valiant missionary who "spake and taught diligently the things of the Lord. . . . And he began to speak boldly in the synagogue." (Acts 18:25–26.)

The Book of Mormon resounds with the words of many faithful, humble, yet confident men who proclaimed the gospel with boldness. After Abinadi was imprisoned for calling King Noah and his followers to repentance, he was summoned before the king's court, "and they began to question him . . . that thereby they might have wherewith to accuse him; but he answered them boldly, and withstood all their questions" (Mosiah 12:19).

As a result of Abinadi's bold and fervent testimony, one of wicked King Noah's priests by the name of Alma was touched in his heart and became a great missionary in his own right. His son, Alma the Younger, also became an outstanding preacher of the gospel, as evidenced by this statement: "I stood with boldness to declare unto them, yea, I did boldly testify unto them" (Alma 9:7).

Ammon, one of the four sons of King Mosiah, was noted for his boldness in defending and protecting the flocks of King Lamoni and in boldly proclaiming the gospel to him (see Alma 17–18).

Nephi's boldness was legendary, not only in teaching the gospel but also in retrieving the brass plates of Laban and in building a ship to cross uncharted waters to the promised land. Six hundred years later, one of the twelve Nephite disciples was also noted for boldness akin to that of his namesake. This latter Nephi sought to prepare the people for Christ's impending visit a few years hence, and he "began to testify, boldly, repentance and remission of sins through faith on the Lord Jesus Christ," and "it were not possible that they could disbelieve his words, for so great was his faith on the Lord Jesus Christ that angels did minister unto him daily" (3 Ne. 7:16, 18). The boldness and courage of Jacob, of Gideon, of Captain Moroni, of Helaman, of Mormon, and of his son Moroni are also legendary.

Bold But Not Overbearing

As important, indeed essential, as boldness is in proclaiming the gospel, Alma gave his missionary son Shiblon some excellent parting counsel prior to his departure for his mission: "See that ye are not lifted up unto pride; yea, see that ye do not boast in your own wisdom, nor of your much strength. Use boldness, but not overbearance; and also see that ye bridle all your passions, that ye may be filled with love; see that ye refrain from idleness." (Alma 38:11–12.)

Alma's cautionary counsel points to the fact that when the

highly desirable trait of boldness remains unbridled, it can easily lead to overbearance, pride, and boasting. An illustration of unbridled passion occurred several weeks before Peter proclaimed the gospel on the day of Pentecost when he boldly cut off Malchus's ear in the Garden of Gethsemane. Though Peter's actions could easily be understood as those of one who loved the Savior and wished to defend Him, the Savior chided Peter, saying: "Put up again thy sword into his place: for all they that take the sword shall perish with the sword" (Matt. 26:52).

Paul's boldness, such a worthy trait, when left unchecked, led to such contention with his faithful missionary companion, Barnabus, that they parted their ways in the company of different missionary companions (see Acts 15:37–41).

Ammon reflected on the fruits of his bold missionary labors among the Lamanites, exulting that "thousands of them do rejoice, and have been brought into the fold of God." His brother Aaron chided him saying: "I fear that thy joy doth carry thee away unto boasting." (Alma 26:4, 10.) Ammon quickly rejoined: "I do not boast in my own strength, nor in my own wisdom. . . . I know that I am nothing . . . ; therefore I will not boast of myself, but I will boast of my God, for in his strength I can do all things." (Alma 26:11–12.) Though Ammon acquitted himself very well in defending his exuberance, Aaron's observation should serve as a gentle reminder to all of us that our boldness and our enthusiasm should not lead to boasting such that we forget whose work this really is and forget by whose power people are really converted to the gospel.

Be Wary of Vainglory

The Apostle Paul cautioned the Philippians about the importance of boldly preaching the gospel, but for the right reasons, as he wrote them:

> And many of the brethren in the Lord, waxing confident by my bonds, are much more bold to speak the word without fear.
>
> Some indeed preach Christ even of envy and strife; and some also of good will:

> The one preach Christ of contention, not sincerely, supposing to add affliction to my bonds:
>
> But the other of love, knowing that I am set for the defence of the gospel. . . .
>
> Let nothing be done through strife or vainglory; but in lowliness of mind let each esteem other better than themselves. (Philip. 1:14–17; 2:3.)

Pride: The Great Stumbling Block

President Ezra Taft Benson has characterized pride, another term for vainglory, as the great stumbling block of Zion.[1] There are many who are bold in declaring the gospel, but their boldness carried to the extreme can readily offend rather than instill a desire to learn more of the restored gospel. So it is that the Lord has declared that "no one can assist in the work except he shall be humble and full of love, having faith, hope, and charity, being temperate in all things, whatsoever shall be entrusted to his care" (D&C 12:8). Temperance holds boldness and impatience in check. Boldness is akin to confidence, a worthy and admirable trait, and the Lord has promised us that when we are filled with love "towards all men" and when we "let virtue garnish [our] thoughts unceasingly, then shall [our] confidence wax strong in the presence of God" (D&C 121:45).

The judicious balance between bold confidence and humble meekness is found in Paul's appearance before King Agrippa. Paul confidently recounted his vision on the road to Damascus, declaring to the king, "I was not disobedient unto the heavenly vision" (Acts 26:19). So persuasive was this Apostle's defense of his beliefs and his missionary activity that King Agrippa told Paul: "Almost thou persuadest me to be a Christian" (Acts 26:28).

But boldness carried to the extreme can lead us to condemn those whom we are trying to convert, and confidence can turn to boastfulness as we brag of those whom we have assisted in the conversion process. One of the most common forms of pride is publicly counting our accomplishments, something which caused Aaron to chide his brother Ammon after the latter had asserted that "we have been made instruments in the hands of God to bring about this great work" (Alma 26:3).

Ingratitude

Pride assumes many other forms more subtle than public boasting. One of these is assuming that we can perform the work of the Lord without the Lord's assistance. Sometimes we become so pleased with our personal progress on the pathway to perfection that we overlook the fact "that it is by grace that we are saved, after all we can do" (2 Ne. 25:23). No matter how pure our thoughts and actions may become, and regardless of how circumspectly we keep all the commandments, and notwithstanding our generosity of time and financial donations, the fact of the matter is that our backlog of sins is so great that, were it not for the grace of the atoning sacrifice of Jesus Christ, we could not be saved.

So it is that the Lord revealed to Joseph Smith that "in nothing doth man offend God, or against none is his wrath kindled, save those who confess not his hand in all things, and obey not his commandments" (D&C 59:21). Ingratitude is an insidious form of pride in which we fail to recognize our total dependence upon our God, who preserves us "from day to day, by lending [us] breath" (Mosiah 2:21). The brother of Jared, a righteous and holy man indeed, was nevertheless chastened by the Lord for three hours "because he remembered not to call upon the name of the Lord" (Ether 2:14). Our prayer life is a reflection of our pride or our humility. When we are humble we pray with gratitude for all of our countless blessings.

Discouragement

It may seem ironic, but discouragement, left unchecked, can lead to an insidious form of pride, though those experiencing discouragement would contend that their feelings are more closely akin to deep humility. But whom do we think about when we are proud? Ourselves! And whom do we think about when we are discouraged? Ourselves!

Without wishing to add to the burdens of those who feel discouraged, and that includes all of us at one time or another, a discouraged person may begin boasting, if you will, about his or her trials and tribulations in life. The discouraged person has the most unruly children, the greatest aches and pains, the most unkind spouse, the worst job, and the cruelest employer. When we are discouraged, we begin to feel that we are the only one on the face of the earth who has had to face disappointment and failure and great inconvenience.

When the Prophet Joseph began to experience some of these feelings while languishing in Liberty Jail, the Lord lovingly promised him "that all these things shall give thee experience, and shall be for thy good. The Son of Man hath descended below them all. Art thou greater than he?" (D&C 122:7-8.)

In countries ravaged by war, famine, and natural catastrophes, discouragement and despair are a normal reaction to very abnormal circumstances. But within a reasonable period of time hope should again be manifested in the lives of the victims of tragic circumstances.

At the conclusion of the fourteen-year war which raged from 74 to 61 B.C., "because of the exceedingly great length of the war between the Nephites and the Lamanites many had become hardened, because of the exceedingly great length of the war; and many were softened, because of their afflictions, insomuch that they did humble themselves before God, even in the depth of humility" (Alma 62:41).

It is interesting that the same war, the same hurricane, and the same earthquake can often evoke opposite reactions from their victims. Some will curse God and lose their faith, while others experience the promises made to and by Jacob that God "shall consecrate thine afflictions for thy gain" (2 Ne. 2:2) and "console you in your afflictions" (Jacob 3:1). Such consecration and consolation provide considerable immunity against depression, discouragement, and despair.

Moroni goes so far as to contend that "despair cometh because of iniquity" (Moro. 10:22). The iniquity may not necessarily involve dishonesty or immorality, but a gradual erosion of faith, hope, and charity (see Moro. 10:20–23). Paul wrote the Romans that "whatsoever is not of faith is sin" (Rom. 14:23). He who is without faith, hope, and charity, the pure love of Christ, often begins to make invidious comparisons with others, to criticize and to complain about his own personal lot in life in contrast with the ease of others. In the process, one's thoughts begin to concentrate more and more upon oneself and less and less upon Jesus Christ, who promised that "if ye have faith ye can do all things which are expedient unto me" (Moro. 10:23).

Discouragement and a lack of charity can be overcome when we "lose ourselves" in the service of others (see Matt. 10:39) and when we pray in gratitude for the things we do enjoy rather than deliberating upon the things we do not have. Part of our baptismal covenant is to be "willing to mourn with those who mourn; yea, and comfort those that stand in need of comfort" (Mosiah 18:9). Each of us who has cause to mourn greatly appreciates the comfort and condolences of others in our hour of need. But when our hour of need stretches into months and even years, there comes a time when we must lose ourselves and overcome our sorrows in order that we may comfort others. And when we are discouraged, "thinking all is lost," when we count our blessings in humble prayers of sincere gratitude, we will arise from our knees armed with greater faith, hope, and charity.

Several years ago a kindly stake president asked me to accompany him to visit a family in his stake in which a great tragedy had taken place. The mother of the family was expecting a child and had planned a birthday party for one of her young daughters just a few days before she was to be delivered. This beautiful, young, faithful mother in Zion walked into a store while a robbery was taking place and she was shot and mortally wounded. She was rushed to the hospital where her baby was delivered, but because of insufficient oxygen, the infant was born with several physical problems.

The stake president and I gave the father and the daughters blessings of comfort, admonishing them to nourish feelings of forgiveness so that this evil deed done to their mother would not canker their souls. A few weeks later I visited a conference in the stake in which this little heartbroken family lived, and I was taken aback by the fact that the stake president had asked this grief-stricken father to offer the closing prayer of the conference. I shall ever remember his gratitude for all our blessings and his plea to "bless those who are less fortunate than we are." Certainly there was to be loneliness and the continual wrestle to overcome vindictive feelings of revenge, but through it all was the pure love of Christ for "those who are less fortunate," and these feelings brought relief from pain and despair.

Unworthiness

When we are called to serve in the kingdom of God, callings are not necessarily confirmations of worthiness as much as they are invitations to improve our lives, as evidenced in the lives of the Apostle Paul or Alma the Younger and the four sons of Mosiah.

Thus, when a calling is extended to us, in humility we may contend that we are truly not worthy to serve. But when we refuse a call we, in essence, say that the Savior's atoning sacrifice and the inspiration of a loving Heavenly Father are not adequate to help us serve ably and well. In short, refusing a calling can be a form of arrogance thinly veiled as humility. Of course there may be times we may need to let the bishop know of some concerns of which he may not be fully aware, but generally speaking, a refusal to serve where called is a form of pride, asserting not *thy* will, but *mine* be done.

A kindred form of arrogance is accepting a call willingly, and perhaps even aspiring to a highly visible calling, and then persisting in our old patterns of behavior rather than striving to undergo a mighty change of heart. Paul made it clear to the Ephesians that callings in the Church are for the "perfecting of the saints," not necessarily for perfect Saints, and we pervert the perfecting process when we resist the need to improve. He who serves without daily repentance and daily prayers of humble supplication for guidance is very proud indeed.

Despite all of the human frailties of the great Apostle Peter, it is well to remember the circumstances surrounding his calling to the holy apostleship. The Savior had entered Peter's fishing boat and "taught the people out of the ship." When He was finished teaching, He instructed Peter to "launch out into the deep, and let down your nets." Peter responded: "Master, we have toiled all the night, and have taken nothing: nevertheless at thy word I will let down the net." After catching a great multitude of fish, Peter, instead of boasting of his prowess as a fisherman, humbly acknowledged the Savior's power by falling to his knees and saying: "Depart from me; for I am a sinful man, O Lord." But the Savior looked beyond the current sins of this humble sinner, proclaiming: "Fear not; from henceforth thou shalt catch men." (Luke 5:1–10.) A calling in the kingdom is not necessarily so much a confirmation of our personal worthiness as it is an invitation to improve our lives.

The Savior called men like Peter and Paul and Alma, not because of what they had done, but because of what they would be able to do with His help, and they remembered the source of their spiritual guidance. By contrast, King Saul had to be reminded by the prophet Samuel of the time "when thou wast little in thine own sight" (1 Sam. 15:17), and King Solomon forgot the time he prayed: "I am but a little child" (1 Kgs. 3:7). The challenge is to grow in confidence while still retaining humility, and increasing in boldness without losing meekness.

A Bold, Yet Meek, Young Man

The Father and the Son ushered in this dispensation through the instrumentality of a bold young man who was later to write: "I had actually seen a light, and in the midst of that light I saw two Personages, and they did in reality speak to me; and though I was hated and persecuted for saying that I had seen a vision, yet it was true." We next observe the balance between young Joseph's boldness and meekness as he continued: "For I had seen a vision; I knew it, and I knew that God knew it, and I could not deny it, neither dared I do it; at least I knew that by so doing I would offend God, and come under condemnation." (JS–H 1:25.) This young prophet in embryo was bold in speaking to the general public, but he was meek before the Father and the Son. This balance between meekness and boldness was exhibited in many subsequent settings throughout the remainder of Joseph's life.

After languishing in Liberty Jail under deplorable conditions amid reports of extreme persecution and abuse of the Saints, Joseph boldly implored the Lord in prayer: "O God, where art thou?" (D&C 121:1.) The divine response was meekly accepted by Joseph: "My son, peace be unto thy soul; thine adversity and thine afflictions shall be but a small moment; and then, if thou endure it well, God shall exalt thee on high" (D&C 121:7–8). During the remaining five years of his life, the Prophet Joseph Smith underwent extraordinary trials and tribulations as he was betrayed by friends whom he had trusted and was persecuted and imprisoned for wrongs he had not committed. Nevertheless, he subjected his will to that of the Father and the Son.

It is interesting to contrast Joseph's boldness before the masses and his meekness before God with Pontius Pilate's boldness before the Savior and His meekness before the masses.

On March 1, 1842, the Prophet responded to an inquiry of Mr. John Wentworth for information about the Church. Wentworth was the editor and publisher of the *Chicago Democrat*. In this very detailed letter, Joseph Smith outlined the thirteen Articles of Faith and boldly set forth a declaration which has since been called "The Standard of Truth" in which he boldly declared:

> Our missionaries are going forth to different nations, and . . . the Standard of Truth has been erected; no unhallowed hand can stop the work from progressing; persecutions may rage, mobs may combine, armies may assemble, calumny may defame, but the truth of God will go forth boldly, nobly, and independent, till it has penetrated every continent, visited every clime, swept every country, and sounded in every ear, till the purposes of God shall be accomplished, and the Great Jehovah shall say the work is done.[2]

There would be some of us who, given the opportunity to explain our beliefs in a public forum, might equivocate, but Joseph declared that the gospel would penetrate every continent at a time when there were approximately thirteen thousand members of the Church located primarily in Nauvoo, Illinois.

Part of the quest in striking the balance between meekness and boldness lies in determining not only *when* to be bold but also with *whom* we are to be bold. There are certain critics of the Church who band together to boldly share their critical comments with one another, but who have little meekness in accepting helpful counsel from priesthood leaders who are sincerely trying to nudge them toward the celestial kingdom.

As bold as the Apostle Paul may have been in declaring the gospel on Mars Hill in Athens, in his letters to the Ephesians and to Philemon he described himself as "the prisoner of Jesus Christ." That is to say, without boasting, Paul declared that he had willingly and meekly, totally and completely subjected his own desires to the will of the Lord. It was the Lord's will that he boldly declare the gospel of repentance and of baptism, and he meekly accepted this divine commission, notwithstanding the fact that he had been whipped thirty-nine times on five different occasions, had been beaten three times with rods, stoned once, been shipwrecked three times, and had spent a day and a night in the chilly waters of the sea, all for the sake of preaching the gospel with boldness (see 2 Cor. 11:24–25).

But the Savior asked no more of the Apostle Paul than he had expected of himself, for "though he were a Son, yet learned he obedience by the things which he suffered" (Heb. 5:8). The Savior's entire life was an exquisite example of the balance between boldness and meekness. His boldness was manifest by His cleansing of the holy temple (see Luke 19:45). His meekness was exemplified in the Garden when He prayed, "Nevertheless, not my will, but thine, be done"

(Luke 22:42), and by his prayer on the cross: "Father, forgive them; for they know not what they do" (Luke 23:34).

Abinadi described the Savior's meekness eloquently and accurately as he prophesied: "After working many mighty miracles among the children of men, he shall be led, yea, even as Isaiah said, as a sheep before the shearer is dumb, so he opened not his mouth. Yea, even so he shall be led, crucified, and slain, the flesh becoming subject even unto death, the will of the Son being swallowed up in the will of the Father." (Mosiah 15:6–7.) This is meekness.

Notes

1. See Ezra Taft Benson, "Beware of Pride," *Ensign* 19 (May 1989): 4–6.
2. *History of the Church* 4:540.

Chapter Thirteen

LOYALTY TO PRINCIPLES AND LOYALTY TO PERSONS

Throughout the scriptures are several recipes for righteousness giving us promises and direction, inspiration and guidance which, if followed, will lead us heavenward. Common to many of these scriptures are references to the godly attributes of faith, humility, meekness, patience, virtue, kindness, and charity. Noticeably absent from various discussions of godly traits is the attribute of loyalty. Loyalty is not mentioned a single time in any of the scriptures ancient or modern. But the attributes of faithfulness, trust, and integrity *are* mentioned numerous times throughout the scriptures, and these are some of the ingredients of loyalty.

An indication of the strength of our testimonies is the degree to which we demonstrate our loyalty to the Savior and our loyalty to the principles which He taught. Loyalty is the test of true friendship, and in this regard the Savior has said: "Greater love hath no man than this, that a man lay down his life for his friends. Ye are my friends, if ye do whatsoever I command you." (John 15:13–14.)

Ruth and Naomi

The scriptures are replete with examples of men and women whose loyalty to one another is legendary. The relationship of Ruth and Naomi is one of the sweetest stories ever told. Elimelech and his wife, Naomi, and their two sons lived in Bethlehem-juda. Because of a famine in the land they emigrated to Moab, and it was there that Elimelech later died. Naomi and her two sons remained in Moab, however, and in due time the sons married two Moabite women by the name of Orpah and Ruth.

After a period of about ten years both of Naomi's sons died, and so she decided to return home to the land of Judah, and she encouraged her two widowed daughters-in-law to "return each to her mother's house" (Ruth 1:8). Orpah kissed her mother-in-law goodbye and returned to her own people, but Ruth turned to Naomi and spoke those immortal words of love and loyalty: "Whither thou goest, I will go; and where thou lodgest, I will lodge: thy people shall be my people, and thy God my God" (Ruth 1:16). As Ruth's life continued to unfold, it is very significant that her loyalties were not only to her mother-in-law but also to the God whom Naomi worshipped. Ruth was true to both a person and a principle.

Abraham and Isaac

One of the greatest tests of loyalty to principle occurred in the life of Abraham. All normal parents dearly love their children, but in the lives of Abraham and Sarah their love for Isaac was enhanced by the fact that "Abraham was an hundred years old, when his son Isaac was born unto him" (Gen. 1:5). I suspect the relationship between father and son may not have involved a lot of one-on-one on the basketball court, but the spiritual maturity of Abraham must have included all the love and concern that one father could have for his son. So when Abraham heard God's command to sacrifice his son as a burnt offering on Mount Moriah, one can only imagine the intense inner conflict between Abraham's loyalty to his God and his loyalty to his own son.

Notwithstanding the conflict between the desire to protect his son and the desire to obey his God, Abraham "rose up early in the morning" and took his young son to Moriah where he fully intended to obey God's command (see Gen. 22:1–12). On that memorable day in the earth's history, Abraham's loyalty to God allowed him to gain great insight into the Savior's forthcoming atonement, for "it was accounted unto Abraham in the wilderness to be obedient unto the commands of God in offering up his son Isaac, which is a similitude of God and his Only Begotten Son" (Jacob 4:5). After that experience Abraham had great empathy for the Father's feelings as His Son suffered in the Garden of Gethsemane and upon the cross at Golgotha.

It may be well to add that, although Isaac asked his father, "Where is the lamb for a burnt offering?" there is no allusion to any resistance on Isaac's part when the moment of truth arrived and Abraham raised his arm with knife in hand, intent on slaying his son. Just as Abraham was loyal to God above, Isaac, too, was loyal to his earthly father and trusted in him, and later the Abrahamic covenant was renewed through Isaac (see Gen. 26).

Joseph of Egypt

It is easy for us to be loyal to an employer who pays us well or to be loyal to a friend who treats us well, but it is much more difficult to be loyal when we know that our loyalty will be misunderstood and could perhaps even be a source of punishment. Such was the case with Abraham's great-grandson Joseph. After being ruthlessly treated by his brothers and being sold to a merchant caravan traveling to Egypt, Joseph eventually found himself in the employ of a man named Potiphar.

Potiphar's wife had evil designs upon Joseph, but Joseph withstood her seductive advances, demonstrating both his loyalty to her husband and his loyalty to his God. Said Joseph: "My master . . . hath committed all that he hath to my hand; . . . neither hath he kept back any thing from me but thee, because thou art his wife: how then can I do this great wickedness, and sin against God?" Then, instead of allowing Satan and Potiphar's wife to weaken his resolve to be true to his master and to God, Joseph fled and "got him out." (Gen. 39.)

Joseph's loyalty was also manifest in his relationship with his family, even his brethren who had betrayed him. His loyalty transcended any inclination for retribution as he gladly furnished them grain in their time of famine.

Loyalty to One's Companion

Some of the best counsel I received as a prospective bridegroom was given to me during a physical examination by old "Doc Cullimore," who practiced medicine in Provo for at least half a century. This wise friend counseled me to be loyal to my eternal companion and never to divulge our differences to others, including parents, and never to disclose details of the boudoir with others.

Of course, there are times when a husband may engage in extreme physically and mentally abusive behavior which necessitates that a distraught wife seek help outside the family. A parent who is trapped in the terrible snare of alcoholism or drug addiction, for example, will stretch the loyalties of spouse and children to the limit. Of such a case, President Brigham Young has said: "It is not my general practice to counsel the sisters to disobey their husbands, but my counsel is—obey your husbands; and I am sanguine and most emphatic on that subject. But I never counselled a woman to follow her husband to the Devil. If a man is determined to expose the lives of his friends, let that man go to the Devil and to destruction alone."[1]

Generally speaking, in the homes of garden-variety Latter-day Saints, keeping confidences within a marriage and within a family is an expression of loyalty to one another. Each time my eternal companion and I have been called into the office of a bishop or stake president or General Authority and searching questions have been asked prior to extending a calling, I have been grateful for Dorothea's unflinching loyalty. Each time a calling has been issued, my angel wife has always responded to their questions about whether I am a good husband and father by saying very compassionately: "He tries hard."

Loyalty to true eternal principles begets loyalty to each other, for as each of us draws nearer and nearer to our Heavenly Father, we draw nearer to each other, as graphically depicted below:

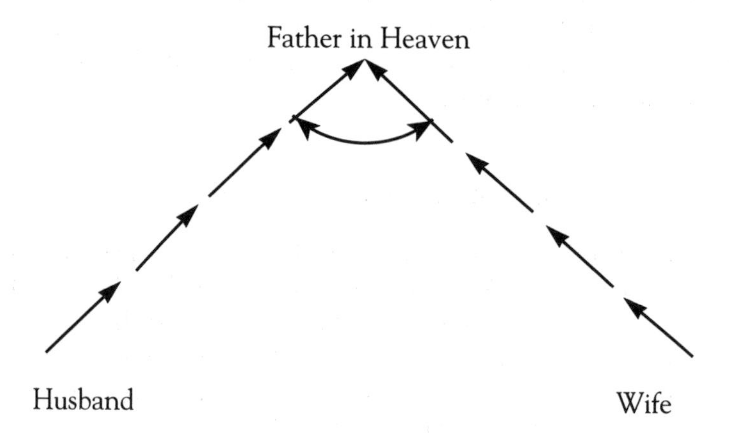

Elder Orson Pratt expressed this thought in these eloquent terms:

> The more righteous a people become, the more they are qualified for loving others and rendering them happy. A wicked man can have but little love for his wife, while a righteous man, being filled with the love of God, is sure to manifest this heavenly attribute in every thought and feeling of his heart, and in every word and deed. Love, joy, and innocence will radiate from his very countenance, and be expressed in every look. This will beget confidence in the wife of his bosom, and she will love him in return; for love begets love; happiness imparts happiness; and these heaven-born emotions will continue to increase more and more, until they are perfected and glorified in all the fulness of eternal love itself.[2]

David, Jonathan, and Saul

A great example of being able to sift through the chaff of conflicting loyalties while retaining kernels of personal integrity is found in the relationship between King Saul, the king's son Jonathan, and Jonathan's young friend named David. At the beginning of Saul's reign it was relatively easy for the Israelites to be loyal to both their king and to godly principles, because their king had been anointed by Samuel, a prophet of God.

But with the passage of time—inasmuch as "it is the nature and disposition of almost all men, as soon as they get a little authority" (D&C 121:39), to soon forget the time when they were "little in [their] own sight" (1 Sam. 15:17)—Saul lost his loyalty both to God's prophet and to the eternal principles he had been taught. Relationships now began to be strained, for the soul of the king's son Jonathan "was knit with the soul of David, and Jonathan loved him as his own soul" (1 Sam. 18:1). After having appointed David as a leader of his armies, "Saul was afraid of David, because the Lord was with him, and was departed from Saul" (1 Sam. 18:12). Loyalties were further stretched when David married Saul's daughter Michal (see 1 Sam. 18:20–28).

Eventually Saul sought to take the life of David, and because Saul's son and daughter were more loyal to true principles than to a father who had abandoned his loyalty to true principles, Jonathan and Michal remained loyal to David. Notwithstanding the fact that Saul had sought to destroy him, David, having the opportunity to kill

Saul while he was asleep in a cave, only cut off a piece of Saul's robe, and then regretted having done so, "seeing he is the anointed of the Lord" (1 Sam. 24:6). After Saul arose and departed from the cave, David confronted his king, saying, "I cut off the skirt of thy robe, and killed thee not . . . ; yet thou huntest my soul to take it. The Lord judge between me and thee." (1 Sam. 24:11–12.) "And Saul lifted up his voice, and wept. And he said to David, thou art more righteous than I: for thou hast rewarded me good, whereas I have rewarded thee evil." (1 Sam. 24:16–17.)

David's loyalty to his king was tested to the limits as King Saul gave "Michal his daughter, David's wife, to Phalti the son of Laish" (1 Sam. 25:44). Saul then chose three thousand men to help him "seek David in the wilderness of Ziph" (1 Sam. 26:2). In the course of events, Saul was once again found vulnerable and at the complete mercy of David, whose servant, Abishai, told David, "God hath delivered thine enemy into thine hand this day: now therefore let me smite him." But the record tells us that "David said to Abishai, Destroy him not: for who can stretch forth his hand against the Lord's anointed, and be guiltless?" (1 Sam. 26:8–9.)

After a series of continuing battles and an ever-deepening iniquity, Saul, the once strong and righteous king of Israel, eventually died by his own hand as he "took a sword, and fell upon it" (1 Sam. 31:4).

There may be some who would criticize David's behavior as blind loyalty and blind obedience, and though David may be judged for his later grievous sins, it cannot be said that he criticized the Lord's anointed servants. As long as King Saul lived, David was loyal to him, but his stronger loyalties were to principles much higher than those lived by Saul.

Cardinal Wolsey

In Shakespeare's *King Henry VIII*, we encounter another collision of loyalties as Cardinal Wolsey is torn between his loyalty to King Henry and his loyalty to the principles of the Catholic church regarding the matter of divorce. Though King Henry's first wife, Catherine of Aragon, had borne five children, only a daughter, Mary, survived, and Henry insisted on a male heir to the throne. The king put considerable pressure upon Thomas Cardinal Wolsey to intercede in his behalf with the pope to obtain an annulment of his marriage to Catherine. But the pope was not persuaded by Cardinal Wolsey's arguments and denied the king's request. Ultimately, Cardinal Wolsey fell into disfavor with both the king and the pope, and the king married Anne Boleyn and laid the groundwork for the formation of the Church of England, independent of the influence from the Roman church.

As Wolsey's once stellar ecclesiastical and political career plummets, Shakespeare has the cardinal lament introspectively: "Had I but served my God with half the zeal / I served my king, he would not in mine age / Have left me naked to mine enemies."[3] Cardinal Wolsey paid the terrible price of remaining loyal to a king who had no loyalty to eternal principles.

Loyalty to Parents and Principles

There are great personally applicable insights to be gained from David's relationship with Saul. David was loyal to the man's office and calling while personally adhering to a loftier set of principles. Though King Saul's behavior was repugnant to David, he rejected the behavior without rejecting the office of the king.

The Prophet Joseph Smith taught that "if children embrace the Gospel, and their parents or guardians are unbelievers, teach them to stay at home and be obedient to their parents or guardians, if they require it; but if they consent to let them gather with the people of God, let them do so, and there shall be no wrong; and let all things be done carefully and righteously and God will extend to all such His guardian care."[4]

The Prophet further taught that "if a man receive not the Gospel, but gives his consent that his wife may receive it, and she believes, then let her receive it. But if a man forbid his wife, or his children, before they are of age, to receive the Gospel, then it should be the duty of the Elder to go his way, and use no influence against him, and let the responsibility be upon his head."[5]

There are many faithful young Latter-day Saints who strive with all their hearts to keep the commandments but whose fathers or mothers may have disregarded previous covenants or may not be members of the Church. I have observed dozens of new converts to the Church who, through persistent example and continual faithfulness and loyalty to parents *and* to eternal principles, have been able to overcome completely any opposition which their parents have had to their belonging to the Church.

Daniel, Shadrach, Meshach, and Abed-nego

Elder Neal A. Maxwell has referred to the Lord's system of "micro-management" through which He divinely maneuvers some of His children to be in the right place at the right time in order to influence the unfolding of great events. Such was the case with four specially chosen young Israelites who were selected by King Nebuchadnezzar to come to the palace to be taught the language and learning of the Chaldeans (see Dan. 1). They were to be treated royally, even to the extent that they would partake of the rich delicacies and wine which the king himself ate and drank.

Here was a wonderful opportunity for these four young men to advance their education and perhaps eventually gain political power, but their loyalty to the king was on a collision course with their loyalty to high principles. Thus, we read that "Daniel purposed in his heart that he would not defile himself with the portion of the king's meat, nor with the wine which he drank" (Dan. 1:8). Notwithstanding the possibility of greatly offending the king by refusing to follow his prescribed diet, after ten days Daniel and his friends appeared fairer and fatter in flesh than all the children which did eat the portion of the king's meat (see Dan. 1:15).

King Nebuchadnezzar next created a large golden image and commanded the people to worship it with the penalty that "who falleth not down and worshippeth shall the same hour be cast into the midst of a burning fiery furnace" (Dan. 3:1–6). This decree, of course, again called into question the loyalty of the Israelites to their earthly king. Exercising their loyalties to a higher, Heavenly King, they refused to worship the image King Nebuchadnezzar had set up, convinced that their God would deliver them. As punishment, Shadrach, Meschach, and Abed-nego were cast into the fiery furnace, and the king himself came to observe the anticipated holocaust. But instead of death by burning, he saw something else. "I see," he said, "four men loose, walking in the midst of the fire, and they have no hurt; and the form of the fourth is like the Son of God." Overwhelmed by what he saw, the king said: "Shadrach, Meschach, and Abed-nego, ye servants of the most high God, come forth, and come hither." He then decreed that his people should do nothing to speak against the God of these three loyal young Israelites, and he promoted them throughout Babylon. (Dan. 3:25–29.)

Sometime later Nebuchadnezzar's rule passed to his son Belshazzar, and it was Daniel who interpreted the writing on the wall which the king had seen. Daniel courageously reported the message: "Thou art weighed in the balances, and art found wanting" (Dan. 5:25–28); and that very night Belshazzar, king of the Chaldeans, was slain, and "Darius the Median took the kingdom" (Dan. 5:30–31).

The new king appointed three presidents to preside over one hundred twenty princes throughout the entire kingdom, and "Daniel was preferred above the presidents and princes, because an excellent spirit was in him" (Dan. 6:1–2). Then began the political intrigue among those who were jealous of Daniel's favored status in the eyes of the king. They lobbied the king to "establish a royal statute" that anyone who would petition any God or man other than the king should be "cast into the den of lions" (Dan. 6:7).

Filled with righteous confidence based on faith in God, Daniel continued to pray to his God, notwithstanding the fact that the windows to his chamber were open, allowing others to see him pray. It was not long before the report reached the king that Daniel had been observed praying to God at least three times daily. Now it was the king who had to wrestle with competing loyalties, but like Pontius Pilate and many politicians in the world today, he yielded to the pulling power of popularity rather than abiding by lofty principles. As Daniel was cast into the den of lions, the king apologetically told him: "Thy God whom thou servest continually, he will deliver thee" (Dan. 6:16).

Let it be said to King Darius's credit that he spent a sleepless night while Daniel languished in the lion's den. Early the next morning the king hurried to see if Daniel was still alive, asking: "O Daniel, servant of the living God, is thy God, whom thou servest continually, able to deliver thee from the lions?" And, to the relief of the king, Daniel replied: "O king, live for ever. My God hath sent his angel, and hath shut the lions' mouths." (Dan. 6:18–22.)

Like Nebuchadnezzar, Darius learned quickly when the instruction involved dramatic visual aids, and, like Nebuchadnezzar, Darius decreed "that in every dominion of my kingdom men tremble and fear before the God of Daniel: for he is the living God" (Dan. 6:26).

One of the lessons to be learned from Daniel and his three faithful brethren is that unstinting loyalty of one person to true and righteous principles encourages others to become loyal to those same principles. And our loyalty to true friends engenders their loyalty to us. Elder Oscar A. Kirkham frequently expressed the sincere assurance to all of his friends that "your name is safe in our home."

Willard Richards

It was a very hot and sultry afternoon on June 27, 1844. Various brethren had come to the Carthage jail to visit and comfort the Prophet Joseph in his final tribulation. At 1:30 P.M. the visitors were asked to leave, and Joseph, Hyrum, John Taylor, and Willard Richards remained in the jail. There was a very somber feeling of impending doom in the air, and the Prophet asked John Taylor to sing "A Poor Wayfaring Man of Grief" to console them. And though he really did not feel like singing, John reluctantly agreed to the Prophet's request that he sing the song a second time.[6]

During the visit from their friends these four brethren were not confined to their cell, but by late afternoon the jailer suggested that, for their own safety, they should return to the cell. "The Prophet turned to Dr. Richards and said, 'If we go into the cell, will you go in with us?'" Then came Willard Richards's reply, demonstrating a loyalty stronger than the bands of death. Said Brother Richards: "Brother Joseph, you did not ask me to come to jail with you—and do you think I would forsake you now? But I will tell you what I will do; if you are condemned to be hung for treason, I will be hung in your stead, and you shall go free." The Prophet replied, "You cannot," but Willard protested, "I will."[7]

False Loyalty

In the spring of 1974, nearly three decades after the war's end, the last Japanese holdout of World War II emerged from the jungles of the Philippines. His name: Lt. Hiroo Onada, age fifty-two. Thirty years previously, Onada's commanding officer, Major Yashimi Tanaguchi, had given his troops an order that they were not to surrender to the Allied forces under any conditions. Unlike other holdouts who simply did not know the war had ended, Onada had known for several years that the hostilities had ended. However, he had been ordered not to surrender, and surrender he would not. He was absolutely adamant in his loyalty to his commanding officer and the Japanese cause.

Hiroo Onada's presence in the Philippine jungle had not been entirely unknown, nor ignored. Over those three decades, he and a comrade in arms (who was later killed) had been credited with the deaths of more than thirty Filipinos and with wounding perhaps a hundred others, as these victims ventured too close to Onada's jungle hideout.

Onada had also pilfered chickens and pigs from the peasants whose farms lay on the periphery of the jungle. These sporadic attacks by Onada had the makings of a potential international incident, so the Japanese government invested over four hundred thousand dollars in a variety of attempts to lure Onada from the jungle. Reconnaissance planes flew at treetop level above the jungle, dropping pamphlets informing Onada that he need not fear reprisals if he would but give up and return to Japan. This attempt met with no success.

Electronic specialists were employed to install expensive loudspeakers which were interspersed throughout the jungle vegetation. Verbal messages were broadcast intermittently at strategic locations, but to no avail.

A group of mercenary adventurers were then outfitted to go into the jungle to track down Hiroo Onada. Finally, one adventuresome young man encountered Onada on a jungle path and explained the purpose of his mission and the necessity of Onada's surrender. Onada adamantly refused unless one condition was met: he would lay down his arms only if ordered to do so by his former commanding officer, Major Tanaguchi.

The retired and aging Tanaguchi was eventually located in Japan and flown to Manila. Onada appeared, wearing the same tattered and torn uniform he had worn for thirty years, and clicked his heels to attention. Major Tanaguchi removed a worn piece of paper from his pocket and in a solemn-sounding voice officially rescinded the order he had given Onada three decades earlier. He then called upon Onada to surrender.

Onada proudly surrendered his weapons and agreed to return home. In Tokyo, Onada was given a "Hiroo's welcome" where he was acclaimed for his intense patriotic loyalty and for his ingenious ability to survive under adverse conditions.

Reporters thronged about in order to interview this extremely unusual person. He had gone into the jungle at age twenty-two. Now, at age fifty-two, surely he must have become a repository of wisdom having spent so much time communing with nature. There had been so many years of solitude and meditation.

But Onada's reply must have been disappointing to the reporters when he said: "Nothing—nothing pleasant happened to me through all these 29 years."[8]

Many alternative lessons could be learned from Onada's experience. We would all do well to strive to emulate his tenacious patriotism and his undying loyalty to his leader. We might also bestow an accolade for his ingenuity and courage in surviving three decades of life in the jungle. But the lesson I wish to draw is this: Many of us venture too near the periphery of the jungles of life. Others become entangled in the undergrowth and, losing a sense of direction, become lost for an eternity. These are they whose loyalties are to false causes and false persons and false principles. These are they who have read and heard the messages entreating them to yield their hearts to Christ, but who doggedly persist on the same jungle paths shielded from the light of the gospel. These are the natural men of whom Paul and King Benjamin spoke.

The Gadianton robbers of Book of Mormon times and the Mafia of today have in common their unholy oaths of loyalty to each other and loyalty to their satanic cause. Occasionally, one of them finally realizes the high cost of loyalty to evil leaders and false causes and agrees to turn state's evidence against his former compatriots. Such an act of disloyalty is pursued against the threat of death, but for some, the peace of conscience derived from shifting loyalties to true friends and true principles is well worth the risk.

Our loving Father in Heaven has invested considerably more than a half million dollars to retrieve us from the jungles of life. He willingly and lovingly sacrificed His Only Begotten Son as a ransom for our sins, to pay the debt required by the law of justice. His Son set the path and led the way—now we must repent and follow Him. We must be loyal to Him, and loyal to the principles He has taught us, and loyal to the covenants we have made with Him and with His Father.

Loyalty to Oaths and Covenants

Participation in priesthood ordinances often involves the making and renewing of covenants. For example, when we are baptized we demonstrate our willingness "to stand as witnesses of God at all times and in all things, and in all places" (Mosiah 18:9). Our loyalty to the baptismal covenant is evidenced by the degree to which we actively share the gospel with others and by the example of our lives.

The sealing ordinance in the temple involves not only a covenant between husband and wife but also a covenant between them and their Heavenly Father.

Thus, when a husband or wife is disloyal to his or her spouse, there is also a lack of loyalty to one's God.

Holders of the Melchizedek Priesthood are expected to be loyal to their priesthood and loyal to their priesthood leaders, and this loyalty is reflected in part by the oath and covenant of the priesthood (see D&C 84:33–42). The Savior revealed to the Prophet Joseph Smith that "all those who receive the priesthood, receive this oath and covenant of my Father, which he cannot break, neither can it be moved" (D&C 84:40). This oath and covenant is a form of contractual loyalty, if you will, between God and man, and our Heavenly Father's commitment to this oath and covenant is immutable. "But whoso breaketh this covenant after he hath received it, and altogether turneth therefrom, shall not have forgiveness of sins in this world nor in the world to come" (D&C 84:41).

For those who remain loyal and true to the covenants they have made and who magnify the priesthood which they hold, the Lord promises that "all that my Father hath shall be given unto [them]" (D&C 84:38).

Loyalty to Leaders

One of the greatest burdens which the Prophet Joseph had to contend with was disloyalty among several of his Counselors in the First Presidency of the Church. Oliver Cowdery was actually designated as "second elder of the Church" in 1830 and as "assistant president of the High Priesthood" in 1834, but four years later he was excommunicated. As he left the Church he predicted that it would fail without him, so proud and so disloyal to the Prophet he had become.

Sidney Rigdon was set apart as First Counselor to the Prophet in 1833, but he, too, was excommunicated eleven years later. Frederick G. Williams was called to be Joseph's Counselor in 1833, and reflecting the fondness and esteem which Joseph had for Frederick, Joseph and Emma named their sixth-born child Frederick G. Williams Smith. But this formerly true and faithful Counselor became engaged in the intrigue against the Prophet, and he was rejected four years later and was eventually excommunicated in 1839.

One of the greatest traitors to the Prophet was William Law, who was set apart as Second Counselor to President Smith in 1841 and was then excommunicated three years later for having been involved in activities subversive to the building of the kingdom and which eventually led to the incarceration and martyrdom of the Prophet. The Prophet Joseph Smith must have gained, through personal experience, great empathy for the Savior's feelings toward Judas Iscariot, who had been called as one of the original Twelve Apostles.

In contrast to the aforementioned men, whose pride led them to believe that they were better suited to lead the Church than the leader they were called to support and sustain, was the Prophet's older brother Hyrum. Hyrum replaced Oliver Cowdery in 1837, and four years later he was ordained as Patriarch to the Church and also as "assistant president." Unlike Laman and Lemuel, who could not sustain their righteous younger brother as their leader, and although Hyrum was nearly six years older than Joseph, his loyalty was never in question. The Lord himself said of Hyrum: "Blessed is my servant Hyrum Smith; for I, the Lord, love him because of the integrity of his heart, and because he loveth that which is right before me" (D&C 124:15).

The relationship between Joseph and Hyrum was eloquently described by Elder John Taylor at the time of their martyrdom: "In life they were not divided, and in death they were not separated!" (D&C 135:3.)

Every stake president and district president, every bishop and branch president, and every president of the Relief Society, Primary, Young Women, and Sunday School is grateful for loyal counselors. A counselor who is truly loyal will carefully warn his or her leader about pitfalls ahead or alert the leader to wonderful opportunities which lie in the future. There is great strength in the presidency principle. Three people take much longer to make a decision than one person acting alone; however, two counselors provide an excellent error-correction function. Each of us has strong personal preferences and talents, and each of us has weaknesses and blind spots. Therefore, it is in the best interests of the kingdom that counselors, including stake high councilors, be selected from a variety of walks of life so that the president can benefit from divergent points of view. A strong presidency, like a beautiful rainbow, can be enhanced by different shades of background experience.

Loyalty to Presidency and Quorum

The French jokingly refer to a statement made several years ago by General Charles DeGaulle, who reportedly complained at how difficult it was to reach a consensus in a country which has six hundred different kinds of cheese! The implication being, of course, that if it takes that many different kinds of cheese to satisfy the general public's tastes, how can one possibly satisfy everyone with one piece of legislation or with only one or two political parties?

But in these latter days the Lord, in explaining the purpose and organization of the Quorums of the Twelve and of the Seventy, has revealed that "every decision made by either of these quorums must be by the unanimous voice of the same; that is, every member in each quorum must be agreed to its decisions" (D&C 107:27).

Sometimes in a bishopric or in a stake presidency, or while serving on a high council, or when serving as an Apostle or Seventy, we are caught in an "Abrahamic test" between our loyalties to principles and people. Sometimes pride intervenes and we may be tempted to be loyal to the death to our own personal principles. But there is a marvelous, wonderful power in unanimous decisions in which individuals with strong personal preferences are given the opportunity to freely express their preferences but who then humbly abide by the will of the entire quorum, presidency, or council. It is at the time of the decision that our loyalty must remain to one another, to our leaders, and to our group decision.

When a stake presidency and high council discuss a matter and arrive at a decision, it is not only very disloyal but extremely disruptive to the work of the kingdom when one or two high councilors spread the word around the stake that "Brother Johnson and I opposed the decision, but the rest of them voted for it." This kind of disloyalty undermines the power and authority of the stake presidency and the other high councilors and does nothing to enhance the esteem in which the two public dissidents are held in the eyes of the members.

The same is true, of course, in a bishopric. The bishop holds the keys. He is the presiding high priest and president of the Aaronic Priesthood. (See D&C 107.) When his counselors counsel with him and present their views, once the decision has been made, any loyal counselor will abide by that decision, support and sustain the bishop, and withhold any criticism of the bishop if the bishop's decision was contrary to the counsel of the counselor. By the same token, bishops should be very, very sensitive to the counsel they receive, and if it seems that a consensus is not immediately reachable, it may be well to postpone the issue for another week or two and give it more prayerful deliberation. But under no circumstances should a counselor tell his wife or other members of the ward, "I told the bishop it was a bad decision, but he wouldn't listen to me." To do so is to follow the folly of Oliver Cowdery, Frederick G. Williams, Sidney Rigdon, and William Law, who were more concerned about governing the kingdom "my way" rather than the Lord's way.

The Savior's plea in the Garden of Gethsemane is an excellent example of loyalty in balance. Though the bitter cup caused Him to bleed from every pore, nevertheless He did the will of His Father. To the end He was loyal to His Father and to His plan. Jesus Christ is described by the Apostle John as "the Word," a very significant title indeed, for not only was the Savior sent into the world to preach the word of God, which is truth, but He was the truth! He lived what He taught and He taught as He lived. (See John 1:1–4 and 1 Cor. 9:14.)

Notes

1. Brigham Young, *Discourses of Brigham Young*, sel. John A. Widtsoe (Salt Lake City: Deseret Book Co., 1977), pp. 200–201.

2. Orson Pratt, "Celestial Marriage," *The Seer* 1 (October 1853): 157.

3. William Shakespeare, *King Henry VIII*, act 3, scene 2, lines 455–57.

4. Joseph Smith, *Teachings of the Prophet Joseph Smith*, sel. Joseph Fielding Smith (Salt Lake City: Deseret Book Co., 1938), p. 87.

5. Smith, *Teachings*, p. 87.

6. *History of the Church* 6:612–15; hereafter cited as *HC*.

7. *HC* 6:616.

8. See "Hiroo Worship," *Time*, 25 March 1974, pp. 42–43.

Chapter Fourteen

COMMUNICATION AND CONFIDENTIALITY

Let Your Light So Shine

When the Lord made his covenant with Abraham, he promised Abraham that kings would come through his lineage, that his posterity would become as numerous as the sands of the sea and the stars of the heavens, that his posterity would receive a land of promise, and that the blessings of the priesthood would flow through his lineage.

Abraham's posterity become partakers of these blessings through their faithfulness, but with every blessing comes a responsibility. In this case, it is the obligation of Abraham's children to share the gospel with the rest of our Heavenly Father's children throughout the earth.

The prophecies of Isaiah and of Nephi (see 2 Ne. 10), Zenos (see Jacob 5), and Ezekiel (see Ezek. 37), to mention only a few, all describe the panoramic process of the scattering and gathering of Israel. Each of us has an obligation to participate in the gathering of the children of Israel. Throughout the entire Doctrine and Covenants the Lord admonishes us to open our mouths and share the gospel with others. He further commands those who have been warned to warn their neighbors (see D&C 88:81). As with all other commandments, obedience begets a wonderful promise: as we share the gospel with others, our sins will be forgiven (see D&C 84:61). The Lord further promised: "How great will be your joy if you should bring many souls unto me!" (D&C 18:16.)

Throughout the world there are courageous full-time missionaries, stake missionaries, and garden-variety members who fearlessly seek out and find friends who are looking for the truth but know not where to find it. The Savior's injunction to "let your light so shine before men" (Matt. 5:16) is followed by countless Latter-day Saints who quietly communicate their testimonies in sharing the gospel with others. Ofttimes the greatest sermons ever preached are the countless kindly acts of service to one's neighbors.

Cast Not Pearls Before Swine

Twenty-seven-year-old Lorenzo Snow shared the following counsel while serving a mission in London, England, in 1841:

> The Savior has commanded not to cast pearls before swine. I am sorry to say that this instruction is not always sufficiently regarded by those to whom our Lord has given, through the Everlasting Covenant, His pearls of wisdom, knowledge, and precious gifts. The consequence is, we lose blessings instead of retaining them—a decrease of the Holy Spirit follows, instead of an increase, and our minds become darkened.
>
> What I allude to is this: we too frequently engage in conversation concerning things of the kingdom of God, with persons of a wrong spirit; and feeling over anxious to make them see, understand, and acknowledge the light presented, we urge on, and persist in the conversation until we partake of the spirit of those with whom we are conversing. We ought to be particularly guarded against falling into errors of this kind.
>
> It is very easy to understand when conversation is attended with profit. We then feel our minds enlightened, and the power of God resting upon us through the Holy Spirit—ideas flow into our minds, and we express them with ease, freedom, and calmness.
>
> Conversation conducted in this spirit proves highly profitable, not only to ourselves, but also to those with whom we converse; and after its close, our hearts are drawn out in gratitude to the Most High for the privilege of imparting the glorious truths of the Gospel to the children of men.[1]

Young Elder Snow articulated in his own words counsel very similar to that revealed in section 50 of the Doctrine and Covenants:

> Verily I say unto you, he that is ordained of me and sent forth to preach the word of truth by the Comforter, in the Spirit of truth, doth he preach it by the Spirit of truth or some other way?

> And if it be by some other way it is not of God.
> And again, he that receiveth the word of truth, doth he receive it by the Spirit of truth or some other way?
> If it be some other way it is not of God.
> Therefore, why is it that ye cannot understand and know, that he that receiveth the word by the Spirit of truth receiveth it as it is preached by the Spirit of truth?
> Wherefore, he that preacheth and he that receiveth, understand one another, and both are edified and rejoice together. (D&C 50:17–22.)

Elder Snow observed that it is difficult to share the gospel with "persons of a wrong spirit," as he put it. The Apostle Paul explains why this is so in his First Epistle to the Corinthians:

> Eye hath not seen, nor ear heard, neither have entered into the heart of man, the things which God hath prepared for them that love him.
> But God hath revealed them unto us by his Spirit: for the Spirit searcheth all things, yea, the deep things of God.
> For what man knoweth the things of a man, save the spirit of man which is in him? even so the things of God knoweth no man, but the Spirit of God.
> Now we have received, not the spirit of the world, but the spirit which is of God; that we might know the things that are freely given to us of God. . . .
> But the natural man receiveth not the things of the Spirit of God: for they are foolishness unto him: neither can he know them, because they are spiritually discerned. (1 Cor. 2:9–12, 14.)

The things of God are to be communicated to the world openly and freely. The warning voice must be raised "to every nation, and kindred, and tongue, and people" (Rev. 14:6), and to those "who are only kept from the truth because they know not where to find it" (D&C 123:12). But this wonderful gospel message must be communicated "in the Spirit of truth. . . . And if it be by some other way it is not of God." (D&C 50:17–18.) Motives must be pure. One must be motivated by a love of the gospel and a love of the person being taught. When such is the case, the "fruit will remain" (John 15:16).

Go Thy Way and Tell No Man

Although the Savior spent his entire life teaching and proclaiming His gospel, there were occasions when certain experiences were so sacred that Jesus commanded those present to maintain the confidentiality of things seen and heard. After healing a leper He charged the man: "See thou tell no man" (Matt. 8:4). Again, after raising a young maiden from the dead, he charged her parents "that they should tell no man what was done" (Luke 8:56).

There was a man in Decapolis who was deaf and suffered from a speech impediment. After restoring the hearing and speech to this good man, Jesus charged those present "that they should tell no man," but human nature being what it is, "the more he charged them, so much the more a great deal they published it." (Mark 7:31–37.)

There were several other sacred experiences which the Savior wished to keep confidential within the group that had experienced them. One such occasion was at Caesarea Philippi when He asked His disciples: "Whom do men say that I the Son of man am?" It was on this occasion that Simon Peter answered: "Thou are the Christ, the Son of the living God." The Savior then responded: "Blessed art thou, Simon Bar-jona: for flesh and blood hath not revealed it unto thee, but my Father which is in heaven." After this confirmation of His divine identity, "then charged he his disciples that they should tell no man that he was Jesus the Christ." (Matt. 16:13–20.)

There would be a time when they would be given the charge to bear witness of the divine mission of Jesus Christ, but now was not the time.

The Savior took Peter, James, and John to a high mountain where He "was transfigured before them," and Moses and Elias also appeared to them, and they heard the voice of God the Father saying, "This is my beloved Son, in whom I am well pleased; hear ye him." As they climbed down the mountain at the conclusion of these marvelous manifestations, "Jesus charged them, saying, Tell the vision to no man, until the Son of man be risen again from the dead." (Matt. 17:1–9.) But after the Savior's resurrection and ascension, on the day of Pentecost, the Apostle Peter bore such a powerful testimony that three thousand people were converted in one day (see Acts 2).

There is a time to speak, and a time to share, and there is a time to meditate and to ponder, and there are times when we should and must treasure certain things in our hearts without sharing them with others. This is true of our personal patriarchal blessings, which are, in the words of Karl G. Maeser, "pages from our book of possibilities." A patriarchal blessing is a kind of personal scripture, but scripture too sacred to be shared with just anyone or everyone. Family members and one's eternal companion may be permitted to read such a blessing, but the contents should not be shared from the pulpit or in circular correspondence which may be unrestricted in scope.

In latter-day revelation the Lord has given us the following excellent counsel: "Remember that that which cometh from above is sacred, and must be spoken with care, and by constraint of the Spirit" (D&C 63:64).

The Message, Messenger, and Receiver

There was a time in certain formerly communist countries when sharing the gospel openly would have resulted in incarceration or loss of housing and employment opportunities, but hopefully these times are past in most of those countries, and what had to be hidden can now be shared openly.

Sometimes constraints are not upon the messenger or the message but upon the receiver, who may not yet be prepared for the message. In the Sermon on the Mount the Savior counsels us: "Give not that which is holy unto the dogs, neither cast ye your pearls before swine, lest they trample them under their feet, and turn again and rend you" (Matt. 7:6).

In another context, the Savior said to his disciples: "Behold, I send you forth as sheep in the midst of wolves: be ye therefore wise as serpents, and harmless as doves" (Matt. 10:16). The lesson is clear. We must be responsive to the Spirit in all of our teaching so that we might be wise in the sharing of spiritual truths (see D&C 50:13–22).

Even prophets of God do not tell us everything they know. After giving us the wise and inspiring admonition to "feast upon the words of Christ," Nephi testified of the doctrine of Christ. He then added, "And now I, Nephi, cannot say more; the Spirit stoppeth mine utterance." (2 Ne. 32:3, 6–7.)

Inadvertent Disclosure

We live in such a highly mobile world with such excellent means of communication and transportation, that each of us must be circumspect in sharing information of a somewhat confidential nature. For example, while teaching a Sunday School class or during a sacrament meeting sermon, we may feel inclined to illustrate a point by sharing a somewhat confidential experience of a brother-in-law, or a neighbor, or other friend who is completely unknown to the audience. We may feel that laying this particular person's life history open to public view is an anonymous act because no one knows of whom we speak. But then, to our great delight this person comes to visit us, and as we introduce him to the Saints within our ward, they say, "Oh, so *you* are the man who used to throw the home teachers out of the house," or, "We heard about all of your tirades as an alcoholic before you joined the Church." What had once been an anonymous story, perhaps shared with a lofty goal in mind, has now become an invasion of privacy. It is always well to have an informed consent from those whose biographies we share. Better still, a good safeguard is to speak merely of "a person I know" without identifying him or her by age or geographical location.

The truths taught in the temple and the sacred ordinances performed therein contain the culminating blessings of the gospel. But notwithstanding their eternal importance, because of their sacred nature they should never be discussed outside the confines of the holy house of the Lord.

Newlywed couples share physical intimacies which begin to weld their marriages into truly eternal relationships as they begin the process of becoming "one flesh." But the sanctity of their relationship must never be shared with others, and to do so can lead to sad consequences. Marital infidelity can often be traced to the unwise disclosure of information which should have been known only to one's marriage partner.

Bishops, stake presidents, and others involved in interviewing married couples must use great discretion in conducting interviews with married couples, so that the sanctity of an intimate marriage relationship is not improperly disclosed. Ecclesiastical leaders should continually teach correct eternal principles and then let married couples govern themselves.

Confession

During an interview with a bishop or stake president, the person being interviewed has an obligation to communicate with his or her ecclesiastical leader any information which would jeopardize his or her qualifying for a temple recommend. We often refer to the bishop as the "common judge in Israel." He is, indeed, a common man with a very uncommon calling. He is called to judge in mercy and wisdom. And in a very real sense, we are also judges of ourselves. When the bishop asks, "Do you fully observe the Word of Wisdom?" in a very real sense, it is I, not he, who judges myself. If I am in doubt, I may ask him for clarification. But in the end, the responsibility for the correct answer is mine.

There is a large difference between admission and confession. Admission is acknowledging our sins and weaknesses in response to an interviewer's question. Confession, on the other hand, involves our taking the initiative in raising the issue of our transgressions and shortcomings. The scriptures are plain that forgiveness occurs from confession: "By this ye may know that a man repenteth of his sins—behold, he will confess them and forsake them" (D&C 58:43).

The Prophet Joseph further admonished the Saints to "be willing to confess all their sins, and not keep back a part."[2]

Criticism

One of the most insidious and destructive forms of communication is criticism. Just because we are able to easily detect character flaws in others does not give us license to publicize such weaknesses. Joseph Smith exhorted the Twelve to "not seek to excel one above another, but act for each other's good, and pray for one another, and honor our brother or make honorable mention of his name, and not backbite and devour our brother."[3] One of the great evidences of true loyalty is to be aware of weaknesses in a friend and not disclose them to others. After all, forgiveness will come to him when he confesses his own sins, not when we confess them in public for him!

However, if I am a truly loyal friend, and I love my friend and want to help him become happy, I may call his bishop and, in very general terms, suggest that the bishop have a heart-to-heart talk with my friend. If my friend takes the opportunity to rid his life of extra baggage, then the suggestion was very worthwhile and I have not disclosed a confidence.

There are some people who, caught up with a feeling of humility and contrition, disclose their own weaknesses before the public, such as in a testimony meeting, rather than confessing their sins in the privacy of a bishop's office. The scriptures tell us that only when sins are widely known should there be public confession (see D&C 42:80–93). Otherwise, our sins should be confessed to our bishop or to our Heavenly Father in prayer.

Joseph Smith assured the Saints, "I do not dwell upon your faults, and you shall not upon mine. Charity, which is love, covereth a multitude of sins, and I have often covered up all the faults among you; but the prettiest thing is to have no faults at all. We should cultivate a meek, quiet and peaceable spirit."[4] In admonishing the Saints to cover each other's sins, he did not indicate that we should "call evil good," rather he was advocating that the Saints look for the good in others and refrain from continual criticism.

The Savior's statement in the Sermon on the Mount is good medicine for all of us: "Judge not, that ye be not judged." He further asks us: "And why beholdest thou the mote that is in thy brother's eye, but considerest not the beam that is in thine own eye?" (Matt. 7:1, 3.) In this same vein, the Apostle Paul wrote the Romans in unmistakable terms that "wherein thou judgest another, thou condemnest thyself; for thou that judgest doest the same things" (Rom. 2:1). In short, our criticisms of others are generally a reflection of our own weaknesses with which we, ourselves, are currently struggling.

The loftier road is found in the Lord's counsel to Brother Lyman Sherman, good counsel to each of us: "Therefore, strengthen your brethren in all your conversation, in all your prayers, in all your exhortations, and in all your doings" (D&C 108:7).

Notes

1. In Eliza R. Snow Smith, *Biography and Family Record of Lorenzo Snow* (Salt Lake City: Deseret News Co., 1884), p. 59.

2. Joseph Smith, *Teachings of the Prophet Joseph Smith*, sel. Joseph Fielding Smith (Salt Lake City: Deseret Book Co., 1938), p. 155.

3. Smith, *Teachings*, p. 155.

4. Smith, *Teachings*, p. 316.

Chapter Fifteen

Remembering and Forgetting

Through His atoning sacrifice, the miracle of forgiveness, the Lord himself has explained in a latter-day revelation: "Behold, he who has repented of his sins, the same is forgiven, and I, the Lord, remember them no more" (D&C 58:42).

It is indeed a great miracle that He who created this earth under the direction of His Father, He who knows all, has promised us that He will forget our sins when we but repent.

Remembering and forgetting constitute a lifelong balancing act. With the passage of time, each of us must deal in good humor with our forgetful acts of failing to remember where we left the car keys, or where we parked the car, or where we left our reading glasses, or where we left the book we were reading. In extreme cases, such as those involving persons afflicted with Alzheimer's disease, the failure to remember relationships with loved ones can become a source of great sorrow in the closing years of life.

Forgetting Past Offenses

But there are others who experience a much more exquisite kind of pain than that caused by senility and chronic forgetfulness. These are they who are unable to forget, and who are also unable to forgive. Some have experienced abuse or neglect in their formative years, leaving their lives scarred and perpetually troubled. Other individuals have been victims of cruel financial scams in which they were intentionally bilked of their life's savings. Still others have been offended or hurt in countless other ways and cannot find it in their hearts to forget or to forgive another.

Still perhaps an even greater burden to bear than past offenses from others are our own offenses toward God. Some people, even after having experienced a kindly, loving, supportive disciplinary council and after having reentered the refreshing waters of rebaptism, cannot forget their past sins, nor can they forgive themselves. But if the Lord is to forget their sins, then they must also forget their own sins.

Few there are who have undergone as mighty a change of heart as did the Apostle Paul. Before his conversion on the road to Damascus, Saul of Tarsus had attended the stoning of Stephen (see Acts 7:58) and had "made havock of the church" (Acts 8:3). Nevertheless, after his conversion, Paul told the Philippians: "Brethren, I count not myself to have apprehended: but this one thing I do, *forgetting those things which are behind*, and reaching forth unto those things which are before, I press toward the mark for the prize of the high calling of God in Christ Jesus" (Philip. 3:13–14, emphasis added).

The conversion experience of Alma the Younger is also very instructive for each of us. Alma recounted to his son Helaman that he was "racked with torment, while I was harrowed up by the memory of my many sins" (Alma 36:17). But upon remembering his father's teachings of the atonement of Christ, and after having prayed for mercy, Alma experienced something else: "I was harrowed up by the memory of my sins no more. And oh, what joy, and what marvelous light I did behold; yea, my soul was filled with joy as exceeding as was my pain." (Alma 36:19–20.) *Remembering* the Atonement had helped him to *forget* his sins, or more accurately said, to be no more troubled by the memory of his sins.

Several years ago one of my students who was a convert to the Church began to relate some of his experiences prior to his baptism. In the course of one of our conversations he began to relate an especially unsavory experience which, I thought, seemed to give him a certain amount of delayed satisfaction in the retelling. I interrupted his account and reminded him that now he had made sacred covenants at baptism, he was to forget his past sins and not to continue retelling them or rethinking them in such a way as to almost experience them again. If he wanted the Lord to forgive and forget his sins, then he must forget his own sins, or, at the very least, remember them with a "peace of conscience" (Mosiah 4:3).

Past Success

While some individuals dwell upon their past failures, others live in a world of past successes. Surely there is no harm in retrieving pleasant memories of the past and in reviewing photo albums and in reading and rereading books of remembrance. Nor is there any harm in recounting pleasant associations with business colleagues or in retrieving feelings of brotherhood and sisterhood toward those with whom we have worked in various Church callings.

But sometimes an occasional bishop or stake president or mission president or Relief Society president has an insatiable desire to dwell in the past and finds it very difficult to cope with the present and to anticipate the future.

Elder Marvin J. Ashton has wisely counseled us to resist the temptation to continually repeat phrases such as "When I was the bishop, . . ." A former stake president who is called as a Regional Representative may well refrain from "When I was . . ." while counseling with stake presidents in his new calling. The plan of salvation is a forward-looking plan as described by Nephi as he admonishes us to "press forward, feasting upon the word of Christ, and endure to the end" (2 Ne. 31:20).

The miracle of forgiveness provides the way for us to be forgiven and a way of forgetting our sins. Humility and meekness would require that we also not dwell unduly upon past accomplishments. The Savior said: "No man, having put his hand to the plough, and looking back, is fit for the kingdom of God" (Luke 9:62).

Looking Backward

President Howard W. Hunter has eloquently explained:

> There is danger in looking backward. . . . The backward glance commences the backward turning, and may be the beginning of our disendowment in the kingdom of God.
>
> As plowing requires an eye intent on the furrow to be made and is marred when one looks backward, so will they come short of exaltation who prosecute the work of God with a distracted attention or a divided

> heart. We may not see clearly the end of the furrow, but we dare not look back. Eternity stretches on ahead, challenging us to be faithful.[1]

There is the returned missionary, for example, who may have enjoyed a bounteous harvest in his former field of labor. As he proudly persists in looking backward upon those plentiful baptisms, he may begin to feel that the Lord will now excuse him from home teaching and other responsibilities because his ledger of past accomplishments indicates a hefty "credit." The satisfaction with previous accomplishments can also begin to serve as the justification for skipping priesthood meeting in order to recover from his previous evening's activities.

Another missionary may look backward with pride on his acquisition of gospel knowledge and his ability to recite innumerable scriptures from memory. But sometimes he forgets the scriptural admonitions to lose ourselves in the service of others. He may also feel a false security that his current scriptural knowledge will last a lifetime and that continuing gospel study is no longer necessary. On occasion, he may feel that his successful mission now entitles him to take certain liberties with the virtuous, lovely young daughters in Zion. Before long, Satan places an unexpected temptation in his path, and because his eyes are ever looking backward, the temptation takes him by surprise, and he learns that hard lesson in life, that "wickedness never was happiness" (Alma 41:10).

Lot's wife is not the only person to have suffered the negative consequences of looking back (see Gen. 19:17–26). Occasionally a young mother with little children will start feeling bored or even trapped by life. Seemingly unable to find anything meaningful to do with her life, though nothing surpasses motherhood for fulfillment, she may begin watching TV soap operas with great relish. Soon she begins to find her husband less dashing and romantic than the handsome television heroes she has come to admire. Slowly, but surely, the borders between illusion and reality begin to blur, and she finds herself looking back, back beyond her temple sealing and the sacred covenants she has made. Her mind wanders back to her high school or college days when she and former boyfriends had some rather exciting experiences together. She begins to ask herself, "What if I had married Fred, or Bill, or Dan? Surely, if I had married one of them I wouldn't be bored and unhappy." Satan begins to fan the flame of evil thoughts, and sometimes these initial thoughts eventually lead to tragic conclusions.

Those who marry should put their hand to the nuptial plough and not look back. Once we have knelt across the sacred altar of the holy temple facing our eternal companion, we must never look back to forgone alternatives. Concerning this matter, President Brigham Young shared the following wise counsel:

> Were I a woman possessed of great powers of mind, filled with wisdom, and, upon the whole, a magnanimous woman, and had been privileged with my choice, and had married a man, and found myself deceived, he not answering my expectations, and I being sorry that I had made such a choice, let me show my wisdom by not complaining about it. A woman's wisdom and judgment has failed her once in the choice of a husband, and it may again, if she is not very careful. By seeking to cast off her husband—by withdrawing her confidence and goodwill from him, she casts a dark shade upon his path, when, by pursuing a proper course of love, obedience, and encouragement, he might attain to that perfection she had anticipated in him.[2]

When times get tough, and surely they will, we must continually look forward with faith and hope and charity and unconditional love. When we continue to pray together, study the scriptures together, attend the temple worthily, practice daily forgiveness, and keep our list of matrimonial misdemeanors small, we will be blessed with a sure knowledge that our marriage has been sealed by the Holy Spirit of Promise—forever! This blessing gives both of us a sense of mutual devotion and security that is foreign to the world in which we live. Such a marriage anticipates eternity with great expectations.

All too often, looking backward includes the frequent use of the condemnatory expressions, "You never do that," or, "You always do this," thus painting our friends and loved ones into an inescapable corner. If we find that others never reach our expectations or that they always give offense to us, there is little hope for change in our future relations. Perhaps *always* and *never* should be reserved for discussions of the eternal verities.

Another insidious form of looking back involves retrieving past memories of the days before we were baptized, or the days before our mission call, or the days before we went to see our bishop to put our lives in order. If in the past we have been guilty of committing a variety of sins, Satan would have us continue to dwell upon them and upon the past. He would have us believe that we have strayed too far to ever return to the presence of our loving Father in Heaven. The devil knows that if we continually look backward we cannot contemplate the future blessings of eternity.

In his great discourse on charity, the Apostle Paul chided the Corinthians about looking back to their younger, immature years. He then urged them to accept the responsibilities of maturity. Said Paul: "When I was a child, I spake as a child, I understood as a child, I thought as a child: but when I became a man, I put away childish things" (1 Cor. 13:11). In the following chapter he admonished his brethren more pointedly to "be not children in understanding . . . but in understanding be men" (1 Cor. 14:20).

Some people have never quite gained an understanding of the basic principles of the gospel because they have never put forth the necessary effort to study the gospel. Thus, the scriptures never become their "life script." They say it is a matter of a shortage of time, but somehow they find time for skiing, television, ball games, escape literature, social events, and videos. As one wag put it: "You can tell the age of the boys by the price of their toys."

Another form of looking back is found in the lives of those who revere prophets of an earlier era but who reject the words of living prophets and Apostles. It seems that it has ever been thus, as evidenced by the mission of Samuel the Lamanite two thousand years ago. Samuel came to the Nephites to admonish them to prepare themselves spiritually for the forthcoming birth of the Savior. He condemned the Nephites, much like the Savior condemned those of His day (see Matt. 23), for reverentially looking backward to the ancient prophets while rejecting the words of the Lord's anointed servants living in their presence. (See Hel. 13–14.)

The ever-expanding and forward-looking nature of the gospel is reflected in the Lord's definition of truth: "Truth is knowledge of things as they are, and as they were, and as they are to come" (D&C 93:24).

Remission of Sins

Sometimes our sins and foolish acts of immaturity have been so painful that it is virtually impossible to forget them entirely. These memories may leave us with an unsettled feeling regarding whether our sins have actually been forgiven. In his great benedictory sermon, inspired by the words given him by an angel, King Benjamin provides us with several benchmarks for helping us determine when we have received a remission of our sins.

First is receiving a "peace of conscience" (Mosiah 4:3). My list of sins is so long I cannot remember them all, but neither can I forget them all. But I can remember them with a peace of conscience without being "harrowed up by the memory of my many sins" (Alma 36:17).

A second indicator of forgiveness is a "great joy" in our souls (Mosiah 4:11). Alma reminds us that "wickedness never was happiness" (Alma 41:10), and thus it is impossible to have true joy and happiness while engaging in evildoing. Righteousness does not guarantee a life of constant sunshine devoid of rain clouds, but wickedness most assuredly robs us of joy, which joy is the design of our existence.

Third, King Benjamin said we will be "filled with the love of God" (Mosiah 4:12) when we have received a remission of sins. He did not say we would have love or feel love, but that we would be filled with love. A soul full of love has no room for anything else. A heart full of love has no place for jealousy or greed or hatred or discouragement or revenge. A heart full of love is full. And how do we experience this love? We must "pray unto the Father with all the energy of heart, that [we] may be filled with this love" (Moro. 7:48).

Fourth, we will "not have a mind to injure one another" (Mosiah 4:13). Our actions toward our companions, parents, children, neighbors, and work associates will be circumspect and governed by the Golden Rule of treating them as we would wish to be treated.

Fifth, we "will not suffer [our] children that they go hungry, or naked," or suffer that they "fight and quarrel one with another" (Mosiah 4:14).

Finally, we will share of our substance in assisting those in need (see Mosiah 4:16–27). When we truly become partakers of the atoning sacrifice of Jesus Christ, we develop a natural inclination to sacrifice for the well-being of others.

Remembering

Just as we can remember our past sins with a peace of conscience, in like manner our increasing humility should help us to review our past accomplishments as we become older and wiser and begin to realize that, compared to the glory of God, our mortal success is puny indeed.

But some things must be remembered. Indeed, we partake of the sacramental bread "in remembrance" of the broken body of Jesus Christ upon the cross. We drink the water "in remembrance of the blood" which the Savior shed from every pore in the Garden of Gethsemane as He took the sins of the world upon himself. As we partake of the sacrament we covenant with the Eternal Father that we will "always remember him," with the promise that we "may always have his Spirit" to be with us. (D&C 20:77, 79.)

Certainly, above all things, we should always keep in remembrance the covenants we have made in the waters of baptism and in holy temples.

Gratitude is an important act of remembrance. In section 59 the Lord revealed to Joseph Smith that "in nothing doth man offend God, or against none is his wrath kindled, save those who confess not his hand in all things, and obey not his commandments" (D&C 59:21). Of all the possible sources of offense to God, it is well to remember that the sin of ingratitude ranks among the highest. Surely we should remember God's countless blessings and endless goodness to us. Criticism and contention persist when people are unable to forgive and forget, but these twin agitants soon disappear when they are surrounded by a sea of gratitude. It is almost impossible to count our blessings and count the faults of others simultaneously.

The ancient Israelites and the Nephites were admonished to remember the bondage of their fathers in Egypt and to remember that it was by the strength of the Lord's hand that they were set free (see Ex. 13:3, 9 and Alma 29:12). Speaking through Isaiah, the Lord said: "I, even I, am he that blotteth out thy transgressions for mine own sake, and will not remember thy sins. Put me in remembrance." (Isa. 43:25–26.) *He* is to be remembered even as our sins are mercifully forgotten. This scripture is a great key to personal happiness in helping us to select that which is to be remembered and that which should be forgotten.

What's in a Name?

There are two schools of thought regarding the naming of children. One school advocates not giving the children the names of their parents so that children may grow up independently and largely unfettered by the good or questionable reputation of their parents. As one who was given the name of my father, as a youth I sometimes wearied of the predictable reaction during formal introductions: "Soooooooo, you're Spencer Condie's son." (In order to explain the "soooooo," perhaps it would be well to mention that my father was an Internal Revenue agent—a fact that sometimes caused mild embarrassment on my part.) On the other hand, because my father has a reputation as an honest and kindly man of integrity, bearing his name has sometimes helped establish relationships with others very quickly.

Helaman the son of Helaman elected not to name his sons after their father or grandfather; instead he named them Nephi and Lehi with the following specific explanation: "Behold, I have given unto you the names of our first parents who came out of the land of Jerusalem; and this I have done that when you remember your names ye may remember them; and when ye remember them ye may remember their works; and when ye remember their works ye may know how that it is said, and also written, that they were good" (Hel. 5:6).

It is extremely significant that, in renewing our baptismal covenants through partaking of the sacrament, we take upon ourselves the name of the Son and we covenant to "always remember him and keep his commandments" (D&C 20:77). When we take upon us the name of Christ this covenant leads us to remember Him and hopefully to become more like Him.

I have been touched by the number of people who name their children after Apostles and prophets of the Lord, sometimes even giving their children the prophet's last name as the child's first given name. As I participated in the reorganization of a stake presidency in eastern Germany a few years ago, I was impressed by the number of brethren I interviewed whose first names may have been Heinrich, Wolfgang, and Rudolph but whose middle names were Nephi, Alma, and Helaman. These men, now in their forties and fifties, had been reared in a social, economic, and political environment very hostile to the free practice of religion. But they had remained true to the faith of their fathers and true to their respective namesake.

A few summers ago I had a wonderful opportunity to participate in a German Scout jamboree attended by four hundred Latter-day Saint youths. At the entrance to each troop's camping site was an arch constructed of long poles bound together by leather lashings demonstrating their camping and construction skills. Above each arch was the name of the troop, but instead of the usual Troop 426 or Troop 18, these young men had selected prominent names from the Book of Mormon. There was the Moroni Troop, the Gidgiddoni Troop, the Liahona Troop, etc. Seldom have I seen or felt a greater spirit on the Sabbath day than among these fine young men whose behavior was consistent with the name of their troops.

Retention of Skills and Knowledge

I grew up in a home in which great emphasis was placed upon learning to play the piano. Both of our parents and all of the children learned how to play the piano, and, I might add, we were grateful for the opportunity to do so, though not at the time. The most marginal player in the family is my elderly father, who couldn't read music too well but who could play by memory rousing versions of "And Here We Have Idaho," "Silent Night," and "My Wild Irish Rose." For years he could be counted upon to play a medley of these three numbers at family gatherings and other occasions. It was especially entertaining for the younger children to hear Grandpa play "Silent Night" in July.

But the children grew older and requests became fewer, and all of us married and left home, and without any requests from the audience there was little motivation for my father to play the medley. And as Dad became seventy and then suddenly eighty, it became apparent that he was no longer able to play. He had forgotten the songs he had known for half a century.

The same can happen to us in terms of our knowledge of the scriptures. We may have an excellent experience in seminary and institute class and serve as successful missionaries, during which time we invest a good deal of time studying the scriptures. But if we are not extremely careful, if we do not persist in searching the scriptures, gradually we will no longer be able to quote the scriptures verbatim, and next we will forget the exact scriptural reference, and eventually we will forget the scriptures entirely.

Happy Family Life

The key to a happy and fulfilling family life is largely found in maintaining a judicious balance between remembering and forgetting. In counseling couples in marriage difficulties, I have been saddened by the steel-trap memory of one or the other of them who, after ten or twenty years of marriage, can retrieve painful memories of several years previously in exquisite detail. On the other hand, when I have asked them what it was that attracted them to each other during their courtship, their memories have become very hazy. Instead of accumulating twenty years of marriage experience, they have had one year's experience twenty times.

Success in a marriage is dependent in large part in forgetting petty differences of the past while remembering the countless acts of kindness and love which have also been part of the relationship. The same holds true in maintaining strong relationships between parents and children. In recent years there have been several biographies on the market written by the offspring of the rich and famous. These sons and daughters reveal the sad details of growing up in a family in which the father or mother was a well-known entertainer, movie star, or political figure. Many of these famous personalities have created a public image over the years as someone who is very affable, generous, and kind, but the children paint a contradictory picture of a tyrannical parent. Even if the details of the book were all true, washing the family laundry in public does little good in "turning the hearts of the children to their fathers," and makes healing the wounds of the past extremely difficult.

The Saving Grace of Selective Perception

Several years ago I took one of our daughters to see her very first football game. I will grant you that American football is a rather complex game to understand, and so it was interesting to overhear her report of her experience at a very exciting game. There was not a word about the kickoff runback for a touchdown, or the sixty-yard intercepted pass, or the forty-yard field goal that was kicked through the goal posts as the crucial seconds ticked away at the close of the game. Instead, she described the antics of Cosmo, the Cougar mascot. When she was asked what the final score was, her report went something like: two hot dogs, one bag of popcorn, and one orange drink.

There were thousands of other football fans whose perceptions varied greatly about the unfolding outcome of the game. As the stadium emptied, several fans concentrated their comments on the fantastic passing on the part of one of the quarterbacks. Others were particularly impressed by the defense of their favorite team, while still others complained about the "lousy officiating" and the "annoying cheerleaders" and about the cost of tickets for such a "crummy view of the field." As one continued walking down the street listening to the various animated comments of the fans as they returned home, one could almost draw the conclusion that many of them had not attended the same ball game we had.

Sometimes a similar phenomenon occurs in families. A favorite topic of discussion in Gospel Doctrine classes has been the question: Why was it that Laman and Lemuel were so rebellious while Nephi was so righteous and they all came from the same family? The fact of the matter is that, in a very real sense, they were not reared in the same family. Laman and Lemuel were reared in a family with at least four righteous younger brothers, while Nephi was reared in a family with two older rebellious brothers. As much as we try to credit or blame Lehi and Sariah with the behavior of their children, one fact cannot be overlooked: each of their sons had his moral agency to be either rebellious or obedient.

Laman and Lemuel had seen and heard the voice of an angel but hardened their hearts (see 1 Ne. 17:45). Nephi and Jacob, on the other hand, responded positively to heavenly messengers, and their receptiveness led to continuing spiritual experiences.

Social psychologists use the term *selective perception* to describe the phenomenon occurring when several people attend the same event and come away with very different impressions. Similar to the variety of reactions to the previously described ball game, within families there are those who are "forgivers" and those who are "faultfinders." Guess which of them have the best relationships with others and which of them live in the happier family. Related to selective perception is the notion of selective retention. For some, childhood is retrieved in memory as a time of wonderment and discovery. For others, this same stage of development was a time of boredom or, unfortunately for all too many, a time of terror and sadness. I am grateful to a great friend for his example of faithfulness and purity of heart in describing his own childhood experiences. His father was an alcoholic who had great difficulty providing for his family. I have heard my friend extol the virtues of his patient and loving mother on several occasions, but not once have I heard a note of bitterness toward his father. This servant of the Lord has selectively overlooked a father's weakness while extolling the virtues of a saintly mother.

Many of the current generation of historians and biographers pride themselves on retelling the lives of their subjects "warts and all." But in the process all too many modern biographies and magazine and news articles contain more warts than good deeds. There seems to be a taste for conquest in subduing the heroic images of Washington, Lincoln, Churchill and other statesmen of their stature. Digging up as much dirt as possible becomes more important than presenting a balanced picture of a person's life.

Many good men of integrity are hesitant to run for public office because of judgmental journalists who take great delight in revealing the human frailties and foibles of youth. Men and women in the public limelight must also be granted opportunities to be forgiven, and their poor judgment of the past must be forgotten or at least be remembered charitably.

It is ironic how forgiving the general public is of athletic stars. Any baseball player who gets a hit one out of every three times at bat is hailed as a hero, notwithstanding the fact that two out of three times he does not get on base. Every quarterback is forgiven for an occasional interception. We have a knack for readily forgetting and forgiving the misses of the stars. Why is it that we establish such exacting standards for people in other fields, for example parenting? I am not advocating a quest for mediocrity, but given the astronomical number of decisions the mother of five children must make in a given day, surely we must give her the benefit of the doubt if a few decisions were not in the best immediate interests of her children. We should forgive her and remember the good that was done, and remember that the intent of the heart was to "bat a thousand."

The Savior's Selective Perception

The Savior's selective perception was evidenced throughout His earthly ministry, as for instance, in His calling simple, ordinary men to serve as His Apostles. Beyond the weather-beaten faces, the leathery hands, and the smell of fish, the Savior perceived divine potential in each of them. The Master's selective perception of Peter's strengths readily outweighed any penchant toward a selective retention of his weaknesses. The importance of selective retention was underscored when Jesus taught Peter that we should forgive others not just seven times but "seventy times seven" (Matt. 18:21–22). There are many memories in life which are best forgotten.

Precisely because selective perceptions are *selective*, they can readily change as fast as hearts can change. A case in point was the Savior's visit to the ancient Nephites. After teaching them at great length, he looked at the multitude and said: "I perceive that ye are weak, that ye cannot understand all my words. . . . Therefore, go ye unto your homes, and ponder upon the things which I have said." (3 Ne. 17:2–3.)

But as Jesus saw that "they were in tears" and that they desired that He would remain with them a little longer, He was "filled with compassion," and He invited them to bring their sick and afflicted to Him, for He saw that their faith was sufficient that all might be healed (3 Ne. 17:5–10).

After inviting the little children to come unto Him, the Savior knelt and prayed "great and marvelous things," and the multitude bore record that "no one can conceive of the joy which filled our souls at the time we heard him pray for us unto the Father" (3 Ne. 17:13–17). The multitude was overcome with joy, causing the Savior to exclaim: "Blessed are ye because of your faith. And now behold, my joy is full." The record continues, "And when he had said these words, he wept." (3 Ne. 17:18–21.)

One important insight to be gained from this inspirational event in the Book of Mormon is the fact that the Savior's perceptions of the people readily changed as their hearts changed.

This was a lesson which took the Apostle Peter a bit longer to learn. In preparation for teaching the gospel to Cornelius, the Italian centurion, the Lord reminded Peter three times: "What God hath cleansed, that call not thou common" (Acts 10:15–16). Nevertheless, as Peter taught Cornelius and his family, "the Holy Ghost fell on all them which heard the word," and Peter's Jewish friends "were astonished" that the gift of the Holy Ghost was poured out upon the Gentiles (Acts 10:44–47).

This experience in preaching the gospel for the first time among those who were Gentiles dramatically changed Peter's selective perception, as he exclaimed: "Of a truth I perceive that God is no respecter of persons" (Acts 10:34).

Through the prophet Isaiah the Lord has promised: "Though your sins be as scarlet, they shall be as white as snow; though they be red like crimson, they shall be as wool" (Isa. 1:18). In keeping with this promise to those who truly come unto Christ and repent of their sins, we remember the Apostle Paul and Alma the Younger for their teachings, inspiring epistles, and missionary labors, *not* for Saul's having "made havock of the church" (Acts 8:3) or Alma's having led many of God's children "away unto destruction" (Alma 36:14).

Within every family each of us must marshal the strength and the charity to forgive parents and brothers and sisters for past offenses and change our perceptions of them as they *were* to a more compassionate perception of what they *are*, garnished with the charitable anticipation of what they *will become*.

We Know You're Trying, Dad

In October 1987 President Howard W. Hunter gave a marvelous general conference address about dealing with adversity. His words offered comfort to many, such as to parents whose children had strayed. President Hunter explained that "our detours and disappointments are the straight and narrow path to Him."[3] The secret to strong family bonds lies in forgetting and forgiving the thoughtless acts of children, especially high-spirited teenagers whose emotions tend to run on the warm side, and in children's forgetting the times they may have been harshly disciplined. Remembering the love and warmth which generally pervades the home is always the loftier course to take. We must allow each other rehearsal time and opportunities to practice our parts.

I have a good friend who arrived home from work just as his twelve-year-old son slugged his ten-year-old brother as hard as he could on the arm. Catching the older boy in the act of aggression, this irate father grabbed the older boy by the ear and ceremoniously marched him to his bedroom with the command: "Now don't you come out until it's time for dinner!"

As my friend returned to the kitchen to give his wife a kiss, she informed him that, while his intentions had been well-meaning, the real offender was the younger boy, who had been pestering his older brother the entire day long. His wife explained that the older son had endured his brother's obnoxious teasing all day long and just lost his composure the precise moment their father walked through the door.

My friend is a very mature individual, and so he walked down to the bedroom prison where the older boy sat in solitary confinement.

Sitting next to his son on the boy's bed, this loving father said, "Mommy tells me I disciplined the wrong boy—I'm sorry I got so upset, son." In response to such a mature apology on the part of his father, this young man proffered an equally mature response: "That's okay, Dad," he said. "We know you're trying." As long as both parents and children remember that all of them are trying to improve, then they will more easily forget the times they are very trying to each other.

Our success in following the plan of salvation lies largely in our attempts at striving to achieve perfection, notwithstanding the fact that "all have sinned, and come short of the glory of God" (Rom. 3:23). The eternal love of our Heavenly Father and of His Only Begotten Son is manifest in the fact that "it is by grace that we are saved, after all we can do" (2 Ne. 25:23).

Notes

1. Howard W. Hunter, "Put Your Hand to the Plow," *Improvement Era* 64 (June 1961): 399.

2. Brigham Young, in *Journal of Discourses* 7:280.

3. Howard W. Hunter, "The Opening and Closing of Doors," *Ensign* 17 (November 1987): 60.

Chapter Sixteen

THE PHYSICAL AND THE SPIRITUAL

Truth Reflects upon the Senses

It was a hot, muggy afternoon with the threat of a late afternoon thundershower. Exhausted, hot, and generally uncomfortable, I found a cool spot on the periphery of a park complete with a miniature forest and a waterfall. The temperature was about 98 degrees and the humidity was oppressive, but as I lay on the cool grass in the shade of a weeping birch, I experienced a refreshing exhilaration I had not appreciated since boyhood days of lying on my back, watching cumulus clouds convulsing into countless configurations.[1]

A great sense of well-being surged through my soul as my physical senses were simultaneously bombarded by the touch of the cool, soft grass, the smell of a blue spruce wafting on a gentle breeze, and the sight of the deep blue sky interspersed with immaculately white, restless clouds. All these sensory inputs were capped with the sound of a few orchestrated songbirds hidden from view.

A sense of gratitude overcame me. I was so grateful that I could touch and feel a variety of textures and temperatures in this world of objects around me. I was thankful for my two nearsighted eyes which allow me to read, and to see the world of nature, and the cheerful faces of the five women in my life and a young son.

I had not given the sense of smell much thought since my last bout with the flu. Here I lay without a flower in sight, and yet my olfactory nerves were overwhelmed by the pleasant smells of this mini-forest. The decaying leaves and pine needles and the smell of dust settled by recent rains helped recall the smell of newly mown hay, sunflowers, sagebrush, and sego lilies on Grandpa's farm.

I felt a sense of shame at having taken my physical blessings for granted. I recalled a stake conference address by Elder Franklin D. Richards many years ago. He related an account of a trip he took with President Kimball after the major throat operation which removed much of his natural vocal cords. That evening as they retired for bed, before praying together, President Kimball asked: "Elder Richards, have you ever thanked the Lord for your voice?"

"No, I haven't," replied Brother Richards.

President Kimball gently suggested, "Would you thank Him tonight that you have a voice, that you can speak and be heard?"

Noise Needers

I reflected upon the way in which our senses of hearing, touch, taste, smell, and sight all represent part of our stewardship of gifts—some spiritual, some physical. I became concerned at what the youth of today are doing with the gift of sound, of hearing. I entered a cultural hall sometime ago in which the level of music (and I use the term rather loosely) was so loud that virtually no one could converse. Even when shouting, communication was impossible. Audiologists have confirmed the fact that youth who persist in frequenting loud discotheques eventually lose much of their capacity to hear normally. What a tragedy to misuse the senses in this way.

Listening to acid rock not only drowns out the still small voice, robbing us of the companionship of the Holy Ghost, but it also impairs our physical capacity to hear. Would that we could be physically fit and so spiritually in tune that we could hear the sound of snowflakes crashing to the ground.

If hearing is attuned to the pianissimo passages of Brahms's Violin Concerto in D, this sense becomes even more sensitive and thus more rewarding. When subjected to acid rock and heavy metal, our hearing becomes dulled and loses its capacity to enrich our lives.

The American naturalist Edwin Teale shared his observations of a very circuitous "19,000-mile journey through the North American Summer." Of this adventure Teale wrote:

> Enjoying the peaceful calm of these mountain heights, I remembered the young barber who had cut my hair in a small town a few days before. His great ambition, he said, was to work in New York. There was a

city! For a good many years, he explained, each summer he had visited his grandfather on his farm in the country. But he couldn't stand it any more. Everything was so quiet! It gave him the creeps. He felt like going out and blowing a trumpet or pounding a drum—anything to make a racket. He represented that new breed, growing in numbers, the Noise Needers.

. . . In step with noisier times, the number of Noise Needers is growing. . . . The metallic clangor of rock-and-roll music is, perhaps, symptomatic of the steady rise in the number of Noise Needers. For them, quiet is somehow unnatural, stillness is somehow unfriendly. They feel better, more at home, when they are surrounded by a din—any kind of din. They do not merely tolerate noise. They like noise. They need noise.[2]

Taste

As one interested in the problems of starvation and providing enough food for a burgeoning world population, I am distressed to see in many magazines and newspapers the large proportion of advertisements for weight-reducing salons, diet pills, and weight-loss paraphernalia, all aimed at salvaging the health and happiness of those who have misused their stewardship of the sense of taste. Oh, I know that there are those with glandular anomalies, but I am speaking of those who have trouble with the appetite gland, those who overindulge their taste buds.

I was traveling with one of the Brethren on one occasion, and he spoke of a stake patriarch he had known. The patriarch had evidently struggled to obtain the spirit of his sacred calling. One day at lunchtime this patriarch opened his lunch box, and there he saw a sumptuous feast before him. As he looked at those thick sandwiches and the rich dessert and all the trimmings, he said to himself: "You glutton, it is no wonder you have difficulty with your calling." From that day onward this good brother began to control his taste buds and curb his physical appetite, and in doing so he said it was much easier for him to have the Spirit as his constant companion.

Sight

We are blessed with such a beautiful universe in which our own earth is a crown jewel that I suspect if we learned that we must sacrifice one of our physical senses in order to retain the others, the last one we would willingly sacrifice would be our sight. And yet, how are we as individuals, and as humankind in general, accounting for this stewardship of sight? Pornographic movies, books, and magazines, and TV-itis are some of the greatest problems facing our society today. How can we stand before the Lord and give him an accounting of our use of this great gift of sight, if it has been prostituted for satisfying our lascivious and prurient desires rather than for edifying our eternal mind and spirit.

We are also blessed to live in the era of the so-called "knowledge explosion" when so many great and challenging books are being written on so many different stimulating subjects, which enlarge our souls and feed our intellects. However as one sage observed: "There is little difference between the person who cannot read and the person who can read but doesn't."

One of the greatest blessings which may come through the gift of sight is this:

"Verily, thus saith the Lord: It shall come to pass that every soul who forsaketh his sins and cometh unto me, and calleth on my name, and obeyeth my voice, and keepeth my commandments, shall see my face and know that I am" (D&C 93:1).

Touch

Of all the senses, perhaps none is more diversified than the sense of touch. As long as our shoes fit, the air conditioning works, and our chicken noodle soup is reasonably warm, few of us make much of a fuss over the minor inconveniences relating to our everyday aches and pains. But one sensation which no one can abide for long is that of itching. Pain is perhaps more easily endured than itching. Just as surrending to the seductive siren of our taste buds can destroy girlish figures or place us on the cardiac candidate list, so also can the itch for things destroy our serenity and peace of mind.

Marya Mannes expressed so eloquently the need for curbing this itching sensation when she wrote:

> The good life exists only when you stop wanting a better one. It is the condition of savoring what is, rather than longing for what might

be. The itch for things—so brilliantly injected by those who make and sell them—is in effect a virus draining the soul of contentment. A man never earns enough, a woman is never beautiful enough, clothes are never new enough, the house is never furnished enough, the food is never fancy enough.

There is a point at which salvation lies in stepping off the escalator, of saying, "Enough: What I have will do, what I make of it is up to me."[3]

The Parable of the Sunburned Sailors

Several years ago there were three young American sailors stationed aboard a ship somewhere between Hawaii and Japan. Observing the beautiful deep-blue sky above the sun-drenched Pacific Ocean, the three of them simultaneously concluded that this would be a wonderful opportunity to acquire a world class suntan. After all, there was not a cloud in the sky and there was no pollution to block the sun's ultraviolet rays.

They located some nice soft bath towels and staked out a place on the upper deck where the sun's rays would be unobstructed. They remembered some good counsel from someone who had told them that in order to get the best results you should turn over every few minutes like a grilled chicken on a turning spit. If you lay on your back a few minutes and then on your stomach a few minutes, then you avoid the peril of becoming severely sunburned. The counsel was good, but it applies best when you don't stay out too long, especially the very first day. Well, boys will be boys, and these young teenaged sailors fell asleep during the rotation process and the warm summer sun turned their white skin from pasty pink to bright red.

When they awakened they began to sense they were in real trouble. Their skin had been so badly sunburned it hurt to put on their shirts, it hurt to move, and it even hurt to breathe. With considerable difficulty they made their way to the lower deck to visit the ship's physician, who gave them some anesthetic ointment to provide some temporary relief from their pain. He suggested that they might even be suffering from first degree burns in a few areas and that they should probably stay in bed for a few days.

These three medium well-done musketeers proceeded to the captain's quarters to report their plight and to request a few days sick leave as recommended by the doctor. They had anticipated some sympathy from the captain, but his reply was totally unexpected. With considerable agitation he said: "Your request for sick leave is denied. When you signed up for the U.S. Navy you agreed to keep yourselves in good physical condition, to be combat ready at all times. You are the property of the U.S. Navy. If we had an emergency aboard ship none of you would be in a position to help. Instead of giving you three days sick leave, I sentence you to three days in the brig (the ship's prison) for misuse and abuse of government property."

As spirit children of our Heavenly Father we are, in a very real sense, His property. The Apostle Paul asked the profound question: "Know ye not that ye are the temple of God, and that the Spirit of God dwelleth in you? If any man defile the temple of God, him shall God destroy; for the temple of God is holy, which temple ye are." (1 Cor. 3:16–17.) "For ye are bought with a price: therefore glorify God in your body, and in your spirit, which are God's" (1 Cor. 6:20).

When we use our eyes to improve our minds and to edify our spirits, we do, indeed glorify God with our body. And when we listen to sublime music and to the spoken word of the Lord's servants, we pay Him honor. When we use our voices to share the gospel, to proclaim the truth, and to comfort and cheer others, we show our gratitude for the price by which our sins were bought. When we adorn our bodies with modest clothing, and when our behavior is also modest, we demonstrate that we are the Lord's children.

Whenever we eat a well-balanced diet (including brussels sprouts and broccoli because we know they'll be good for us) and when we follow a program of physical exercise we are, in essence, paying tribute to our Father who created us all. When we take care of our eyes and ears and skin and cardiovascular and muscular-skeletal systems, we not only enjoy better health and vigor of mind and body now, but we are also better prepared to "waste and wear out our lives" in building the Kingdom of God. May each of us take good care of the Lord's property—our bodies—the temples of our spirits.

Dual Nature of Man

Our senses can be either a great blessing or dire curse in our lives depending upon our development and control of them. We need not subdue our physical senses in monastical ascetism, but we do need to strike a spiritual balance in our lives where spiritual senses and sensitivity come first. Our physical senses are a great blessing as the Lord Himself proclaimed in this dispensation: "For man is spirit. The elements are eternal, and spirit and element, inseparably connected, receive a fulness of joy; and when separated, man cannot receive a fulness of joy." (D&C 93:33–34.)

Latter-day Saint theology is unique in its conception of God the Father as an immortal, celestial being with a glorified body of flesh and bone. Other major religions contend that in order for God to be perfect he could not be clothed in flesh. The lesson is clear: Godhood and eternal joy require control of the senses, not the complete abandonment of them.

Perhaps no principle of the gospel places the dualistic—physical and spiritual—nature of man in such contrast as the principle of fasting. As we exercise self-control in overcoming the demands of our physical body, with our physical senses held in check, our spiritual senses develop at an accelerating rate.

When fasting in the proper spirit, our inward strivings are to "seek first the kingdom of God," and we gain a growing realization that the gospel is not just true, it is important—indeed, it is a matter of spiritual life and death. Our life develops a sense of spiritual urgency and a sense of kinship with a loving Father in Heaven.

The Lord has promised that when we engage in fasting and prayer in a spirit of rejoicing and "with cheerful hearts," then "the fulness of the earth is [ours]" (D&C 59:14–16). "Yea, all things which come of the earth, in the season thereof, are made for the benefit and the use of man, both to please the eye and to gladden the heart; yea, for food and for raiment, for taste and for smell, to strengthen the body and enliven the soul" (D&C 59:18–19).

Perspective

We should develop a sense of balance, a sense of perspective. This sense is worth more than dollars. We must beware of Satan's favorite tomfoolery of forging fickle fantasies which are merely substitutes for spirituality. When faced with a choice between pursuing an immediate physical sense of pleasure and a long-range sense of spiritual joy, remember, oh remember "wickedness never was happiness" (Alma 41:10), no matter how enticing it may seem at the time.

We must not give way to discouragement, Satan's counterfeit of humility and meekness. When struggling to reach those plateaus of impeccable performance, we can ponder upon the perspective that "no one can make us feel inferior without our consent."

We must gain a sense of mission, a sense of perspective of our own place in the eternal scheme of things. When we "seek learning, even by study and also by faith" (D&C 88:118), we will acquire a sense of belonging that supersedes the loneliness of an autistic world of materialism. Thereby we learn that we "are a royal priesthood, an holy nation, a peculiar people" (1 Pet. 2:9)—yes, children of God.

We should gain a sense of kinship with God. This sense of membership in an eternal family with infinite future possibilities should humble us to the dust while simultaneously inspiring us to attain the loftiest heights within our own family, our chosen profession, and within the kingdom of God.

Notes

1. This chapter is a modified version of an address delivered at the commencement exercises of the Brigham Young University College of General Studies, August, 1976.

2. Edwin Way Teale, *Journey into Summer* (New York: Dodd, Mead and Co., 1960), pp. 21–22.

3. *Reader's Digest*, June 1974, p. 207.

Howard W. Hunter

To the membership of the Church in every country of the world and to people everywhere I extend my love... I pray that we might treat each other with more kindness, more courtesy, more humility and patience and forgiveness.

...I would invite all members of the Church to live with ever-more attention to the life and example of the Lord Jesus Christ, especially the love and hope and compassion he displayed.

-President Howard W. Hunter

M-21 Joseph Lyon & Associates dba Magazine Printing Co.

Chapter Seventeen

TEACHING AND LEARNING

A few summers ago our family took a vacation to California which included a visit to the world-famous San Diego Zoo. The species on display were informative, entertaining, and inspiring. We attended a very fascinating demonstration by two young animal trainers who had tamed a number of normally wild birds and animals. Of particular interest was an impressive demonstration of falconry in which a young falcon obediently heeded the signals of its trainer in swooping down from great heights at a speed in excess of ninety miles per hour, meeting its target each time with great precision. This experience readily brought to mind William Butler Yeats's prophetic poem "The Second Coming," which I quote in part:

> Turning and turning in the widening gyre
> The falcon cannot hear the falconer;
> Things fall apart; the center cannot hold;
> Mere anarchy is loosed upon the world,
> The blood-dimmed tide is loosed, and everywhere
> The ceremony of innocence is drowned;
> The best lack all conviction, while the worst
> Are full of passionate intensity.[1]

Information Theory

Claude Shannon, the father of information theory, may well have been interested in the reasons the falcon could no longer hear the falconer, because information theory attempts to describe and measure the transmission of information through a given communication channel.

The main elements of information theory can be graphically depicted as follows:[2]

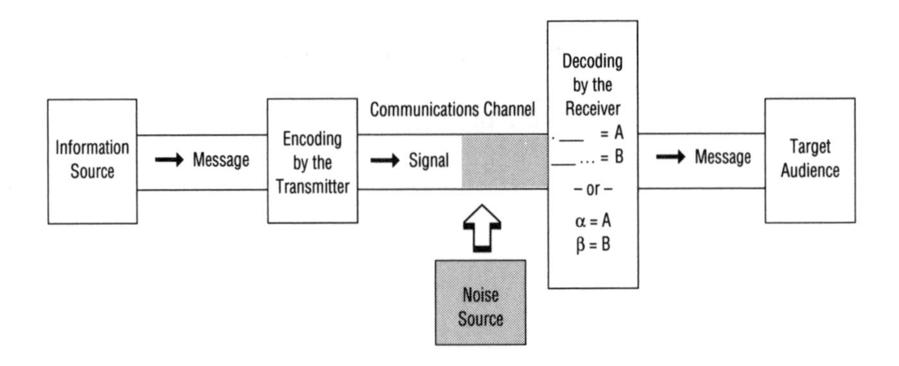

An information source may range from Moses on Mount Sinai to a cub reporter covering a meeting of the city council. The message, in turn, may be as immortal as the Ten Commandments or as trivial as a classified ad. Generally, the original message is encoded into a signal which is transmitted on stone tablets, by radio waves, by lights flashing in Morse code, as a TV signal, as printed news media, or as a handwritten letter. It is assumed that on the opposite end of the communications channel there will be a receiver with a capability of decoding the signal and of transmitting the message further to the target audience.

Within information theory, any distortion of a message is referred to as "noise." Car-radio listeners readily recognize noise as the static which interferes with the message one attempts to receive while traveling in an automobile near some high-voltage power lines. When a broadcast is disturbed by noise, the message will be unclear, and one is uncertain as to whether thirty or thirteen people were injured in an explosion.

Although we generally associate the word *noise* with unpleasant audible sounds, within information theory "noise" can also refer to the snowy picture on a television set, to typographical errors in a news article, or to illegible words in a handwritten document. In short, noise refers to anything that detracts from the true content of a message and causes uncertainty in the mind of the receiver.

The embellishment of a story with too many details can create more noise than information, so that the receiver is uncertain of the central message and is confused regarding the most pertinent information. On the other hand, too few details also leave the listener in a state of uncertainty. This may be the case in our communications with a child, a companion, or a colleague when things left unsaid leave them in a state of unintended uncertainty.

Reducing Noise

It is reassuring to know that when one encounters the perpetual problem of noise in a given channel there are means for reducing uncertainty within a message. One method is simply increasing the amplitude or volume. Another method is repeating the message until it is finally understood. We call this redundancy. A rule of thumb in radio advertising suggests that the announcer mention the brand name of a given product three times to avoid its confusion with another product.

In theology one kind of redundancy is the law of witnesses. When a loving Heavenly Father wishes to communicate with His children through His prophet on earth, it is not uncommon for a given message to be repeated several times until the intended receiver unmistakably understands its form and content.

Teaching and Learning

Such was the case with the Apostle Peter, who initially resisted the notion of taking the gospel to the Gentiles. Three times the voice of the Lord implored him: "What God hath cleansed, that call not thou common" (Acts 10:15–16; 11:9–10).

Following the great destruction in the land, signifying the crucifixion of Jesus Christ, the ancient Nephites were gathered together around the temple at Bountiful when "they heard a voice" as if it came out of heaven, but "they understood not the voice which they heard." A second time "they heard the voice, and they understood it not." But "the third time they did understand the voice which they heard." (3 Ne. 11:3–6.)

In this latter dispensation the Lord has reiterated the law of witnesses anciently given to the children of Israel. To the Prophet Joseph Smith the Lord said: "In the mouth of two or three witnesses shall every word be established" (D&C 6:28; 128:3; see also Ether 5:4; Deut. 19:15; 2 Cor. 13:1). It is not incidental that on the evening of September 21, 1823, when Joseph Smith supplicated the Lord for an assurance of his spiritual standing, the angel Moroni appeared to him three times. Joseph recounted that during Moroni's second appearance that night "he commenced, and again related the very same things which he had done at his first visit, without the least variation" (JS–H 1:45). During the third visitation on that evening Joseph reported that Moroni repeated "the same things as before" (JS–H 1:46). A fourth angelic appearance occurred the next morning while Joseph worked in his father's field.

Redundancy of Doctrine

My study has led me to conclude that, generally speaking, there is no major doctrine or teaching that is not expounded at least twice, either within the same volume of scripture or within two or more different volumes of scripture. For example, the Lord revealed through Isaiah that "they that wait upon the Lord shall renew their strength; . . . they shall run, and not be weary; and they shall walk, and not faint" (Isa. 40:31), a poetic, prophetic promise also found in section 89 of the Doctrine and Covenants.

The law of tithing was taught anciently by the prophet Malachi (see Mal. 3:8–11) and also repeated verbatim by the Savior himself as He visited the ancient Nephites and taught them and blessed them (see 3 Ne. 24:8–11). Isaiah carefully taught the law of the fast (see Isa. 58:3–11), and this law is again explained in D&C 59:12–14.

Some critics of modern revelation attempt to dismiss contemporary prophets as plagiarists of ancient scriptures who pass off their work as new or continuous revelation. A case in point is the great redundancy between the Sermon on the Mount as contained in the Gospel of Matthew and the Savior's sermon contained in 3 Nephi of the Book of Mormon. Others may claim that Mormon's eloquent exegesis on charity as "the pure love of Christ" is simply an edited version of the same message in Paul's First Epistle to the Corinthians (see 1 Cor. 13).

Skeptics may speak of prophetic plagiarism, but an information theorist recognizes repetition as a key to understanding. A practitioner in the field of communication is interested in reducing as much noise in the channel as possible in order to get the message through. To him, it is self-evident that the originator of a message would repeat information as many times as necessary until it is completely understood by the intended receiver. To a Latter-day Saint, the fact that an epistle of Paul may be similar to the writings of Mormon or Moroni is easily understood: they received their revelation from the same source.

The use of inverted parallelism in the chiastic literary form of scripture is another means of reducing noise and uncertainty through redundancy of the message.[3] In *The Art of Biblical Narrative*, Robert Alter discusses at length various techniques of repetition found in the scriptures. He concludes that "man may repeat and fulfill the words of revelation, repeat and delete, repeat and transform; but always there is the original urgent message to contend with, a message which in the potency of its concrete verbal formulation does not allow itself to be forgotten or ignored."[4]

Our English word *information* is a derivative of the Latin root *informare*, which means to form, as in becoming a formative principle which shapes one's character.[5] Unfortunately, just because a message is repeated several times does not assure that the receiver will always act upon it. Such was apparently the case with Eli, the temple priest and father of two wayward sons. You will recall that the Lord was greatly displeased with Eli "because his sons made themselves vile, and he restrained them not" (1 Sam. 3:13). The lyrics of James D. Burns's hymn "Hushed Was the Evening Hymn," set to music by Arthur Sullivan, tenderly contrast Eli's failure to listen with the sensitive ear of the boy-prophet Samuel:

> Hushed was the evening hymn;
> The temple courts were dark;
> The lamp was burning dim
> Before the sacred ark;
> When suddenly a voice divine
> Rang through the silence of the shrine.
> The old man, meek and mild,
> The priest of Israel slept;
> His watch the temple child,

The little Levite kept;
And what from Eli's sense was sealed,
The Lord to Hannah's son revealed.

O give me Samuel's ear,
The open ear, O Lord,
Alive and quick to hear
Each whisper of thy word,
Like him to answer at thy call
And to obey thee first of all.

O give me Samuel's heart,
A lowly heart, that waits,
Wherein thy house thou art
Or watches at thy gates,
By day and night, a heart that still
Moves at the breathing of thy will.

O give me Samuel's mind,
A sweet unmurmuring faith,
Obedient and resigned
To thee in life and death,
That I may read with childlike eyes,
Truths that are hidden from the wise![6]

Decoding

A crucial element within information theory is the decoding of a message by the receiver. Even if a message is repeated several times through a noise-free channel, there is still no guarantee that it will be perfectly understood by the receiver. An example of the process of decoding is the mapping of Morse code messages into alphabetic characters. A knowledge of English grammar and great literature will be of little avail if one is unable to decode the dots, dashes, and appropriate pauses.

Decoding is also necessary in merely trying to understand a typical inter-office memo. One of my colleagues has a plaque on his desk which aptly describes this problem in these terms: "I know you believe you understand what you think I said, but I am not sure you realize that what you heard is not what I meant."

In communicating information, the content of a given message may remain the same even though it is communicated through several different forms. A message can be presented as a formal verbal statement at a press conference, as a printed newspaper article, as a radio broadcast, or as a televised interview involving rehearsed answers to prepared questions. Regardless of the form of the signal, the content remains virtually the same. Sometimes noise and uncertainty enter into interpersonal relationships when individuals fail to say what they mean or, conversely, fail to mean what they say.

Speaking as a scientist, surgeon, and Apostle, Elder Russell M. Nelson reminds us that "the truth isn't 'relative.' It is only man's understanding of the truth that is 'relative.'"[7] He cautions us against the use of negative information solely for the purpose of furthering "negative ends."[8] On the other hand, he reminds us that "if the true and righteous people are silent, those who use truth in unrighteousness will prevail," or, as Yeats puts it: "The best lack all conviction, while the worst are full of passionate intensity."

The dilemmas surrounding the disclosure of truth are sensitively resolved by Elder Nelson as he advocates "a commitment to truth *and more*," which includes a self-searching sensitivity not only to the form and content of the truth, but also an awareness of our motives for disclosing the truth.[9]

Such is the challenge in decoding messages from on high when the Sender himself has said: "For my thoughts are not your thoughts, neither are your ways my ways, saith the Lord. For as the heavens are higher than the earth, so are my ways higher than your ways, and my thoughts than your thoughts." (Isa. 55:8–9.)

How, then, is one to decode the meaning of personal revelation from God if His thoughts are not our thoughts? And how are we to understand the words of His living prophets or the messages in the holy writ of prophets of a bygone age? The Apostle Paul provided a decoding formula to the Corinthians when he explained that "the Spirit searches all things, yea, the deep things of God. For what man knoweth the things of a man, save the spirit of man which is in him? even so the things of God knoweth no man, but the Spirit of God." (1 Cor. 2:10–11.)

During our excursion to the zoo a few years ago, we strolled alongside the caged animals and were delighted with the animated antics of the African monkeys and their tree-climbing cousins. But when we reached the area where the lions and tigers were kept, our then twelve-year-old son, Craig, was extremely disappointed. It did not seem quite right to him that all the lions were lounging in the sunshine. Nudging me with his elbow, he said: "Give 'em your shrill whistle, Dad, and wake 'em up." Not wanting to disappoint him, I quickly obliged, and, with all due humility, I do have a very shrill whistle. But the lioness didn't even stir. I turned to Craig and said: "Now watch this." I then began my imitation of a tiger growl, in a very deep and quiet voice. To Craig's amazement the lioness pricked up her ears, raised her head, and then began to prowl around.

Just as the lioness responded to the soft growl in spite of the noise of the crowd, we receive communication from our Heavenly Father when we are sensitive to the whisperings of the still small voice.

Nephi assures us that "when a man speaketh by the power of the Holy Ghost the power of the Holy Ghost carrieth it unto the hearts of the children of men" (2 Ne. 33:1). The Lord asks an important question in this regard: "Therefore, why is it that ye cannot understand and know, that he that receiveth the word by the Spirit of truth receiveth it as it is preached by the Spirit of truth? Wherefore, he that preacheth and he that receiveth, understand one another, and both are edified and rejoice together." (D&C 50:21–22.)

Decoding Lehi's Dream

Few passages of scripture have greater symbolic density and richness than Lehi's dream in the Book of Mormon (see 1 Ne. 8). Contained within nineteen brief verses of scripture are at least ten symbols expressing the essence of earth life. These symbolic expressions include, of course, the dark and dreary waste, a large and spacious field, a tree, the fruit of the tree, a river of water, a rod of iron, a straight and narrow path, the head of a fountain, a mist of darkness, and a great and spacious building. When one decodes the meaning of these symbols, and also the symbols included in the Savior's allegory of the true vine (see John 15) and Zenos' allegory of the olive tree (see Jacob 5), one will have discovered a marvelous blueprint for understanding the meaning and purpose of earth life.

Developing an ability to decode sacred symbolic messages is absolutely essential to finding the way back to our heavenly home. Elder Dallin H. Oaks has identified "eight different purposes served by communication from God: (1) to testify; (2) to prophesy; (3) to comfort; (4) to uplift; (5) to inform; (6) to restrain; (7) to confirm; and (8) to impel."[10] Sometimes a divine message may appear to be uncertain to us, as receivers, because we anticipate a message of comfort while the intent of the Sender is to transmit a message impelling us to action. Or, we wish to gain a quick glimpse of our future while the Lord wishes to try our patience and our faith.

Nephi shared an important observation with his wayward brethren which is also instructive for each of us. Said Nephi: "Ye have seen an angel, and he spake unto you; yea, ye have heard his voice from time to time; and he hath spoken unto you in a still small voice, but ye were past feeling" (1 Ne. 17:45).

Nephi interpreted divine injunctions in the hope that "the truth shall make you free" (John 8:32), whereas his rebellious brothers reacted with the knee-jerk mind-set: "The truth shall make you mad."[11]

Of the Lamans and Lemuels and the Pharisees of the world, the Savior said: "Therefore speak I to them in parables: because they seeing see not; and hearing they hear not, neither do they understand. And in them is fulfilled the prophesy of Esaias, which saith, By hearing ye shall hear, and shall not understand; and seeing ye shall see, and shall not perceive: for this people's heart is waxing gross, and their ears are dull of hearing, and their eyes they have closed." (Matt. 13:13–15.)

The decoding of spiritual messages involves more than the mind and ears—one must also feel the message. So it was that King Benjamin began his benedictory address with the following prefatory preparation of his people: "Open your ears that ye may hear, and your hearts that ye may understand, and your minds that the mysteries of God may be unfolded to your view" (Mosiah 2:9).

Channel Capacity

In addition to addressing the problems of uncertainty, encoding, decoding, and noise, information theory is also concerned with the transmission capacity of the communications channel. When I was a young boy our family telephone was on a party line involving as many as half a dozen other families. We children learned at a very early age that long conversations with our friends were very seldom private conversations. The communications channel could handle only one coherent conversation, but the number of listeners knew no bounds.

Once a channel has reached its maximum capacity, sending additional information through that channel will merely increase the noise and uncertainty, as illustrated in this diagram:[12]

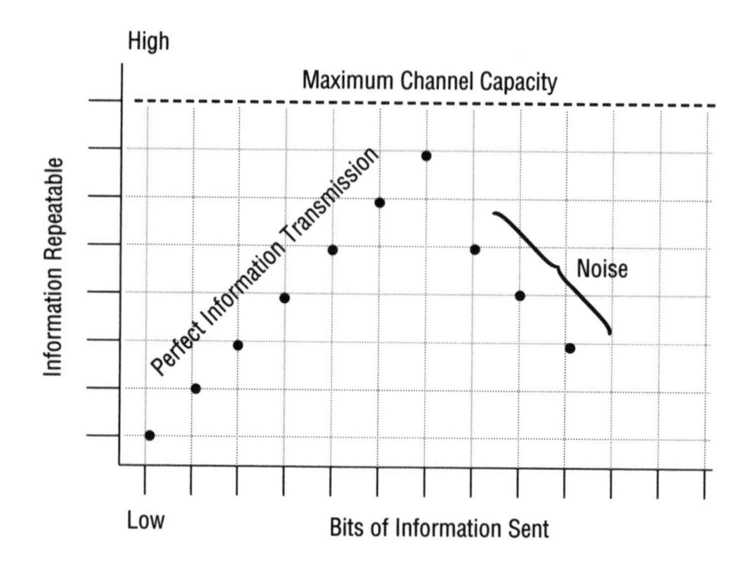

So it is that a patient Father in Heaven reveals His will to His children on earth in piecemeal fashion, as we read in the Book of Mormon: "Thus saith the Lord God: I will give unto the children of men line upon line, precept upon precept, here a little and there a little; and blessed are those who hearken unto my precepts, and lend an ear unto my counsel, for they shall learn wisdom; for unto him that receiveth I will give more; and from them that shall say, We have enough, from them shall be taken away even that which they have" (2 Ne. 28:30; see also Isa. 28:9–13; D&C 98:12).

Many of us desire to know certain information before we are either prepared or able to act upon that knowledge. Elder Boyd K. Packer has eloquently addressed such concerns as follows:

> You cannot force spiritual things. Such words as *compel, coerce, constrain, pressure, demand* do not describe our privileges with the Spirit.
>
> You can no more force the Spirit to respond than you can force a bean to sprout, or an egg to hatch before its time. You can create a climate to foster growth; you can nourish, and protect; but you cannot force or compel: You must await the growth.

> Do not be impatient to gain great spiritual knowledge. Let it grow, help it grow; but do not force it, or you will open the way to be misled. . . .
>
> . . . Should we stand in need of revealed instruction to alter our course, it will be waiting along the way as we arrive at the point of need.[13]

On a later occasion, Elder Packer shared this observation:

> All things not only *are not* known but *must not* be so convincingly clear as to eliminate the need for faith. That would nullify agency and defeat the purpose of the plan of salvation. Tests of faith are growing experiences. We all have unanswered questions. Seeking and questioning, periods of doubt, in an effort to find answers, are part of the process of discovery. The kind of doubt which is spiritually dangerous does not relate to *questions* so much as to *answers*.[14]

In examining our channel capacity for receiving divine inspiration, it would be well to review the Apostle James's counsel regarding any attempts to listen to two competing messages simultaneously. Said James: "A double minded man is unstable in all his ways" (James 1:8).

Perhaps we can also learn an important lesson from communicating with audible dots and dashes in Morse code. As important as the short and long bursts of sound may be, the silent pause between each signal is indispensable. Thus we read the identical instruction in two separate "handbooks" on decoding divine communication: "Be still and know that I am God" (Ps. 46:10 and D&C 101:16). It is often said that the teacher learns more than his or her students. But much can be learned by listening. President Marion G. Romney once observed, "I can always tell when I am speaking under inspiration—I learn something new as I speak."

It is encouraging and comforting to receive the assurance of the Lord that our channel capacity for understanding eternal truths may ever increase, as our obedience increases. Said the Lord: "And the Book of Mormon and the holy scriptures are given of me for your instruction; and the power of my Spirit quickeneth all things" (D&C 33:16). Modern scripture further assures us that "no man receiveth a fulness unless he keepeth his commandments. He that keepeth his commandments receiveth truth and light, until he is glorified in truth and knoweth all things." (D&C 93:27–28.)

Disobedience and sin constitute noise which clogs the

communications channel, but as noise is removed from our lives, our channel capacity increases. Alma described this process in these words: "He that will harden his heart, the same receiveth the lesser portion of the word; and he that will not harden his heart, to him is given the greater portion of the word, until it is given unto him to know the mysteries of God until he know them in full" (Alma 12:10).

A cardiologist friend tells me that hardening of the heart is attributable to four major factors: diet, lack of exercise, stress, and pollutants. I suspect that if the hardening of one's heart is a reversible process, and the scriptures give us hope that it is, then one's heart can also be softened through altering one's diet to include more spiritual food, exercising greater faith, and subsequently reducing the stress of anxiety and guilt through sincere repentance. Finally, when a wide range of pollutants are removed from one's environment, the combined result should be a softening of one's heart and the opening of celestial channels allowing room for "the greater portion of the word, until it is given unto him to know the mysteries of God until he know them in full" (Alma 12:10).

Perpetuation of Eternal Values

The specific application of information theory deals with the communication of a message between one transmitter and one receiver. However, these same concepts lend themselves to a more general application dealing with the transmission of traditional values from one generation to the next. In his best-selling book *The Closing of the American Mind*, Allan Bloom bemoans the increasing erosion of the common core values of Western civilization reflected in part by a growing disregard for the Bible.[15] This seems to be part of the problem addressed by Yeats in his poem "The Second Coming": "Turning and turning in the widening gyre / The falcon cannot hear the falconer." Intergenerational noise is drowning out many of the time-tested messages of the ages.

Reaching the Limits

We live in a day when human limits are rapidly expanding in all areas through the knowledge explosion, technological innovations, the field of medical science, and in the performance of human feats of athletic prowess. Fifty years ago the four-minute mile was considered to be an impossible barrier, but the current record is 3:46, and a 1988 magazine article projects the maximum human limit to be 3:34.[16] But there are other limits which also have been extended, expanded so far in fact that the words of Yeats ring ever louder in our ears:

> Things fall apart; the center cannot hold;
> Mere anarchy is loosed upon the world,
> The blood-dimmed tide is loosed, and everywhere
> The ceremony of innocence is drowned.

I speak now of the limits of human morality, decency, and propriety. Just as our society and culture have broken land speed records and opened up the frontiers of neurosurgery and super conductivity, so have we also opened up the Pandora's box of pornography in unimagined multi-media proportions. Thirty years ago the word *abortion* was generally an unspeakable word and an unthinkable thought, but since the *Roe v. Wade* decision in 1973, which legalized abortion, "the blood-dimmed tide is loosed, and everywhere / The ceremony of innocence is drowned."

The Supreme Court of the United States must not shoulder all the blame for upholding the constitutionality of that landmark decision. After all, the court often reflects the preferences of the general public. Now, in most major cities in the United States, the number of abortions performed surpasses the number of babies born, and "the ceremony of innocence is drowned [as] / The best lack all conviction, while the worst / Are full of passionate intensity."

Sobering evidence of disintegrating core values in our present-day society is also provided by a survey of the main concerns of public school officials. In 1940, a number of American educators were asked to indicate the major discipline problems they faced in their schools. Their responses included chewing gum, making noise, running the halls, getting out of turn in line, wearing improper clothing, and not putting paper in the waste basket. Four decades later, in 1982, another group of public educators were asked to identify their major disciplinary problems. Now their main concerns included rape, robbery, assault, burglary, arson, bombings, murder, suicide, absenteeism, vandalism, extortion, drugs, alcohol, gang warfare, pregnancy, abortion, and venereal disease.[17]

The Rising Generation

Our generation and Western culture can learn an indispensable lesson from the Book of Mormon regarding the necessity of very consciously and systematically and repetitiously transmitting eternal values to each succeeding generation. We read that following King Benjamin's righteous reign, "it came to pass that there were many of the rising generation that could not understand the words of king Benjamin, being little children at the time he spake unto his people; and they did not believe the tradition of their fathers. They did not believe what had been said concerning the resurrection of the dead, neither did they believe concerning the coming of Christ." (Mosiah 26:1–2.)

We currently live in a very noisy world, so noisy in fact that we live in peril that the messianic and millennial messages of the ages will not get through, or the signal will become so distorted that these messages are no longer recognizable by the rising generation.

It is true that repetition is helpful in transmitting information accurately and completely, but if decoding formulae are lost, or encoded messages become distorted by excessive noise, the message simply will not get through to the next generation. But the message must get through, and it must get through with as little noise and uncertainty as possible. We must extend the channel capacity of our youth, and to do so, several sources of noise must be removed from the channel. It is very difficult for the still small voice to guide our lives if we seldom stop to listen (see D&C 131:6).

President Hugh B. Brown was wont to say that it is well to know the gospel is true, but it is even better to know the gospel. In the early days of the Restoration, in fact a year before the Church was organized, the Prophet Joseph received the following counsel for his brother Hyrum: "Seek not to declare my word, but first seek to obtain my word, and then shall your tongue be loosed; then, if you desire, you shall have my Spirit and my word, yea the power of God unto the convincing of men" (D&C 11:21).

Sometimes there is noise in our message when we are uncertain of its content, or, as the Apostle Paul put it, "if the trumpet give an uncertain sound, who shall prepare himself to the battle?" (1 Cor. 14:8.) We must learn to listen if we are to learn our lessons well.[18]

On the other hand, once we are armed with a clear understanding of our message, the Lord reminds us that: "Ye are not sent forth to be taught, but to teach the children of men the things which I have put into your hands by the power of my Spirit" (D&C 43:15).

Precious Promise of Primary

The quest for teaching by the Spirit is one enterprise which requires a judicious balance between faith and works, prayer and preparation. Teaching must never be pursued as an attempt to impress others with our knowledge, but should rather be an effort to edify, inform, inspire, and to change others for the better (see D&C 99:2).

In my early youth I soon learned just how long a mile was, because that is precisely the distance my little white-haired grandma and I would walk down the gravel road together to Primary. She was a slightly built woman and scarcely more than five feet tall. She didn't walk fast, but she had great endurance.

Both Grandma Condie's parents were Danish immigrants, and though they were honest, hardworking folk, survival took precedence over education. Although Grandma's formal education ended with the sixth grade, she was nevertheless one of the best teachers I have ever known. Her success was not attributable to a command of a large or eloquent vocabulary. As I think back on the seeds that were sown and the lessons that were harvested each week, I think her success lay in the fact that she followed a formula which all good teachers pursue:

Preparation. The foundation for any lesson is preparation. Grandma knew that a well-delivered lesson needs time for incubation, just as eggs need time between fertilization and hatching. She realized the Lord's promise that "if ye are prepared ye shall not fear" (D&C 38:30). She continually studied the scriptures and Church magazines looking for appropriate enrichment ideas and materials for a future lesson. There were no last-minute "Saturday night specials" in Grandma's repertoire of gospel discussions. Each lesson had been prayed over and prepared well in advance.

Her widening eyes or creeping grin or occasionally furrowed brow all added to the suspense and excitement of every lesson. An occasional tear or a catch in her voice underscored the eternal importance of her message.

Grandma was very much aware of the Savior's promise to his disciples that "the Holy Ghost . . . shall teach you all things, and bring all things to your remembrance" (John 14:26); and she felt that this meant the Holy Ghost would help her remember things she had been studying during the previous week rather than help her remember things she had never read before.

Use of Illustrations. Grandma realized that, especially for young children, a picture is worth a thousand words. I don't know why Grandma did not use a two-dimensional flannel board for visual aids, but she used something even better. My uncle sawed narrow parallel slits in a piece of wood a little smaller than a breadboard. Into each of these slits Grandma would slide her little pictures so that the visual presentations were always three-dimensional, with the most prominent figures in the foreground and the supporting cast in the background.

The picture board had an oval hole in one end to make it easy to carry, and it was always an honor to have the chance of carrying it for her. After all, she wasn't too much larger than the children she taught, and so she appreciated a little extra help carrying all of her materials to Primary.

Inspiration. Grandma knew that when a lesson is taught by the Spirit "the Holy Ghost carrieth it unto the hearts of the children of men" (2 Ne. 33:1). Under these circumstances a word is worth a thousand pictures! The compound interest which accrued to her lessons was evidenced by the countless letters she received from young women and young men serving on missions, thanking her for the truths she had taught them in Primary a dozen years earlier.

Another great teacher, the Apostle Paul, explained that his sermons were "not with enticing words of man's wisdom, but in demonstration of the Spirit and of power" (1 Cor. 2:4).

Power of Example. Grandma followed the counsel of the Apostle Paul: "Even so hath the Lord ordained that they which preach the gospel should live of the gospel" (1 Cor. 9:14). This little lady lived the gospel that she preached. Her life exemplified every gospel principle from consecration to enduring to the end. Though she never held positions of high visibility and leadership, one of her most treasured possessions was the pin she received recognizing her forty years of continuous service as a Primary teacher. After teaching for several additional years, she was released as a Primary teacher three weeks before she died of cancer at age seventy-nine.

Elevating a Child's Self-Esteem. Regardless of how a little child looks, acts, or smells, a great teacher continually reaffirms his or her eternal identity. One of the greatest messages in all of Latter-day Saint hymnody is the simple yet eloquent song, "I Am a Child of God." When this message is adequately internalized before the age of ten or twelve, the temptations of the teens and the subsequent heartbreaks of later years can largely be avoided.

A great Primary teacher continually points children toward celestial goals: "Now, Suzy, *when* you are married in the temple . . ." And, "Johnny, *when* you go on your mission . . ." There is no room for *if* statements when one is contemplating eternity.

Loving Them All. There is a shop-worn cliché which is nevertheless a truism: "They don't care how much you know, until they know how much you care." Those whose attendance is sporadic, because support from home is lacking, deserve an even greater measure of love and attention. Each child should begin to feel the power of the Lord's revelation wherein he likens his church to a body which "hath need of every member, that all may be edified together, that the system may be kept perfect" (D&C 84:110). Should they ever be absent, they should feel that the class is just not the same without them.

This same feeling of reaching out to every member should pervade the prayers of auxiliary presidencies and bishoprics in search of new teachers, choristers, organists, and secretaries to staff their organizations. I am indebted to Elder Sterling W. Sill for pointing out a great lesson in leadership contained in 1 Samuel. The Lord instructed the prophet Samuel to go to the house of Jesse and there he would find the new king of Israel. After interviewing Jesse's seven older sons, Samuel told Jesse: "The Lord hath not chosen these." He then asked Jesse, "Are here all thy children?" Jesse then explained that the youngest son, David, was out in the fields with the sheep. After David had been fetched from the fields the Lord told Samuel, "Arise, anoint him: for this is he." (1 Sam. 16:1–12.)

There are many "Davids in the fields" who don't attend our classes regularly, whom we need to bring safely into the fold. There are other "Davids in the fields" whom we often overlook as we consider the staffing needs of various organizations. For example, we sometimes automatically exclude women in their sixties and seventies because "they probably don't have enough patience to be around young children."

When I was eleven, my Primary teacher was Sister Nash, a dignified, elderly widow who spoke with an authoritative yet quivering voice. Her head rested unsteadily upon her neck and shoulder muscles weakened with age. Her teaching was not very animated, but her best visual aids were her moistened eyes as she frequently bore her sweet testimony to us. As tears welled up to the brim, we knew that she knew that what she said was true. Even for the rowdiest of our "dirty dozen," somehow it would have been a great sacrilege to have ever interrupted her class. When we were in her presence, irreverent acts became unthinkable thoughts.

Sometimes we also overlook the men who are electricians and lawyers who have the gift of being able to reach young children. We should always keep in mind that the purpose of the Church is "for the perfecting of the saints" (Eph. 4:11–14) and that Primary and Sunday School teachers do not have to be perfect; they mostly have to be interested in attaining perfection and be willing to feed His sheep.[19]

Feasting on the Word

The Lord's sheep should be able to feast upon the words of living prophets and the scriptures, which are filled with "recipes of righteousness." Such recipes include the Sermon on the Mount (see Matt. 5–7 and 3 Ne. 12–14), declared by President Harold B. Lee to be the Lord's constitution for a celestial life. The Ten Commandments (see Ex. 20:3–17) are another invaluable recipe. Though they do not contain the complete gospel, universal obedience to them would eliminate most of the ills of the world.

King Benjamin's benedictory sermon on overcoming the natural man (see Mosiah 2–5) is indispensable to our happiness. Alma's interrogatory sermon to the people of Zarahemla consists of forty-one soul-searching questions which provide several easily understood standards for elevating our current level of spirituality and worthiness (see Alma 5). His words to the people in Gideon also provide us with a list of godly attributes which we can and should graft into our lives (see Alma 7).

Paul's reference to the fruit of the Spirit is a succinct statement of the godly attributes which invite the Holy Ghost to be our constant companion (see Gal. 5:22–23).

The Apostle Peter's prescription for becoming partakers of the divine nature provides us with a road map leading to the celestial kingdom (see Pet. 1:4–8).

In this latter dispensation the Lord has revealed numerous additional recipes of righteousness in the Doctrine and Covenants, including section 4 on the preparation for preaching the gospel. Section 88:118–26 is a virtual catalogue of principles which, if followed, will assure that our homes may become a corner of heaven on earth. The first verse of section 93 is all-encompassing in both its requirements and its promise that "every soul who forsaketh his sins and cometh unto me, and calleth on my name, and obeyeth my voice, and keepeth my commandments, shall see my face and know that I am."

All the Scriptures in One

It is recorded that as the Savior ministered to the ancient Nephites He "expounded all the scriptures in one" (3 Ne. 23:14). His teaching was understandable in its form yet broad and deep in its content. He had no pet doctrines which He taught to the exclusion of other teachings. He taught the fulness of the gospel and "all the scriptures in one."

The Old Testament is replete with stories of faith and devotion and also contains graphic examples of the consequences of disobedience. It foretells the scattering and gathering of Israel and the birth and messianic mission of the Son of God.

The four Gospels of the New Testament help us to know and love the Savior. They testify of the divine mission of Jesus Christ, and in this regard President Gordon B. Hinckley has urged us to pay special attention to the Gospel of John and, from the Book of Mormon, 3 Nephi.

The epistles of Paul provide us with great counsel on a wide range of gospel topics upon which he preached, "not with enticing words of man's wisdom, but in demonstration of the Spirit and of power" (1 Cor. 2:4; see also D&C 99:2).

The Book of Mormon is another witness for Christ which has come forth at a crucial time in the history of the world when many have lost any knowledge of the Bible. It is a special witness of Jesus Christ in our day, and the doctrines taught and the historical events which are described within its pages are as current and relevant as today's news. The Lord has strongly admonished us to "remember the new covenant, even the Book of Mormon" (D&C 84:57).

The Pearl of Great Price, though brief in length, is an all-encompassing book of scripture that includes our premortal existence, the purpose of our mortal life on earth, the signs of the second coming of Christ, and the sacred record of the restoration of the gospel in our day.

And finally, let us remember and be grateful that whatsoever living Apostles and prophets "shall speak when moved upon by the Holy Ghost shall be scripture, shall be the will of the Lord, shall be the mind of the Lord, shall be the word of the Lord, shall be the voice of the Lord, and the power of God unto salvation" (D&C 68:4).

The Savior "expounded all the scriptures in one." In this mortal sphere He alone lived all of the godly virtues in perfect balance. A balanced approach to reading the scriptures will also be conducive to our living balanced lives.

Notes

1. William Butler Yeats, "The Second Coming," in Stanley B. Greenfield and A. Kingsley Weatherhead, eds., *The Poem: An Anthology* (New York: Appleton-Century-Crofts, 1968), pp. 309–10.

2. This diagram is a modification of the same scheme first published by Claude E. Shannon, "A Mathematical Theory of Communication," *Bell System Technical Journal* 27 (1948): 379–423. For additional insight and applications of information theory, see David Slepian, ed., *Key Papers in the Development of Information Theory* (New York: Gordon and Breach, 1973); M. Tribus, "Thirty Years of Information Theory," in R. D. Levine and M. Tribus, eds., *The Maximum Entropy Formalism* (Cambridge Mass.: The M.I.T. Press, 1978), pp. 1–14; D. S. Jones, *Elementary Information Theory* (Oxford: Claredon Press, 1979); Masud Mansuripur, *Introduction to Information Theory* (Englewood Cliffs, N.J.: Prentice-Hall, 1987).

3. See John W. Welch, "Chiasmus in the Book of Mormon," *BYU Studies* 10 (Autumn 1969): 69–84; see also Noel B. Reynolds, "The Political Dimension in Nephi's Small Plates," *BYU Studies* 27 (Fall 1987): 15–37.

4. Robert Alter, *The Art of Biblical Narrative* (New York: Basic Books, 1981), p. 112.

5. See Paul Young, *The Nature of Information* (N.H.: Praeger, 1987), p. 6.

6. James D. Burns, "Hushed Was the Evening Hymn," *Hymns*, 1948, no. 252.

7. Russell M. Nelson, "Truth and More," *Ensign* 16 (January 1986): 69.

8. Nelson, "Truth and More," p. 72.

9. Nelson, "Truth and More," p. 73.

10. Dallin H. Oaks, "Revelation," in *Brigham Young University 1981–82 Fireside and Devotional Speeches* (Provo, Utah: University Publications, 1982), p. 20.

11. This expression is borrowed from Henry C. Link, *The Return to Religion* (New York: Macmillan Co., 1939).

12. This is an extensive modification of a diagram included in Wilbur Schramm, "Information Theory and Mass Communication," *Journalism Quarterly* 32 (1955): 131–46.

13. Boyd K. Packer, "*That All May Be Edified*" (Salt Lake City: Bookcraft, 1982), p. 338.

14. Boyd K. Packer, "'The Law and the Light,'" in *The Book of Mormon: Jacob Through Words of Mormon, To Learn with Joy*, ed. Monte S. Nyman and Charles D. Tate, Jr. (Provo, Utah: Religious Studies Center, Brigham Young University, 1990), p. 8.

15. See Allan Bloom, *The Closing of the American Mind* (New York: Simon and Schuster, 1987), pp. 56–61, 65, 374.

16. See *U.S. News & World Report*, September 19, 1988, p. 52.

17. See Maurine Ward, "The Disappearing Child," *This People*, Fall 1988, p. 22.

18. Revision of Spencer J. Condie, "Be Still and Know," *Sixth Annual Harman Lecture*, sponsored by the Brigham Young University Division of Continuing Education, January 3, 1989.

19. The section "Precious Promise of Primary" was delivered at the Granger Regional Primary Leadership Training Conference, March 18, 1988.

Conclusion

Jesus and the Quest for Perfect Balance

In His great intercessory prayer the Savior said: "And this is life eternal, that they might know thee the only true God, and Jesus Christ, whom thou hast sent." He then prayed for us: "Holy Father, keep through thine own name those whom thou hast given me, that they may be one, as we are." (John 17:3, 11.) If we are to know the Father and the Son and to become one with them, then we must strive to become like them (see 1 John 3:1–2 and Moro. 7:48).

A living prophet has indicated that Jesus Christ acquired all of the godly virtues and attributes and lived them in perfect balance. Balance, or temperance, is critical in the development of the traits of godliness, for, as Elder Dallin H. Oaks has put it, "Our strengths can become our downfall."[1]

Sometimes those with admirable reputations for "getting the job done" test the tolerance and the faith of those around them, often leaving ruffled feathers and injured feelings in their wake. There are others who are loving and kind but whose affection borders on Eli's indulgence of his wayward sons (see 1 Sam. 3:12–14).

The Savior created this earth under the direction of His Father (see Mosiah 4:2); He atoned for our sins and is our advocate with the Father (see D&C 29:5). He is "the author and finisher of our faith" (Heb. 12:2). He got the job done! In humility He could honestly and sincerely declare to His Father: "I have finished the work which thou gavest me to do" (John 17:4).

Perhaps we could briefly highlight some of the events of the Savior's earthly ministry to examine how He did His Father's will while maintaining a perfect balance in His life.

In addition to His divine nature, it may well have been His unflinching love and loyalty to His Father and His love for us which provided the motivation and the eternal perspective in maintaining godly attributes in balance, as He "continued from grace to grace, until he received a fulness" (D&C 93:13).

Throughout His earthly ministry "the weightier matters of the law, judgment, mercy, and faith" (Matt. 23:23), held sway over the demands of the law. His mercy stood betwixt those who repented and the demands of justice (see Mosiah 15:9).

His life was one of meekness, yet He boldly "overthrew the tables of the moneychangers" and drove them from the temple (Matt. 21:12).

At age twelve He confidently discussed the gospel in the temple, and the doctors "were astonished at his understanding" (Luke 2:47), yet He humbly acknowledged, "My doctrine is not mine, but his that sent me" (John 7:16).

He frankly forgave brokenhearted sinners, such as she who bathed His feet with tears (see Luke 7:36–50), yet He could not abide hypocrites or hypocrisy (see Matt. 23:23).

He compassionately healed sin-sick souls and made the lame to walk and the blind to see, yet He also held Peter accountable to convert his brethren (see Luke 22:32) and to feed His sheep (see John 20:15–17), and He reminded the Nephites of events which should have been included in their records (see 3 Ne. 23:9–13).

The Savior resolved the tensions between the letter of the law and the spirit of the law by revealing to His prophets "a more excellent way" of developing a pure love for others (see Ether 4:11; 1 Cor. 12–13; Moro. 7:45–48).

He had a vision of His mission—the big picture—"to bring to pass the immortality and eternal life of man" (Moses 1:39), yet He also considered the lilies of the field (see Matt. 6:28), the mustard seed (see Matt. 13:31–32), the leaven in the loaf (see Matt. 13:33), and the lost coin (see Luke 15:8).

The Son of God created the earth (see John 1:1–14), and blessed little children (see Matt. 19:14–15).

He gladly went to weddings (see John 2:1–10) and to visit people's homes, but He also assured himself some time alone (see Matt. 14:23).

Though He himself had "not where to lay his head" on earth (Matt 8:20), He promised others mansions in heaven above (see John 14:2).

He was the Master Teacher, and His words were scripture, and He quoted prophets of old, and was easily entreated as He grew from grace to grace. He was humble yet confident, exacting yet forgiving (see D&C 1:31–32).

"Though he were a Son, yet learned he obedience by the things which he suffered" (Heb. 5:8). He subjected His will to the will of the Father. Even in His hour of greatest agony in the Garden, He declared: "Nevertheless not my will, but thine, be done" (Luke 22:42).

The tension between loyalty to people and loyalty to principles was previously discussed in this book. But there is no tension when we are loyal to Jesus Christ, because He embodies eternal principles. Not only did He teach the word on earth, and not only does He reveal the word today, but He *is* the Word, full of grace and truth (see John 1:1–14).

He lives all the virtues in perfect balance, and if we are to become like Him we must seek to do the same.

Notes

1. See Dallin H. Oaks, "Our Strengths Can Become Our Downfall," *BYU Today* 46 (November 1992): 34–43.

INDEX